# The
# Questions
## Within

This book is dedicated to all the men and women
who devote their lives to healing, caring and
supporting the milions who are suffering
through man's inhumanity to man.

JHS Books
P.O. Box 613, Dorking RH4 9JT
www.jhsbooks.com
(Further copies can ordered from the above address or website)

A CIP catalogue record for this book is available from the British Library

ISBN: 978-0-9956802-6-5

Designed and typest: by janie louise hunt
Cover photograph: janie louise hunt

Printed and bound in Great Britain by
Biddles Books, Kings Lynn, Norfolk PE32 1SF
www.biddles.co.uk

JHS Books is a non-profit publisher.
A donation of £5 per book purchased will be made
to your nominated registered Charity or your church
who support men, women and children in the world
who are in desparate need of help.

# The
# Questions
## Within

J O H N   S A H L

# CONTENTS

# Foreword

"I met John nearly 30 years ago in a business context in the City of London. Gradually over the following years I came to know him as a person and as a friend. He is an unusual man in many ways: very thoughtful, quietly and invisibly generous in the extreme with all that he is and has to offer, gentle but courageous beyond the norm, happy not to be in the limelight and with an integrity that shines brightly.

John writes in *The Questions Within* on some of the topics on which anyone worth their salt will want to spend a lifetime reflecting. Socrates it was, or so Plato tells us, who said that an unexamined life is not worth living and yet we seem to be surrounded today by an indifference, a passivity, a complacency, a shallowness, a carelessness even, that is hard to find so embedded in other times and generations. Even the youth, so full of the passion and the fury that is theirs by right, do not seem to want to address the real issues we face on this earth. A surprisingly militant secularism has spread very rapidly across our land these last few decades, with cheer leaders who, in the main, have taken it that Jesus Christ was no more than a good but deluded man at best. They might well be encouraged to read this book. It is simple, straight-forward and exudes a joy and an earnest desire to see others come to a Christian faith, that can only come from a place of deep experience of the transformative power of Jesus.

St Francis of Assisi once said that 'learning is not even knowledge because facts have to be experienced to be known whereas love can teach in an instant what a hundred volumes cannot'. If the Enlightenment could really be so-named, we would live in a world very different to the dark and sombre one that threatens our very existence in these days. Yet, the pages of this book describe a love for his fellow man, an understanding of the human condition. Above all, they proclaim a Hope which can but be very attractive: that there is a God of love and a God of justice by Whom all our actions will one day be weighed and Who has made a pathway to eternity with Him that is open to anyone who chooses it.

Here is a man you can trust: he has no axe to grind; he is, as he says himself, approaching the end of a long life; he does not need to prove anything to anyone. I recommend  John's meditations to you unreservedly".

**James Odgers**
Founder
The Besom

# Introduction

"If God is the creator of the world
and loves everyone, how do you explain
pain and suffering?"

That is a good question. How do we answer other basic questions or objections to belief and practice of the Christian life in following Jesus Christ?

That opening Question relates to one of seven subjects in this book for which I attempt to give some guidance, explanation and thoughts for you to consider. This is not a scholar's book for we have hundreds, if not thousands, of those already available, often giving somewhat complex answers to questions which Jesus dealt with in simple terms.

Complexity was not a feature of Christ's teaching as He preached the 'Good News' of the Gospel. When 3000 people committed their lives to following Christ on one day after His resurrection (Acts 2 v.41), loving God, each other and their neighbours, it was not because they had all gained a scholar's degree in theology.

There are, however, many great Christian authors who have contributed so much to my own understanding, beliefs and trust in the faith we share and to whom I owe a great debt. You will find relevant quotations from them as you read through the book.

This book is non-denominational. I write simply as a Christian trying to follow Jesus who offers us truth, forgiveness, hope and a love that has the power to change our lives forever.

 ## Acknowledgements

There are some friends who have been kind enough to give me the benefit of their advice in regards to the writing of this book, principally Martin & Maire S., Alison M., Jeni G-S., Rachel S., Peter S., Laura P., Chris E., Godfrey S.,  Jane W. and Cathy F.

Thank you all so much.

The book design by janie louise hunt has been of immeasurable value to me, a collaboration in every aspect and for which I cannot express enough thanks.

My very grateful thanks to my family for their love, encouragement, support and understanding during the four years of research and writing I took to complete this book.

"…learning is not even knowledge because facts have **to be experienced** to be known, whereas **love can teach** in an instant what a hundred volumes cannot."

ST FRANCIS OF ASSISI

# 1. Which Love Makes the Real Difference to Life?

"Many years ago, when I worked as a volunteer at a hospital, I got to know a little girl named Liz who was suffering from a rare & serious disease. Her only chance of recovery appeared to be a blood transfusion from her 5-year old brother, who had miraculously survived the same disease and had developed the antibodies needed to combat the illness. The doctor explained the situation to her little brother, and asked the little boy if he would be willing to give his blood to his sister.

I saw him hesitate for only a moment before taking a deep breath and saying, "Yes I'll do it if it will save her." As the transfusion progressed, he lay in bed next to his sister and smiled, as we all did, seeing the color returning to her cheeks. Then his face grew pale and his smile faded. He looked up at the doctor and asked with a trembling voice, "Will I die right away, or how soon?" (1)

True love can be measured by what we are prepared to sacrifice for the people we love. This small five-year old boy thought the doctor had meant that he would lose his life in order to save his sister from dying and he was willing to do that for her. I read that story quite by chance on the internet and found it both moving and humbling.

If someone asked you to define the word 'love', what response might you make? What love would the questioner be referring to? Love for your wife, husband or children, for your parents, other family members, close friends or, perhaps, God. Unfortunately, we use only one word in English to express – 'love' - and it is frequently used quite indiscriminately to cover a variety of relationships with people, animals, nature and even material possessions, like homes and cars. To illustrate how the word 'love' can be devalued, my purchase of waste-bin liners featured the command, 'Don't Waste Love'.

The Greeks do not have this problem for they have four words to express different kinds of love. 'Agape' is first and foremost because it denotes a pure love specially related to the love of God.

Then for immediate family love they use the word 'Storge' and for important friendships 'Phileo' is most appropriate. Last, but not least, is the word 'Eros' which refers to romantic love including sexual relationship.

These are all serious human relationships which require commitments to one another but 'Eros' is the only word which includes a sexual union. What society has done is to reduce the meaning of 'Eros' to just a physical event and so 'having sex with someone', is referred to as 'making love' when it is often simply sexual lust with no 'love' commitment on either side between the couple concerned. Indeed, we introduced a new phrase to cover some of this behaviour, namely, 'one-night stands'.

Some children are growing up with little sense of what true love means and the commitments it involves, with casual sex being promoted and portrayed through films, plays, magazines and television productions as one of the key experiences in life. In 2015 I saw posters in hospitals advertising free contraceptives to anyone aged between 13 and 21 years. What message does that give to school children who see the posters?

Even more sophisticated means of contraception and if that fails, abortion, effectively on demand, have largely removed the fear of unwanted pregnancies.

But where has this supposed sexual freedom led us? In recent years the NHS has reported abortion levels of more than 180,000 children per year in England & Wales. There are five legal 'grounds' on which an abortion can be authorised by two registered medical practitioners. "In 2013 the vast majority (97% 180,680) of abortions were undertaken on ground 'C' condition which states: "the pregnancy has not exceeded its twenty-fourth week and that the continuance of the pregnancy would involve risk, greater than if the pregnancy were terminated, of injury to the physical or mental health of the pregnant woman (section 1(1)(a)). About four-fifths (81%) of abortions in 2013 were carried out for single women, a proportion that has risen slowly from 76% since 2003." [2]

The decline in sexual morality has been reflected in the decline of fully committed loving relationships. The Daily Telegraph featured a report on the reality of the problems produced by side-lining traditional marriage as the basic foundation for family life:

"Couples who marry before having children are nearly twice as likely to stay together as those who do so after, research claims. Other factors often linked to family stability, such as parents' ages or their level of education, had only a "marginal", if any, effect on their chances of staying together, the study by the Marriage Foundation think tank concluded.

The research also suggested that those who started families but never wed were almost three times as likely to separate from their partners by the time their first child was 14 or 15 than those who married before child-rearing. Sir Paul Coleridge, the former High Court family judge who set up the foundation in 2012, said the study showed that it was a "myth" that cohabitation was as stable as marriage". [3]

The effect of public acceptance of this myth has also affected the re-action of many married couples who run into trouble. Divorce rates in recent years have declined from the previous peak earlier this century, but the UK still has the highest rate of divorce in Europe, despite the increasing trend of civil partnerships and the reducing trend of marriages.

The extent of our love for anyone can best be measured by what we are prepared to sacrifice for them. Nowhere is this more apparent than in most parent relationships with their own children. Protecting, caring, educating and encouraging their children are first requirements of loving their children, whatever sacrifices that love may demand.

Like all true love for others this springs from people's hearts which is where committed love flows from.

I have a distant memory of a 'news' story about a terrorist who walked into a crowded Middle-Eastern restaurant one lunchtime and threw a hand grenade on to the small dance floor in the centre of the dining room surrounded by dining tables. In the few seconds before it exploded, two fathers rushed from their near-by tables and hurled themselves over the grenade. They paid the ultimate sacrifice endeavouring to protect their families.

But, loving relationships and self-sacrifice are not the hallmark of every family. We know from the media that there are many families living with substantial personal problems for individual members and without committed love for each other.

For children who need love, affection and protection, most of all from their families, the effect can be nothing short of disastrous. Is it any wonder that some children living without the love they need from their parents question why they were born in the first place. Even worse is the terrible effect on children who have suffered any type of abuse in their homes.

The homes where families care for one another, who share both joy and sadness, riches or poverty, success and failure can only do so because they truly love and respect each other. Children who have lacked this committed love from their parents, siblings and other family members often suffer severe long term damage. They can suffer loss of confidence in themselves and lack of trust in other people extending into their adult lives. When affected in this way they can easily become depressed and insular as they look at their future wondering what they are going to do in life and how other people will be treating them. They observe a world which is full of the greed by those who have too much already – not just millionaires, but billionaires – and on the other side, families and many others who are unable to pay for the basic necessities of life.

At a Christian house party in the 'nineties', the late

Sylvia-Mary Alison, a founder of Prison Fellowship, gave a talk about their work. She reported that the majority of prisoners were under 25 years of age and most of them had never experienced genuine love from anyone.

This was confirmed more recently by one prisoner who wrote, "It would be easy to shut myself away and not have anything to do with the outside world, but I know it is important for me to have communication. I never knew what family was when I was growing up and I never learnt how to love." [4]

It was also interesting to learn from their website that prisoners who were visited by family and friends during their time in prison were 25% less likely to re-offend than the prisoners who received no such support. Once again, love points the way.

In other areas of life, relationship counselling is not only available but can be very helpful in offering people support and advice on how to deal with breakdowns in personal relationships. 'How could this friend not love me anymore after all we have meant to each other?' might be the question.

But, if the 'friend' who had broken the relationship was asked how it happened, he or she would usually have no difficulty in providing reasons to justify their decision. It seems self-evident that most human love is conditional upon required responses to the demands made upon each other. Since we are all self-centred to some degree and generally want our own way, it becomes clear from our personal and observed experience of relationships that we are seemingly unable and unwilling to provide that love which is without any limits even to our dearest loved ones, not least when their behaviour in thought, word or deed is unacceptable to us. Forgiveness is not always a first thought in our minds for anyone whom we feel has hurt us and so we fail to offer that love which is sacrificial.

All of us build up our own lives based on a variety of attitudes towards different aspects of life which we acquire over the years. We might think our close friends will support our views, but they do not always do so. But, disagreement with our view need not signify any reduction in their love or affection, but a reflection that their boundaries and experience are different to our own. Their own character profile may also require time and deep thought, or even hesitation, if we are proposing something considered 'new or different' by them, before reaching the support or decision we would like from them.

If we accept everyone is selfish to some degree then people will endeavour to protect their own position and reputation, as a priority, before giving their consent to any proposal.

Although self-interest is part of our nature, it is often

the case that we cannot understand why other people, including close friends and relations, do not see 'things' the way we do or agree the actions we think should be taken in a particular situation.

They are not necessarily being deliberately difficult to agree to our way of thinking or action. They may be simply expressing their views on the particular subject in accordance with their own thinking and, perhaps, practical experience of similar situations they have encountered.

But there is also another side of the coin. How often do we get requests to do this or that, to help or support someone or something which in our heart of hearts we do not wish to do. Nevertheless, we often do agree to the requests because we feel that any refusal will prejudice our relationships with the people concerned and, perhaps, reported to others.

This last point is important for some very generous people who seemingly can never say, 'No, sorry', when asked to help and who, in consequence, can wear themselves out. 'Why do they always ask me?' they complain, to which the honest answer might be 'Because you never refuse'. Taking advantage of such volunteers when things need to be done is quite common because they, themselves, have not set any limits to the help they are willing to give. If that is the case, perhaps it will be difficult for them to understand why other people have set limits to the help they are prepared to offer.

Many of us have heard of people sometimes complaining about the demands made upon them, even by their own family members. They are asked because the requests are unlikely to be refused because of the love they have for one another. If people do not know where our boundaries are, that is our fault, not theirs. Or is it? Some of us don't feel they have a right to say no, or it maybe fear of rejection. It is not about fault but learning, coming to terms with the understanding that we can and are allowed to say no. That fear of rejection is an ultimate human trait, part of our fragile human nature.

Everyone would like to be loved unconditionally, of course, but that seems unlikely in the great majority of our human relationships. But there are men and women down the years who have demonstrated their total commitment to love others, whatever the cost to themselves, sometimes their own lives.

How does one explain this? We sometimes call these people 'saints' indicating they are not ordinary people like us and that is true. These saints are generally people who have utmost trust and belief in God's love for us all which they express in their own lives.

The problem is we usually take more notice of the love people can offer us than God's love which is unsurprising if people do not believe in God – but, perhaps, surprising if they do. The love we share with others is nearly always conditional upon some return of that love in a form we expect.

God gives us something far more than even the closest human relationship we can probably experience. He does not give us a list of requirements to satisfy him before he loves us. He already does, whatever we think, say or do. What God wants is our free-will offering of love for him and obedience to his commands.

When Jesus Christ was asked which commandment was the greatest in the Law, He answered, "Love the Lord your God with all your heart and with all your soul and with all your mind(...)Love your neighbour as yourself".[5] What a difference it would make to our lives if everyone tried to love each other. If only....!

But, there seems to be little likelihood that this will happen any time soon for evil is, and always has been, a dominant force in the world since humanity began. As John, the Apostle, wrote to his own Christian community towards the end of the first century: "We know we are children of God and that the whole world is under the control of the evil one." [6].

He was, of course, confirming what Jesus had said those many years before, that all manner of bad times people had experienced in the past would continue. We would not be free from wars, hunger, persecution or any other of the miseries people have suffered throughout history and, above all, man's sin against his own kind.

In countries such as nominally Christian England and America, slavery was practiced up to the 19th Century as one example, and slavery in other forms is still practiced around the world in our own time.

People of evil intent have often hidden behind the false cloak of a faith in God or as a member of a particular religion in order to perpetrate their crimes against their fellow men, women and children. Why, after all these centuries, can some women still be treated as second-class citizens and of little value except as servants to man's will? How can people misuse or abuse children for their own gain or advantage?

Personal power can be a corrupting influence on any life, but a person's standing in society or public life does not finally rest on what they have said, written or done, but on what character they have shown. After the end of life,

> "Your friends, if they can, may bury you with some distinction and set up a monument(...)and when that is done, all is done. Your place is filled up by another"[7],

but tangible expression of a person's love for others will be remembered. Is that not the reason why the nation poured out so much heartfelt emotion when Princess Diana died? True love is our most important human emotion and when expressed and received it makes a real difference to our lives, whatever our circumstances.

Reading about the encounters Jesus Christ made in the Bible, one cannot be other than amazed at the different kinds of people he met and loved and the compassion he expressed for those people whom we would probably consider disreputable, such as a prostitute or a thieving tax collector.

He met and often healed some of the people who were ignored or banned within their own communities like the lepers and individuals who were blind or beggars and a woman who had suffered from constant 'bleeding' for years. His love and practical support for them changed their lives and gave an example of loving care for others to follow.

Whether people were rich or poor was of no consequence to him – he loved them all, as in the case of the rich young ruler who stated he kept all God's commandments, but could not accept Christ's request to sell his possessions, give them to the poor and follow him.

Jesus was fiercely opposed to hypocrisy, deception, violations against the poorest and those in authority who were exploiting their power for personal gain. Not many unbiased historians are likely to deny that Jesus Christ is the most influential person who has ever lived. It was estimated in 2010 that more than 30% of the world's population claimed to be Christians. Jesus was not, and never aspired to be, a king or ruler on earth, but his life, example and teaching has changed the world. He had a servant heart, totally concerned for the well-being of all people, expressing God's love and forgiveness for all who would turn away from their sins. His teaching and example showed us how to express our love for God and for other people who are in need.

If we are to follow Christ and understand 'the real meaning of love' many of us, as individuals, and many churches, may need to consider changes to some of the priorities in life. It is vital to God's kingdom that all Christians continually demonstrate their love and commitment in practical terms to the poor, the sick, the disadvantaged, the homeless, the unemployed, victims of war, violence, persecution and for many others in the world whose suffering is so great. Jesus was crystal clear in his illustration of what was required of his followers – the people called out by God – when he related his parable about the sheep (the saved), and the goats (the damned), in Matthew's gospel:

"When the Son of Man comes in his glory(....) All the nations will be gathered before him and he will separate the people one from another as a shepherd separates the sheep from the goats. He will put the sheep on his right and the goats on his left. Then the King will say to those on his right, 'Come you who are blessed by my Father; take your inheritance(.....) For I was hungry and you gave me something to eat, I was thirsty and you gave me something to drink, I was a stranger and you invited me in, I needed clothes and you clothed me, I was sick and you looked after me, I was in prison and you came to visit me.

Then the righteous will answer him, 'Lord, when did we see you hungry and feed you, or thirsty and give you something to drink? When did we see you a stranger and invite you in, or needing clothes and clothe you?

When did we see you ill or in prison and go to visit you? The King will reply, 'Truly I tell you, whatever you did for one of the least of these brothers and sisters of mine, you did for me.'(....)

Then he will say to those on his left, 'Depart from me, you who are cursed'(....) Truly I tell you, whatever you did not do for one of the least of these, you did not do for me'"[8].

The lack of emphasis on the need for all Christians to recognise and support Christ's command to look after those in need has been a problem over the centuries. It is one of the problems of man-made organisations. For nearly three hundred years after Jesus died, Christians had no churches and little organisation, but these early followers of Christ were empowered by the Holy Spirit to preach the good news of Jesus Christ, salvation and helping those in need.

Elders, who were experienced, knowledgeable and faithful followers of Christ were appointed in their small groups to nurture new converts and to provide teaching, support and encouragement to all Christ's followers. But the common problem for successful and expanding organisations is man's ambition and desire to control everything and everybody. When Jesus lived the Jews had more than 600 rules and regulations for their brethren to follow. Christianity was about to experience the same fate.

The Christians had been so successful in carrying out Christ's command to preach the gospel everywhere they went that the Roman Emperor, Constantine, decided to convert Christianity into a State religion. He was a worshiper of the pagan Gods, which he did not abandon, and brought into Christianity many of the pagan traditions such as paid clergy, choirs, processions and church buildings. [9]

For Christians at the time, this adoption of their faith by the Roman Emperor must have been considered a huge blessing. Persecution of Christians had been prevalent and bloody under some of the former Emperors and now they were free of that danger and free to tell many more people about Jesus and their faith.

But, they little realized how state sponsorship of their faith would change the practice of Christianity in the future. Up to that time, Christians would be paying their taxes to Rome and sharing their care, money and goods with those in real need. Today, we pay taxes, but we are also able to give to Charities of all descriptions to help those who are suffering greatly. There are thousands of good 'causes', not only for those in our country, but all over the world, many of which Christians support with donations, goods and services as well as giving to their denominational church. Getting the individual balance right between these two demands can be difficult, not least when many churches are suffering declining numbers often resulting in reduced income, whereas overheads can remain high. As a result, it may not be possible to give more than 10% - 20% of their church income to those who are suffering.

The possible dilemma for some Christians is that they might reasonably expect any Charity to be using at least 80% of the donations they receive for the benefit of those they are supporting. Not all Charities achieve that percentage. However, their accounts can be easily checked on 'The Charity Commission' website showing details of their income, expenditure and giving for the last 5 years and how much they consider their necessary cash reserves should be for their work and future projects.

In a world where millions of adults and children are suffering from malnutrition, disease, inadequate water supplies, homelessness, persecution and many other afflictions, Christians need to be showing God's love in their giving and service to those in need. Our loving 'service' in supporting and caring for people who are suffering illness, mental or physical disabilities, unemployment and bereavement, to name just a few more adverse human conditions, is also our Christian responsibility.

But no one is suggesting expression of that love and care for those who are suffering is always easy. For example, in terms of supporting and caring, many people are concerned they will not be able to speak the 'right words' to the suffering people they know and to whom they wish to show their love and support. Nowhere is this more evident than when we are speaking to a friend who is in mourning for the loss of a loved one. I remember one young friend and mother telling me that after her husband committed suicide some of her friends would actually cross the road in order to avoid speaking to her. When she decided one day to cross the road herself to ask why this particular close friend was avoiding her, the friend replied that she simply did not know what to say to her.

We do not necessarily need to say very much when trying to support someone who has lost a loved one, still less to talk about one of our own bereavement periods in life. This can be very unhelpful to the person whose sad heart and mind is naturally concentrating on their own immediate loss. Nor is the bereaved person necessarily looking for immediate advice on how to deal with their loss or what to do or to plan for the future.

Silence is not to be confused with indifference. I think it was the deaf composer, Beethoven, who visited a bereaved widow friend with little or no ability to converse with her. Instead, he simply went to her piano and played some beautiful music expressing his loving concern and grief for her.

Jesus never asked his followers to create yet another 'religion' – he asked them, as he asks us, to follow him, to be his disciples, or rather his 'students', which I understand is the correct translation of the Greek word. We may not entirely succeed, but surely we should be trying to follow his example as countless people have done in every century since then, demonstrating God's love through their selfless love and service for people who needed meaningful help and support.

"Strangely, perhaps, it is the very focus upon Jesus Christ that naturally leads his followers into the world of God beyond religions. That is where the only justifiable pluralism is to be found. Beyond religion! What this Christian pluralism says is that, because God is who

Jesus Christ shows him to be, any person who in God's eyes it seems right for him to accept certainly will be accepted by Him(.....)Christian pluralism thus concedes that people of 'other' religions or no religion at all may be 'right with God'.(....)It will not be because of their religion.

Rather, it will be because their lives are centred on that same love that is expressed in the person and teachings of Jesus and of his people at their best. It will be because God is love". (10)

Jesus had no hesitation in condemning evil wherever it existed, but his key message to everyone was his love, God's love, for every person whatever they might have done and wherever they might be in life's journey. No one is barred from that love – not even the worst sinner, providing he or she is prepared to repent, i.e. to change their ways.

People generally realize that being positive and joyful or feeling down at heart does not depend on what we know or do not know, what we have or do not have, but on whether we love, and on whether we are loved. But, loving unreservedly, no matter what the outcome, is challenging.

I share this struggle. Perhaps you do as well. But I think Paul, the Apostle, was right when he wrote to the first Christians in Corinth: "No matter what I say, what

I believe, and what I do, I'm bankrupt without love". [11] The late, beloved Christian evangelist and leader, John Stott, listed in Time Magazine's "100 Most Influential People" in April, 2005, beautifully describes why this kind of love is the most important requirement in our lives:

> "God is love in his essential being, and has revealed his love in the gift of his Son to live and die for us. Now he calls us to be a community of love, loving each other in the intimacy of his family - especially across the barriers of age and sex, race and rank - and loving the world he loves in its alienation, hunger, poverty and pain. It is through the quality of our loving that God makes himself visible today". [12]

How well, I wonder, are we doing that? God's love is the love that makes the real difference to our own lives and to other people's lives as we express it to them.

"…the most beautiful

thing that man can do,

is to *forgive* a wrong."

ELEAZAR OF WORMS IN 13TH CENTURY GERMANY – A JEWISH RABBI

# 2. Do we Need to Forgive?

I was a young child during the Second World War, but I recall the absolute horror of it all. In the area in which we lived at the time we never suffered bombing raids as such. But towards the end of the war, I still remember seeing the German V1 guided missile bombs in the skies before their engines ceased. They fell indiscriminately on helpless men, women and children with devastating effect and loss of life.

Then, after the war, we were exposed through news-reels in cinemas to the nightmare images of hundreds of emaciated dead bodies lying on the ground in Nazi concentration camps. On the Allied side, UK and US bombers dropped thousands of tons of high-explosive bombs and incendiaries on Dresden in Germany in February 1945, destroying the city and killing many thousands of civilians and children. The carnage was so great that the British Prime Minister, Winston Churchill, denounced such bombing of cities as "mere acts of terror and wanton destruction", but later withdrew the remark. These are but two examples of the trauma, loss and cruelty suffered by people in so many nations during World War 2.

For many people 'forgiveness' for those who had carried out all the war atrocities was never even considered. Corrie ten Boom was a Dutch woman who, with her family, risked their lives in order to help persecuted Jews escape occupied Holland. Corrie and her sister were eventually caught and sent to a concentration camp where they suffered greatly and where her dear sister, Betsie, died. She writes movingly of one post-war experience:

"I traveled all over Holland, to other parts of Europe, to the United States. But the place where the hunger was greatest was Germany. Germany was a land in ruins, cities of ashes and rubble, but more terrifying still, minds and hearts of ashes. Just to cross the border was to feel the great weight that hung over that land. It was at a church service in Munich that I saw him, the former S.S. man who had stood guard at the shower room door in the processing centre at Ravensbruck.

He was the first of our actual jailers that I had seen since that time. And suddenly it was all there—the roomful of mocking men, the heaps of clothing, Betsie's pain-blanched face.

He came up to me as the church was emptying, beaming and bowing. 'How grateful I am for your message, Fraulein.' he said. 'To think that, as you say, He has washed my sins away!' His hand was thrust out to shake mine.

And I, who had preached so often to the people in Bloemendaal the need to forgive, kept my hand at my side.

Even as the angry, vengeful thoughts boiled through me, I saw the sin of them. Jesus Christ had died for this man; was I going to ask for more? Lord Jesus, I prayed, forgive me and help me to forgive him. I tried to smile, I struggled to raise my hand. I could not. I felt nothing, not the slightest spark of warmth or charity. And so again I breathed a silent prayer. Jesus, I cannot forgive him. Give me Your forgiveness. As I took his hand the most incredible thing happened. From my shoulder along my arm and through my hand a current seemed to pass from me to him, while into my heart sprang a love for this stranger that almost overwhelmed me.

And so I discovered that it is not on our forgiveness any more than on our goodness that the world's healing hinges, but on His. When He tells us to love our enemies, He gives, along with the command, the love itself."[1]

I find it quite amazing that Corrie could offer her hand of acceptance to this guard who had played his part in the suffering she had endured and the death of Betsie. I would have no confidence in my own ability to do the same in a similar situation. You may agree that Corrie's act of forgiveness for this man is against all natural instincts, but the results of her response both for the man and herself were quite wonderful. For the ex-guard who expressed his gratitude for Corrie's message of forgiveness, the weight on his conscience for his past cruelties to prisoners must have been terrible to bear and he is overjoyed that he has found forgiveness for those sins.

But what of Corrie – not least in that time between the man holding out his hand to her and she refusing to take it as she felt again the pain of her sister's death and her own suffering in that concentration camp?

She could not forgive the man in her heart in those moments. Few of us would have blamed her, but Corrie, in her trauma, still had the belief that it is not for her to judge this man and so she prays to Jesus to give his forgiveness through her, for she knows that Jesus died for this man and every other repentant man or woman to cover their sins. She beautifully expresses how she felt as she took his hand knowing her prayers had been answered.

It is difficult enough for most of us to forgive others who have offended us in any way – even small offences – and that difficulty usually grows with the severity of the sin against us. "I will never speak to her again"; "He has ruined my life," are examples of what we may say in the heat of the moment, but too often, people mean what they say. Family feuds can be maintained for years and what of 'sector' divides where leaders claim religious or nationalistic grounds for indiscriminate condemnation of everyone who opposes their views or beliefs.

This necessity to forgive others for the pain or suffering they may have caused is a problem for many people, not least for those who still bear the scars and deep memories of betrayal of love or abuse. I remember hearing the story of one lady who felt her life had been ruined by a trusted friend's actions. Many years later she still harboured her anger for this person and her own well-being was suffering to the point where she was advised to get some Christian counselling in order to deal with her very negative view of life and herself.

Towards the end of her sessions she told the counsellor about her terrible experience with this ex-friend and she was advised not only to forgive the friend, but to tell her. So she wrote a letter offering her forgiveness, but many days passed because she could not find it in her heart to post it. She told of the day much later on when she walked up to the post box and hesitantly placed her letter inside. As she did so, she felt a wave of positive emotion run through her body and she, herself, was subsequently healed.

It is important to recall Christ's warning to those who accept God's forgiveness for themselves but refuse to forgive those who have wronged them. In Matthew's gospel Jesus tells the story of the Unmerciful Servant, who fits that profile. His Master says to him:

> "You wicked servant," he said, "I cancelled all that debt of yours because you begged me to. Shouldn't you have had mercy on your fellow servant just as I had on you?" In anger his Master turned him over to the jailers to be tortured, until he should pay back all he owed. This is how my heavenly Father will treat each of you unless you forgive your brother from your heart." (2)

We sinners need to receive forgiveness for our wrongs, even though we may try to hide or forget what has been said or done, and Jesus gave advice for this when he said:

> "Therefore, if you are offering your gift at the altar and there remember that your brother has something against you, leave your gift there in front of the altar. First go and be reconciled to your brother; then come and offer your gift."(3)

Jesus Christ was also quite clear about our personal responsibilities when he said:

> "But I tell you, love your enemies and pray for those who persecute you, that you may be children of your Father in heaven. He causes his

sun to rise on the evil and the good, and sends rain on the righteous and the unrighteous. If you love those who love you, what reward will you get? Are not even the tax collectors doing that? And if you greet only your own people, what are you doing more than others? [4]

And Jesus also says,

"Do not judge, or you too will be judged. For in the same way as you judge others, you will be judged and with the measure you use, it will be measured to you."[5]

What does all this mean? Corrie knew what it meant at a very deep level, deeper than most of us would experience in a lifetime. We need to extend genuine love for everyone regardless of their faults or misdemeanors. That love does not condone evil at any level or in any form and it is right to condemn all such acts. But Jesus makes the essential point that this does not give us the right to judge or condemn the person who sinned. The two requisites for us to show those who have sinned against us are forgiveness and love which may help to encourage their willingness to change their behaviour towards others. Why?

It is because forgiveness is the most important signal we can show that we are offering our unconditional love. For people who may never have experienced much love or forgiveness, if any, the impact can be of enormous value to them. For some people this seems too much to ask of them when the hurt they have received has been so great, but in those cases it may be that they think that forgiving someone means the same thing as forgetting the offence ever happened. Not even Jesus indicated 'forgetting' was required and it is rarely possible to achieve. The distinction between forgiving and forgetting is an important one. Most people will have difficulty in forgetting the harm they have suffered through another's actions – perhaps they never will! It is not possible to wipe out the memory of our bad experiences in life in the same way that you can 'delete' and forget an item on a computer.

Our natural emotions so easily take over our minds when we are hurt because we all live 'in the moment' – the only time we can live. The past has gone and the future is yet to come. We cannot live in either the past or the future – only the here and now. The result is that anger, revenge, resentment or at worst, hate, may thrust themselves forward as responses to the damage we have suffered, mentally, physically or both. If these emotional re-actions are not rejected, then any thoughts of forgiveness will automatically be cast aside.

One of the major reasons why these confusions exist is because we fail to distinguish between sinful acts which should be condemned and the sinners to whom we should show love and the possibility that there is another way to live, which includes love for our neighbour in its broadest sense. For most non-believers, Christ's command to 'love our enemies' is often beyond reason since many believe it runs counter to every natural instinct for self-preservation and security.

Generally, at national level, any potential or actual threat to safety or security is met by an equal threat of retaliation to the aggressor. And it cannot be said that many national leaders of countries, known as 'Christian', have been less aggressive in their pursuit of territory, power and riches over the centuries, even fighting each other with both sides claiming 'God on their side'. Of course, it was always a false claim, but believable by many. Where was forgiveness after the First World War? Was not the treatment of post-war Germany one of the causes leading to the Second World War? Forgiveness can be denied so easily and love so hard to find at every level of society and in every nation.

And what of our own sinful acts whether major or minor? Apologising for our mistakes or for causing harm in some way to other people is difficult for most of us. There is our pride, sometimes our authority and usually our self-image at stake when we admit we have been wrong in thought, word or deed. To counteract this, good reasons, and blaming others, are often given in response for our offences, but are they 'good reasons' or just excuses to minimise the possible damage to our perceived reputation?

Yet, we know most people will see through that defence. Why should we have this difficulty in admitting faults of any kind and saying 'sorry' for, in general experience, we know genuine apologies are seldom refused and usually accepted with goodwill, sometimes even understanding, by those we may have wronged?

Henri Nouwen was a Dutch priest who left his renowned academic life to look after people with mental disabilities at the L'Arche Community in Toronto. He also wrote many books. One of his great books is entitled, 'The Return of the Prodigal Son'.

The book cover depicts the painting by Rembrandt in c.1667 based on the bible story Jesus told of the self-centred younger son who persuaded his loving, rich Father to give him his future inheritance, then left home and squandered everything in loose living leading eventually to his own imminent starvation.

His only option is to return to his Father's house, where he hopes to express his regret to his Father for his wrong doing and subsequently be able to earn his keep as a worker, if not as a disgraced son. His Father sees his son coming from afar and rushes out to welcome him home, blessing him and later organising a banquet to celebrate his return. But, what of his elder brother's feelings when he comes home to find this party going on? Jesus continues the story:

"Meanwhile the older son was in the field. When he came near the house, he heard music and dancing. So he called one of the servants and asked him what was going on. 'Your brother has come', he replied, 'and your father has killed the fattened calf because he has him back safe and sound. The elder brother became angry and refused to go in. So his father went out and pleaded with him.

But he answered his father, 'Look! All these years I've been slaving for you and never disobeyed your orders." Yet you never gave me even a young goat so I could celebrate with my friends. But when this son of yours who has squandered your property with prostitutes comes home, you kill the fattened calf for him!

'My son', the father said, 'you are always with me, and everything I have is yours. But we had to celebrate and be glad, because this brother of yours was dead and is alive again; he was lost and is found." (6)

How many of us would have sided with the older son who had been loyal, obedient, and hard-working all his life and received no recognition from his father remotely like the banquet his errant brother was receiving. But his father was right wasn't he? The faithful older brother would inherit all that the father owned and was clearly loved.

The parable of the 'Prodigal Son' is one of the most

poignant stories Jesus told. He is telling us, in the parable, how much God, the Father, loves us whatever we may have thought, said or done, if we love him and truly repent of our sins. Many people think that 'repenting' means being sorry for what we have said or done. This is important, but only the first stage of repentance. The word 'repent' means that we need to change our attitude and behaviour in contrast to our previous sinful ways. If we are not prepared to do so, what is our regret really worth? It is, perhaps, analogous to a thief stealing an item, then apologising to the owner, but keeping the stolen goods and continuing to steal.

When some Pharisees, teachers of the law, who were seeking to lay a trap in some way for Jesus to fall into, they brought a woman into the Temple courts who had been caught in the act of adultery for which the Jewish penalty was to stone to death both the woman and the (absent) man, according to Moses law. But, that was not their first objective:

> "Teacher, this woman was caught in the act of adultery. In the law Moses commanded us to stone such women. Now what do you say?" they asked Jesus in relation to what penalty he would call for this sinful woman. They were using this question as a trap, in order to have a basis for accusing him. But Jesus bent down and started to write on the ground with his finger.

When they kept on questioning him, he straightened up and said to them, "Let any one of you who is without sin, be the first to throw a stone at her." At this, those who heard began to go away one at a time, the older ones first, until only Jesus was left, with the woman still standing there. Jesus straightened up and asked her, "Woman, where are they? Has no-one condemned you? No-one, sir," she said. Then neither do I condemn you" Jesus declared. "Go now and leave your life of sin."[7]

If we do repent of our past sins, asking God for forgiveness and with a firm resolve to change our past sinful behaviour, then Jesus is telling us that God, the Father, will forgive us with no record of our offenses being kept by Him. Within my own knowledge, I know of no other faith which defines God as 'love' in the same way and which offers God's complete pardon, if true repentance for sin is made. But, that possibility of free pardon through his act of redemption on the cross is exactly what Jesus taught us.

There are two sides of the coin denoting forgiveness. On one side the all encompassing love and forgiveness of God freely given to each one of us who truly repent of our sins. On the other side, our forgiveness for all who have offended against us. Jesus could not have made this clearer than he did in The Lord's Prayer – 'Forgive us our sins as we have forgiven those who have sinned against us'. One is dependent on the other.

God's good purposes for mankind have been and are continually upheld by ordinary Christian people who demonstrate their faith in so many practical and loving ways to others, who may be family members, friends, neighbours and those in real need. In fact I often think of Jesus looking at our world rejoicing in the fact that so many people on this earth claim to be Christians.

Thank God we know that the most important requirement of Christian faith is our personal relationship with Him. This requires people to follow Jesus through His teaching and commands, being guided by the Spirit and for each one of us to love God and to love other people, forgiving them for any offences against us and sharing our faith with anyone who will listen.

"Therefore, as God's chosen people,
holy and dearly loved,
clothe yourselves with

# compassion,

## kindness,

### humility,

#### gentle patience.

Bear with each other and

## forgive one another

if any of you has a
grievance against someone.

## Forgive as the Lord forgave you." [8]

"What Christians need is

a little **more** of Christ's Christianity,

and a little **less** of man's."

A RELIGIOUS HINDU'S OBSERVATION AFTER VISITING ENGLAND AND AMERICA
IN THE LATE 19TH CENTURY TO EXAMINE CHRISTIANITY

# 3. Why Would You Believe in Jesus Christ?

The 'Spectator' magazine published an article in 2012 written by Matthew Parris which took my interest because it compared the position of the corporate 'church' in his mind with the person of Jesus Christ with these words:

"One of the reasons we can be pretty sure Jesus actually existed is that if He had not, the Church would never have invented Him(...) As an unbeliever my sympathies are with the fundamentalists. They seem to me to represent the source, the roots, the essential energy of their faiths. They go back to basics. To those who truly believe, the implicit message beneath 'never mind if it's true, religion is good for people' is insulting. To those who really believe, it is because and only because what they believe is true, that it is good. I find David Cameron's remark that his faith, 'like Magic FM in the Chilterns, tends to fade in and out', baffling. If a faith is true it must have the most profound consequences for a man and for mankind. If I seriously suspected a faith might be true, I would devote the rest of my life to finding out". [1]

That opinion may be shared by others. But, I wonder why so many people do not want to find out why these millions of people 'believe their faith is true, that it is good'. Why is it that they are not prepared to investigate Christ's claims, his teaching and the evidence for His resurrection from the dead - the latter being the foundation stone of the Christian faith?

One reason may be that they have observed the practices, pronouncements and organisation of the institutional church, together with its failings, a common factor with all man-made organisations, and decided against belonging to the church. But Jesus is the founder and centre of Christianity – not the church. The profound effect Jesus has had on the world in thought, word and deed that we find from the New Testament times of 2000 years ago up to the present time is unequalled. We need to look at who Jesus Christ was - his character; how he lived, what he taught, what responses he made to some serious questions and what actions he took when faced with people who were suffering. And what was Christ's attitude to other areas of life we generally think are important? Jesus has been portrayed in paintings and writings by many artists and authors, but how far are these accurate profiles of the man who changed the world? Here, perhaps, is a more realistic understanding of Christ's character from Rev'd Dr. Alison Morgan:

"Jesus, then, was profoundly at odds with the

world into which he came. Far from being the meek and humble stereotype with a star-spangled, angel-attended and really rather magical stable birth whom we are taught to revere in school, Jesus was a difficult and uncooperative revolutionary who so threatened the established order of the day that there seemed to be no option but to have him executed. By turn irascible, compassionate, exhausted and stubbornly silent, Jesus was(....) abrasive, rude and cuttingly clever when confronted with the religious leaders of the day; he regarded the existing political order as an irrelevance; he paid astonishingly scant attention to the binding nature of the laws of the physical universe; and wherever he went he brought an explosion of light into darkness and a release of people from the unseen powers that had bound them. This is the man who told a rich young ruler to give away all his wealth, and who taught that the kingdom of God would belong to the poor. This is the man who insisted on the importance of giving food, drink and clothing to the destitute; who warned his disciples to lay up treasure in heaven rather than on earth; and who said that if a beggar asks you for your coat, you should give him your shirt as well. This is the man, indeed, who inspired Mother Teresa. And yet it wasn't quite as simple as that. The rich young ruler was told to give away all he had; but Zacchaeus, the dishonest tax collector, was apparently permitted to keep half his considerable capital. The disciples were taught to donate their money to the poor; and yet immediately afterwards a woman who had spent a vast sum on a jar of costly ointment was praised for pouring it over Jesus' head as an act of homage.

Mary, Joanna and Susanna used their wealth to support Jesus and the other disciples, and Joseph of Arimathea provided Jesus' tomb out of his means; there is no suggestion that Jesus had asked them to give away their money.

So whatever it was that he was advocating, it wasn't the restructuring of society on the basis of the simple redistribution of wealth to the poor."[2]

Some people might argue that some of these attitudes appear to be contradictory, but this is not the case. For example, Jesus is emphasizing that we all have an obligation to help those who are in real need. And for those who are well-off, he is more interested in how that wealth is shared with those in need than the riches they possess. Jesus is the most extraordinary person in history. His teaching and his actions sprang from a heart of true love for everyone, rich and poor, good or bad. He spoke to everyone in ways they could understand whether intellectuals or poor working people.

"Where can you find in the teaching of Jesus anything that strikes you as wrong? How do you account for the fact that there have been no moral advances on His teaching from that day to this? How did He get His matchless teaching without ever having been to college? How is it that it fits all people in every culture? What was the unrepeatable factor in His heredity and environment that produced such a remarkable teacher?

Yes, the teaching of Jesus was very special indeed! If you could improve on it you would be on the front page of every major newspaper in the world(.....) The character of Jesus was special. Never has there been a character like His, so humble and yet so strong, so prayerful and yet so down to earth, so peaceful and yet so energetic, so loving without sentimentality, so dynamic without being hearty. Nobody has been able to hold a candle to that matchless life, and nobody has been able to trash it either. Jesus is the only fully balanced person who ever lived. He had no strong points because He had no weak ones. He embodied all the virtues we associate with both men and women and none of the vices. In all the world He has no equal."[3]

Many scholars, authors and historians echo these views.

The foundation for all our lives needs to be 'love' because it will seek to help, in any way we can, the lives of those who are suffering and conduct our lives with others on the basis of fairness and equality taking into account their circumstances, whether good or bad.

We might also refrain from making judgements on other people because we seldom know all the circumstances surrounding the accusations. How did Christ show this love for everyone regardless of their position in life?

"Jesus did not let any institution interfere with his love for individuals. Jewish racial and religious policies forbade him to speak with a Samaritan woman, let alone one with a chequered moral background; Jesus elected one as a missionary. His disciples included a tax collector, viewed as a traitor by Israel, and also a Zealot, a member of the superpatriot party. He praised the counter cultural John the Baptist.

He met with Nicodemus, an observant Pharisee, and also with a Roman centurion. He dined in the home of another Pharisee named Simon and also in the home of an "unclean" man, Simon the Leper. For Jesus, the person was more important than any category or label.

The issues facing society are pivotal, and perhaps

a culture war is inevitable. Jesus declared that we should have one distinguishing mark: not political correctness or moral superiority, but love. Paul added that without love nothing we do— no miracle of faith, no theological brilliance, no flaming personal sacrifice—will avail." [4]

We might agree Jesus gave us very good examples of how we should act in love for other people of all descriptions at all times. But what if we will fail to meet these standards because of our self interest and lack of concern for those in real need? Jesus did not hold back in his judgement on anyone who fails the standards of conduct required in thought, word and deed, when our lives claim to be based on love for God and other people. Without that love the charge of hypocrisy is justified.

Jesus insists that nothing less than love will fulfill our lives and he pointed to some important actions and attitudes resulting from that love when he said:

"Again, you have heard it was said to the people long ago, "Do not break your oath, but fulfill to the Lord the oaths you have made."

"But, I tell you, do not swear an oath at all(...)All you need to say is simply "Yes" or "No"; anything beyond this comes from the evil one."[5]

He is emphasizing that people should be able to rely on

the truth and reliability of our word, without any reservations which will somehow let us off the hook if we should change our minds for any reason. Jesus goes on to say:

> "If anyone slaps you on the right cheek, turn to them the other cheek also.(....) If any one forces you to go one mile, go with them two miles. Give to the one who asks you and do not turn away from the one who wants to borrow from you."[6]

Romans had the right in those days to command any of their subjects to carry their personal bags for one mile in whatever direction they were going. But, Jesus is making the point that when forced to carry out any task, going the 'extra mile' ought to be our normal response, not an exception. He gave many other examples which naturally flow from a heart of love for people, regardless of their actions, demands or circumstances. Following Jesus Christ's ministry to thousands of people, mainly fellow Jews, in towns around the country for three years or so, He knew He had to face the final trial of His life on earth in human terms which would end in his gruesome and horrific execution on a wooden cross.

But, Christ's entry into Jerusalem on a donkey was greeted by crowds of cheering people, some spreading their cloaks before him on the road and shouting, 'Blessed is He who comes in the name of the Lord'. We are told that when He entered Jerusalem, the whole city was stirred. But that welcome did not last very long.

It could not, for as already pointed out, 'Jesus was a difficult and uncooperative revolutionary who so threatened the established order of the day that there seemed to be no option but to have Him executed'.

Many of His actions and parables following His arrival, bear witness to the danger he posed to those in religious authority who quickly sought to have Him arrested and sentenced to death. And so we see an example of the frailty and indecision of people when faced with the choice between good and evil. Self-interest and survival are the order of the day.

There were crowds welcoming Him to the city and only days later, crowds demanding the Roman Governor, Pontius Pilate, to have Jesus executed. Pilate asked the crowd what crime had Christ committed. Their only answer was to shout, 'Crucify Him, crucify Him'. Although Jesus had told His disciples that He would rise from the dead, not one of them seemed to believe it. The only recorded close witnesses to Christ's crucifixion were Mary, His mother, His disciple, John, and the women from Galilee who had followed and cared for Him. Cambridge Professor, John Polkinghorne, in his book "Quantum Physics & Theology" writes:

"On the face of it, the final episode of Jesus'

life had been one of utter failure. If that had been the end of his story, not only would it put in question any claim that he might have had to any special significance, but I believe that it would have made it likely that He, someone who left no personally written legacy, would have disappeared from active historical remembrance in the way that people do who are humiliated by being seen to have had pretensions above the sober reality of their status.

Yet we have all heard of Jesus, and down the subsequent centuries He has proved to be one of the most influential figures in the history of the world. Any adequate account of Him has to be able to explain this remarkable fact. Something must have happened to continue the story of Jesus.

Whatever it was must have been of a magnitude adequate to explain the transformation that came on His followers, changing that bunch of frightened deserters who ran away when he was arrested, into those who would face the authorities in Jerusalem, only a few weeks later, with the confident proclamation that Jesus was God's chosen Lord and Messiah."[7]

Many, if not most, people in the world either believe

or want to believe in some form of life after death. But which 'religion' or faith is likely to be true or do they all point to the same end? The basic fundamental claim for Christianity is Christ's resurrection. Can that be proven beyond reasonable doubt?

We generally decide what is true or false on the evidence provided, and the obvious starting point for verifying the resurrection of Jesus is whether He was dead when taken down from the cross.

There is no evidence, in the history of the first century AD, that anyone questioned the death of Jesus on the cross or the empty tomb and no one was ever expected to survive a Roman crucifixion and nor do any seem to have been reported at that time.

Both the Jewish leaders and the Romans would have done everything possible to find his body in order to nullify Christ's prophesy before He arrived in Jerusalem when He told his disciples:

> "We are going up to Jerusalem, and the Son of Man will be delivered over to the chief priests and teachers of the law. They will condemn Him to death and will hand Him over to the Gentiles to be mocked and flogged and crucified. On the third day he will be raised to life!"[8]

There is other evidence in the Bible pointing to the fact of Christ's resurrection, but let us suppose that the Gospel writers wanted to deceive the world, if Jesus had not died, by lying about His resurrection from the dead. Why would they tell us that women were the first witnesses of the resurrection? In those days women were forbidden in law to give evidence of any kind. Even the disciples did not accept their word without checking the empty tomb for themselves.

And why, if they were perpetrating a lie, would the gospel writers indicate that people did not immediately recognize the resurrected Jesus straight away? Mary Magdalene did not do so, thinking she was talking to the gardener outside His tomb on Easter morning, until Jesus spoke her name. Neither did the disciple, Cleophas and his companion, recognize Jesus as he joined them on their long walk to Emmaus until the evening, when He broke bread with them at supper.

Why would the Apostles write that these friends and others were unable to immediately recognize someone with whom they had been close friends and disciples? Since this evidence does not initially support Christ's resurrection for, 'seeing is believing' and need not have been written about at all, it is almost certainly because it was true. Christ was no longer 'flesh and blood' after his execution, as we normally identify any person, but as Jesus described Himself - "Look at my hands and feet. It is I myself! Touch me and see; a ghost does not have flesh and bones, as you see I have."[9]

The Christian belief is that Christ, who led a perfect life, was God's only son and suffered that dreadful death on the cross to redeem us from our sins. Everyone bears the responsibility for putting Jesus to death. We are all sinners, but His sacrifice is not for the accumulated sin of all people, it is for the redemption of the sins of each and every person whom God accepts.

Some years ago I had an experience which I will never forget. I was thinking about sin and the cost of our redemption suffered by Jesus on that cross for each individual person. Whether in a dream or vision, I do not know, but I was transported in my mind, to Jerusalem on the day of Christ's crucifixion. The whole scene was like the depictions we have seen in films and paintings of Jesus on that day apart from me, wearing a modern shirt and trousers.

But I was not standing in the crowd shouting for His death. The wooden cross was lying on the ground with Jesus bound to it and I was kneeling down hammering a rusty iron nail through Jesus' wrist to the cross. As I finished the ghastly task, I turned to Jesus and he was looking at me. His face was utterly contorted and twisted with pain, but as his eyes met mine I saw they were full of love for me. And I believe they are full of love for everyone, regardless of how one's journey in life has been.

Nothing else so draws people to Jesus as the time when they see and recognize His love for them on the cross. Some years ago I was told of a past Bishop of Paris who related the story during his sermon about three atheist students at university who decided to have a laugh at the expense of any priest in the Cathedral who would hear a false confession from one of them. They drew cards to decide who would confess and also agreed a'bet'.

But the old priest soon recognized this was no genuine confession. However, he continued to listen and at the end he instructed the student to carry out a penance for his 'sins'. The priest told the young man to go to the large carving in the church which depicted Jesus nailed to the cross and said he would have to kneel in front of that cross and say three times, "Jesus, I'm told you died like this, for love of me, but I couldn't care less". When he came out of the confessional, his other two friends insisted that he must do the penance to win the bet and so he went and knelt down in front of this cross and said, "Jesus, I'm told you died like this, for love of me, but I couldn't care less."

After a pause he repeated it a second time. The third time, he looked at the figure on the cross and he found he could say nothing. And the Bishop told the congregation, 'I know this story is true, because I was that young student'.

This spiritual experience for that Bishop was a decisive moment in his younger life and the reason for it was his meeting with Jesus on that cross. Is that type of experience possible for all – even today?

"Yes, it is possible to meet with Christ for ourselves. Sometimes, however, this seems to be one of the 'best-kept secrets' within the Church! All sorts of impressions are given as to what will help people come to faith or what will make them a true Christian'. People are encouraged to read books or study theology, to attend church regularly or do good to their neighbour.

"All of these are indeed strongly to be encouraged! But not one of them actually makes a person into a Christian. They are a means to an end, not the end itself. What makes a person a Christian is, as it was for the disciples, an encounter with the Risen Christ himself". [10]

That quote is important because it points to the fact that our relationship with God is not established by whether or not we attend any church or belong to any particular denomination, but it depends on each person's individual relationship with God through Jesus Christ and the power of the Spirit. This will be clearly expressed in our love for other people. This attitude of love for God and people has been clearly expressed:

"Above all, one has to find by thought and

experience that love can be trusted as a way of life. This can be learned by interaction with Jesus in all ordinary and extraordinary circumstances. He can bring it to pass that we rely on love; and that is why he boldly asserted that the only mark of being his student or apprentice in life was how his students love one another. And it is, again, why one of his best students could say, on the basis of a lifetime of experience: "Everyone who loves is born of God and knows God". (11)

However, even when we are regarded as loving people, our self-will and self-interest can periodically re-assert themselves, especially when our personal circumstances are difficult or under pressure. Our inherent belief that self-preservation is the first law of nature needs no second opportunity to invade our hearts and minds again. The idea of a faith in God and his love bringing joy to life is sometimes beyond comprehension, but it offers this re-assurance to those who sincerely seek the truth:

"For some people the Christian faith may seem very complicated; 'I'll never be able to understand it all!' they say. Others may view themselves in a negative light; 'God would never be interested in me!' they think. But the Good News is that anyone can meet with this Jesus.

No one is 'beyond the pale'. And when people

do so, Jesus automatically takes them right into the very heart of the Christian faith. It all then begins to make sense. Why? Because they themselves know in a personal way the One who is at the very centre of it all - the very one around whom the rest of the Christian faith is built". [12]

This is one of the reasons why arguments between people both for and adamantly against belief in God usually bear little fruit because there is no common ground between the two. The Christian has this personal experience of faith which is not based on some intellectual assessment. The non-believer demands proof for that faith generally knowing that absolute proof would not be possible.

I was told about the time two Christians at a University decided to ask other Undergraduates and Masters if they believed in God or not, and their reasons why in either case. One Master declared he did not believe in God and proceeded to give five reasons for his refusal. One of the students then asked him, 'If I can give you answers to all those reasons why you do not believe in God, would you re-consider?' The Master's response was instantaneous, 'No', he replied, 'because I can give you five more reasons why I do not believe'. He was not, of course, interested in changing his mind at all, whatever the evidence provided. In that respect he represents the disinterest of many people over the generations which is very sad and the partial blame for this must rest with we Christians who have not been prepared, willing or able to share the good news with others, when we may have had the opportunity to do so.

G.A. Studdert Kennedy (1883-1929) wrote this moving poem describing the utter sorrow Jesus must undergo continuously as He watches all the people who still pass Him by without even noticing Him, nor realising His love and sacrifice for them:

## "INDIFFERENCE"

*"When Jesus came to Golgotha*
*They hanged Him on a tree,*
*They drove great nails through hands and feet,*
*and made a Calvary;*
*They crowned Him with a crown of thorns,*
*red were His wounds and deep,*
*For those were crude and cruel days,*
*and human flesh was cheap.*

*When Jesus came to Birmingham*
*they simply passed Him by,*
*They never hurt a hair of Him,*
*they only let Him die;*
*For men had grown more tender,*
*and they would not give Him pain,*
*They only just passed down the street,*
*and left Him in the rain.*

*Still Jesus cried, 'Forgive them,*
*for they know not what they do',*
*And still it rained the wintry rain*
*that drenched Him through and through;*
*The crowds went home and left the streets*
*without a soul to see,*
*And Jesus crouched against a wall*
*and cried for Calvary.* "* [13]

"How can a mother

*trust* and **love** a God

who let her baby die."

PETER KREEFT, PROFESSOR OF PHILOSOPHY IN USA

# 4. How on Earth Does a Loving God Allow Pain and Suffering?

Our 27 year old son, Martin, and his wife, Sue, were staying with us after our Christmas celebrations. It was about 5am in the morning on the 28th December, 1991 when our daughter, Deborah, burst into our bedroom to wake us.

'Come quickly', Debs shouted to us, 'Martin has stopped breathing!' My wife, Margaret, immediately rang for an ambulance whilst I rushed to their bedroom. Sue and I gave Martin artificial respiration, whilst waiting for the ambulance men to arrive, but with no result. They gave him shock treatment, again with no result, before taking him to the hospital where the staff confirmed, as kindly as they could, that Martin had been dead on arrival. The cause had been sudden death resulting from heart failure. Our hearts broke then and will never mend because we loved him so much and still do.

I have related the loss of our dear, truly wonderful son, brother, and loving husband to Sue, because we, as a family, experienced such a tragic loss. We share that suffering and pain with so many others who have experienced the unexpected loss of a loved one. In 2008 I read that in the UK, an average of twelve apparently fit and healthy young adults under age 36 died every week from undiagnosed cardiac conditions – often referred to as 'sudden death syndrome'.

We all have to die from some cause which may strike at any time in our lives from the moment we are born. I doubt many elderly people would like to live forever on this earth as the years take their toll, for pain, disabilities and suffering are always difficult to deal with, to understand and to accept. 'Why has this happened to me?' is a common cry from the heart when someone is unexpectedly faced with a serious illness or accident.

Pain and suffering are often naturally linked together as meaning the same thing – but, in fact, they are not. When we talk about suffering it is generally true we associate pain with whatever our condition is, but pain related to our physical body is also a necessity. Many more people would be seriously at risk of premature death if we did not experience pain.

It is built into the structure of our bodies to act as a warning signal that something is wrong. For example, you feel an acute, perhaps spasmodic pain in the pit of your stomach, attend your doctor who sends you to hospital to have an appendix removed and you are well again. Without pain, you would not have seen the doctor and the appendix could have erupted causing peritonitis and you might now be dead. We also know how the absence of pain so tragically affects those people suffering from leprosy.

"Except in very early stages, the leprosy patient does not feel physical pain. That, in fact, is the problem: after leprosy bacilli deaden nerve cells, patients no longer alert to danger, proceed to damage their own bodies. A leprosy patient may walk all day on a sharp metal screw, or use a splintery hammer, or scratch an infected spot on the eyeball. Each of these acts destroys tissue and may eventually lead to loss of limb or vision, but at no point does the leprosy patient hurt.

Though they may not hurt, leprosy patients surely suffer, as much as any people I have ever known. Almost all the pain they feel comes from outside, the pain of rejection imposed on them by the surrounding community."[1]

In the UK people have demonstrated time and time again their practical support for those in need, men, women and children who are suffering greatly, whether in this country or abroad and the need is everywhere and continuous in one place after another.

For example, the CBM charity points out that around 1.4 million children are blind, and yet in half of these cases their sight could be saved by treating diseases early or

CBM (*formerly Christian Blind Mission*)

correcting conditions such as cataracts. An operation to remove cataracts and restore eyesight to a child costs around £95, as long as it is done early enough to prevent blindness becoming irreversible. Distressing isn't it, when you think how such a relatively small amount of money given can completely change a child's life?

The reason why the majority of seriously suffering people in poorer nations are not being looked after and healed is because of mankind's greed and self-interest – not because it cannot be done.

God has provided, but too many people, not least in governments, corporations and businesses in the world do not make the commitment to act fairly for all the people, especially those who are in great need. Why is it that there are millions of people, especially children, who are suffering and dying every day who receive only periodic media attention, but if some accident or outrage occurs resulting in a number of people dying or injured the media often create news headlines for days on end? People are thereby persuaded to think there is a tragic 'sum total of all the loss and suffering' endured by those who died through the same cause, at the same time.

It is right and natural we should mourn those deaths, particularly when a tragedy has occurred, but there is no such thing as 'a sum total of human suffering'. The various degrees of suffering for every person during their life and eventual death, however caused, are a unique experience for each and every person. Why does the media persuade us that people who died in an air crash one week is so much worse than the deaths of the far greater number of individual men, women and children in the same nation who died in hospitals, in their homes or in other accidents in the same week?

The grief in the loss of a loved one is no less for the widow whose husband has died in a car accident than the widow whose husband was killed in a plane crash. The Office for National Statistics registered deaths of 501,424 in England and Wales in 2014 (506,790 in 2013), which is the equivalent of 9,642 deaths each week. The answer to my media question above is probably, and sadly, the old adage that 'bad news' sells.

How did Jesus respond to the suffering of other people? When he met a suffering or dead person, he was always deeply moved. When his friend, Lazarus died, he wept. He often went against the general codes of conduct for the society of that time as when he touched and healed the woman who was haemorrhaging blood. He also healed many skin diseases, including people with leprosy who were avoided at all costs by others.

Jesus' response to suffering should convince us that God does not wish us to suffer. Look how Christ recoiled from the thought of his own imminent, excruciating death on a wooden cross, asking His Father God to take that suffering away, but only if it was God's will.

However, Peter Kreeft, a professor of philosophy at Boston College and The King's College, does not hold back in making this opening challenge to everyone:

"The case against God can be quite simply put like this: How can a mother trust and love a God who let her baby die?(.....) the strongest case against God comes from the billions of normal lives that are full of apparently pointless suffering. It is not just that the suffering is not deserved; it is that it seems random and pointless. For every one who becomes a hero and a saint through suffering, there are ten who seem to become dehumanised, depressed, or despairing.

And the universality of it - there's the rub. Your neighbour, your best friend, your doctor, your mechanic all have deep and hidden hurts that you don't know about, just as you have some that they don't know about. Everybody out there is hurting. And if you don't know that, you're either very naive and believe in people's facades, or so thick-skinned that you don't hurt yourself and don't feel other people's hurts either(....) Most people go through seventy or eighty years with less than half a dozen occasions of really agonising, unendurable physical pain. A hundred years ago you were lucky to get through a single year without pain that today we would call terrible. Think of a world without anaesthetics. Yet people are hurting far more psychologically and spiritually today than ever before. Suicides are up. Depression is up. Mindless violence is up. Boredom is up. (In fact, the very word boredom does not exist in any premodern language!) Loneliness is up. Drug escapism is up."[2]

When he writes this, he points us to the fact that the vast majority of people living before the 20th Century faced many prevalent life-threatening diseases of the times, such as consumption, smallpox and so on, for which there were no cures available. In the 19th Century, parents could fear up to half their children might die before they were 10 years old. Adult deaths were common under age 40. Many causes of death in those days have been eliminated now and we have the means of diagnosis, drugs, medical competence and relevant operations to deal with most of those historic diseases in the wealthiest countries of the world.

Atheists sometimes use suffering as an example of why there can be no God – least of all a loving God. They have a problem here, themselves. If they deny any God exists, their own answer must be that pain and suffering is simply a natural outcome of the evolutionary process for which they can offer no further explanation. But on what basis does an atheist bring a non-existent God, (from their point of view), into any discussion on suffering?

Pain and suffering are separate entities, though often linked together, as previously mentioned. The ethical and caring atheists might therefore claim that the majority of suffering in the world is caused by other people who are either evil or immoral and they would be correct. But, who is to decide what is evil or immoral and on whose credentials?

For example, cannibalism, hopefully now in the past, was morally justified by those tribes who practiced it. When faced with this problem of how morality standards should be set and by whom, the well-known atheist, Bertrand Russell, apparently responded in a radio interview, that one knew what was right or wrong by how one 'felt' about an issue. Well, people practising cannibalism clearly had no problems of conscience about it at the time. There are many other current examples of practices justified and carried out in the world, not least in relation to women and children, which can be categorized as inhuman, degrading and immoral, not only by 'believers' in God, but also by non-believers, .

But it is the 'believers' who have the problem of explaining pain and suffering, particularly Christians, because they claim that God is love as well as just. Loving God and 'loving your neighbour as yourself' are the two great commands given by Jesus Christ.

American author, Philip Yancey, surely one of the most inspiring Christian writers of our age, illustrates some differences in the attitudes people have, both with those who seek fame, money and status, and those who choose to give their lives to helping others:

> "In my career as a journalist, I have interviewed diverse people. Looking back, I can roughly divide them into two types: stars and servants. The stars include NFL football greats, movie actors, music performers, famous authors, TV personalities, and the like.

> Yet I must tell you that, in my limited experience, these 'idols' are as miserable a group of people as I have ever met. Most have troubled or broken marriages. Nearly all are hopelessly dependent on psychotherapy. In a heavy irony, these larger-than-life heroes seem tormented by incurable self-doubt. I have also spent time with servants. People like Dr. Paul Brand, who worked for twenty years among the poorest of the poor leprosy patients in rural India. Or health workers who left high-paying jobs to serve with Mendenhall Ministries in a backwater town of Mississippi. Or relief

workers in Somalia, Sudan, Ethiopia, Bangladesh or other such repositories of world-class human suffering(....) I was prepared to honor and admire these servants, to hold them up as inspiring examples. I was not, however, prepared to envy them. But, as I now reflect on the two groups side by side, stars and servants, the servants clearly emerge as the favored ones, the graced ones. They work for low pay, long hours, and no applause, 'wasting' their talents and skills among the poor and uneducated. But somehow in the process of losing their lives they have found them. They have received the 'peace' that is not of this world.

When I think of the great churches I have visited, what comes to mind is not an image of a cathedral in Europe. These are mere museums now. Instead, I think of the chapel at Carville, of an inner-city church in Newark with crumbling plaster and a leaky roof, of a mission church in Santiago, Chile, made of concrete blocks and corrugated iron. In these places, set amidst human misery, I have seen Christian love abound."[3]

But pain and suffering do pose a very large problem. Philip Yancey went through a period of doubt about God's love in relation to the suffering problem before his trust returned.

"For a good portion of my life, I shared the perspective of those who rail against God for allowing pain. Suffering pressed in too close. I could find no way to rationalize a world as toxic as this one. As I visited people whose pain far exceeded my own, though, I was surprised by its effects. Suffering seemed as likely to reinforce faith as to sow agnosticism.

And as I visited those with leprosy, particularly, I became aware of pain's underlying value(.....) My anger about pain has melted mostly for one reason: I have come to know God. He has given me joy and love and happiness and goodness. They have come in unexpected flashes, in the midst of my confused, imperfect world, but they have been enough to convince me that my God is worthy of trust. Knowing him is worth all enduring."[4]

There are good and essential reasons why pain exists in our world related to our mental and physical conditions and capabilities already referred to in this chapter. But, if God is the Creator and all powerful, people may ask why he could not have made us free of possible suffering. That might be a good fundamental question to ask, but...

"As soon as we introduce the question of what would have been better, we again invoke an absolute point of reference, and that we can only introduce if God exists. In the final analysis, our world is the only one where love was genuinely possible. The love of a mother for her child. The love of a man for his wife. The love of a friend for a friend. The love of a man or a woman for God. We must recognize that love is the supreme ethic that we know of, and where love is possible, freedom and the possibility of suffering accompany it(....) In turning our back upon God, we lose the source of defining love, live with the pain of unholiness, and suffering remains an enigma—leaving our blemished characters in search of a moral law and our finite minds crying out for an answer. Which of us does not hurt when we see a pure love abused and despised? Our hearts reveal a hunger for a love that is pure, and in this world we have lost both definitions because we have denied their source."[5]

To know you are loved by God is to change your whole attitude to life in any of the circumstances you find yourself in and that knowledge is the power which enables people to give their practical expression of love to others, if they choose. Remember Mother Teresa in India sharing God's love by her own total loving commitment to the poorest of the poor facing deprivation and death. Despite all the suffering she had witnessed her attitude to all misfortune was summed up when she said:

"From heaven the most miserable earthly life will look like one bad night in an inconvenient hotel!" Philip Yancey relates this very moving experience from one of his travels:

"I have seen evidence of God's presence in the most unexpected places. During our trip to Nepal, a physical therapist gave my wife and me a tour of the Green Pastures hospital, which specialises in leprosy rehabilitation.

As we walked along an outdoor corridor, I noticed in a courtyard one of the ugliest human beings I have ever seen. Her hands were bandaged in gauze, she had deformed stumps where most people have feet, and her face showed the worst ravages of that cruel leprosy disease. Her nose had shrunk away so that, looking at her, I could see into her sinus cavity. Her eyes, mottled and covered with callus, let in no light; she was totally blind. Scars covered patches of skin on her arms(....) I'm ashamed to say my first thought was, she's a beggar. She wants money.

My wife, who has worked among the down-and-out, had a much more holy reaction. Without hesitation she bent down to the woman and put her arm around her. The old woman rested her head against Janet's shoulder and began singing a song in Nepali, a tune that we all instantly recognised: 'Jesus loves me, this I know, for the Bible tells me so'.

'Danmaya is one of our most devoted church members', the physical therapist later told us(....) She loves to greet and welcome every visitor who comes to Green Pastures, and no doubt she heard us talking as we walked along the corridor'.

A few months later we heard that Danmaya had died. Close to my desk I keep a photo that I snapped just as she was singing to Janet. Whenever I feel polluted by the beauty-obsessed celebrity culture I live in - a culture in which people pay exorbitant sums to shorten their noses or plump up their breasts to achieve some impossible ideal of beauty(.....) I pull out that photo. I see two beautiful women: my wife, smiling sweetly, wearing a brightly coloured Nepali outfit she had bought the day before, holding in her arms an old crone who would flunk any beauty test ever devised except the one that matters most. Out of that deformed, hollow shell of a body, the light of God's presence shines out."[6]

How wonderful that Philip and his wife should stop and see the beauty inside the heart and soul of this amazing woman. How many of us might have done our best to avoid any contact with Danmaya based on her deformed appearance. We so often form opinions and criticisms of people on the way they look, not on their inner self – their character and willingness to give out of love whatever they can offer to others.

But, the question 'How does a Loving God allow Suffering?' remains. Perhaps one answer might be, 'How could a loving God do anything else?'

Out of His infinite love for each one of us, God has given every person the free will to decide everything within their own power – the right to choose for ourselves, a most precious gift. We cannot expect God to suspend that right every time we make the wrong choices or bad decisions for our lives, our beliefs or anything else in life. Nor can we expect God to stop the free will decisions of those who are intent on gaining their own selfish desires, whatever the harm, fatal or otherwise, caused to other people. God gave us free will to choose love and obedience to Him and His commandments or to refuse.

That is the only way our love for God and for others can be shown to be genuine in our beliefs and our lives. I remember many years ago a scientific study was made to try and establish the root causes of avoidable suffering in the world. The result turned out to be a rather simple answer – the vast majority was attributed to man's inhumanity to man, firstly by inflicting harm and evil on people. Secondly, in neglecting to give medical, material or financial resources, and care to those who were suffering. The small remainder was due to natural disasters.

I heard in a radio broadcast in 2015 that some agency or other at the United Nations had calculated that if, as a first priority, feeding everyone in the world adequately was agreed and implemented, the world's total food production would only require 75% of what we currently consume. If correct, there is no reason for anyone, anywhere to be starving, is there? We have the resources to put an end to so much suffering caused by lack of proper food, adequate water, medical protection, shelter and so on for the poorest people who are most in need, but not, apparently, sufficient will or the necessary love to do so.

If 'Love your neighbour as yourself', seen in its wider context, was actually practiced by the majority of people in the world, not least by the leaders and peoples of all the wealthy nations, there would be a dramatic reduction in the suffering endured by millions of men, women and children every day of their lives, both at home and abroad.

I am generally a positive person, but I cannot see this happening any time soon. But, individually, we can all contribute to this command, if we choose, by showing genuine love for all who are suffering in our world. This might be financial support for worthy charities. It might also be in giving practical help to those in need in our own communities. Thousands of people already do so, which should be an encouragement to all of us to help make a real difference to the millions who are suffering, including those who are nearby.

Whether our hearts are in the right place depends not only on our word, but on what we are prepared to give, to do and to sacrifice for those who are suffering.

Not enough in my case, but how is this challenge reflected by wealthy Governments around the world who should bear some share of responsibility for looking after the starving, the homeless, the poorest children and so on, around the world? I looked up the Overseas Aid contributions made by countries on the Wikipedia website. Payments, listed as 'Official Development Assistance (ODA)', by countries as a percentage of their Gross National Incomes (GNI) are provided for 2014. This seems to be a relatively fair figure to compare the aid provided by participating countries.

It was good to note that the UK came 6th in the table with a contribution of 0.71% of our GNI in overseas aid. The highest percentage contributions were made by Sweden 1.4% and Norway at just over 1% of GNI. But might not all wealthy nations contribute at least 1% of GNI? The responsibility for that decision lies in the hands of Governments and there is substantial variation in their ODA payments. America contributed 0.17% of GNP and only 6 countries met the United Nations target of 0.7% of GNI in 2014 – one more than in 2013.

The problem of suffering is huge and you might agree unfairly distributed according to whether you live in a rich country or a poor one.

> 'The very sharp edge of pain and death is felt universally, and every religion or philosophy of life has to deal with it. A philosophy that espouses no belief in God cannot even justify the question, let alone provide an answer except for the hope of extinction. If this gap in human knowledge could only be filled, just think of how it would redefine everything. Honesty of mind drives every generation to seek an answer that does not smack of ignorance or arrogance, and life's passages demand something better for each life before the curtain falls. For the Christian there is an answer."[7]

God does not have responsibility for allowing pain and suffering. Apart from the accidents of natural disasters, mankind, in its selfishness, is the primary cause and has that responsibility.

*"If anyone has material possessions*
*and sees a brother or sister in need*
*but has no pity on them,*
*how can the love of God*
*be in that person?*

*Dear children,*
*let us not love with words or speech,*
*but with*
**actions** *and* **in truth**."[8]

"Runaway *inequality* has created a world where 62 people own as much as the *poorest* half of the world's population".

Oxfam press release January 2016

# 5. Living with
# Hope or Just Surviving?

The French priest, Michel Quoist, was, at one stage in his life, a researcher and practitioner in Advanced Studies at the Institute of Social and Political Sciences. He also wrote a thesis on Sociology. In 1954, age 33, he published a book, "Prayers of Life", which has been very successful with sales of c.2.5million copies all over the world. Michel also asked some very pertinent questions in his book, "Meeting God", which are still relevant today, not only for young adults making their way in life, but for all of us:

"Why are we alive? Why do we train for a profession? Why do we get up each morning and go to work? Why do we get married, create a home, have children? And then, later in life, sit in an armchair waiting for death? Why, my friends? What is our life? What is man?

Where do we come from? Where are we going? Are we just hanging in space? Do we come from nowhere and are we going nowhere? Are we just little sparks of life that came about by chance, sufficiently conscious to know that we are alive and

that our life is absurd? What a terrible fate!(....)
May I confide in you? When I was a young man,
I tried to find an answer to these fundamental
questions. I looked at 'man' and tried to discover
the deepest and most universal force present
in him. As soon as I have found that, I thought,
I shall go upstream and find the source of life.

My first reaction was that it all depended on a
will to live and a fundamental need to defend life
and help it to develop.

But gradually I discovered another force in
man's heart that was much stronger than the will to
live – 'Love'. So strong was the power of that love,
I found, that man was able to sacrifice his life". [1]

Michel Quoist is right, isn't he? There is nothing in the
world more important than love. When are people most
content and joyful with life? Surely, when they know they
are loved.

This is why so many people feel depressed and
wretched when that love is lost by separation - resulting
from breakdowns of relationships with people whom they
have loved. Why do these 'breakdowns'' occur if the love
was so valued by the people concerned?

Some may simply reply, 'For many different reasons,

I expect......' but on closer, honest examination, the main cause, perhaps more often than not, is the self-interest of one or sometimes both parties. If we begin to experience lack of our required response from loved ones, it is all too easy for our love for them to lessen as our own attitude towards them changes.

That is not the 'strong power of love' Michel refers to, which is capable of the supreme sacrifice of one's life. It is conditional love for which we expect an appropriate and acceptable response to be made by our loved ones. Some people may ask, why not? If this life is all there is, then it follows that each one of us should get as much out of it as we can without being burdened by other people's problems, needs or demands and there are some people who seem to have that attitude.

I still remember the day my grandfather was reluctantly carried out of our small flat by the medics taking him to a nursing home where he later died. I was about 12 years old at the time and his parting words to me were, 'Don't forget, John, self-preservation is the first law of nature!' He was right, of course, but belief in a loving God and an after life makes a difference to that attitude with love and care for others becoming a very important concern in our daily lives.

It seems evident that the majority of the world's people do believe in a God or 'Force/Power' outside of our planet and it has generally always been so. There are also millions of people who are unsure whether a 'God' exists or not, known as agnostics. A relatively small percentage of the world's population – the atheists - claim no God or spiritual power exists at all.

Mankind's knowledge and understanding of our world in all respects increases from one generation to the next and will continue to do so. The atheist argument rests on the claim that there is a lack of absolute proof that God exists.

Lack of 'absolute' proof for an idea, belief or concept, at some point in time, is not justification for declaring its invalidity. In the 17th Century, scientists maintained the theory that the earth was flat and the sun revolved around the earth.

Then Galileo in 1632, the Italian mathematician, astronomer and physicist, confirmed the findings of Copernicus who died in 1543 that the Sun was the centre of our Solar System, not the earth, which evidence was dismissed by many authorities at that time.

If God exists, he would be beyond human comprehension and although we are fully accustomed to reaching decisions on the basis of the evidence available, whether right or wrong, there can never be any absolute proof that God does exist. That belief is a matter of faith, based on strong evidence and the personal experience of believers, themselves.

But not for the atheists – they state categorically that no God or other 'power' outside of our earth exists so it is, perhaps, not surprising that one unknown writer defined the atheist in these terms, 'An atheist is a person who claims infinite knowledge that there is no one in the universe with infinite knowledge'.

What is some of the strong evidence referred to which suggests that God does exist? In his book, "One World", Cambridge Professor John Polkinghorne, a Quantum Physicist, gave a compelling argument, including an illustration, on why it is difficult, if not impossible, to explain the order in the universe on any other basis than the existence of God. One example he gives is an indicator of the evidence for God provided by composite scientific observation and further analysis of how the universe operates, with the reasonable conclusion that this order in the world did not just happen, but required a 'creator' in the first place.

'In the early expansion of the universe there has to be a close balance between the expansive energy (driving things apart) and the force of gravity (pulling things together). If expansion dominated then matter would fly apart too rapidly for condensation into galaxies and stars to take place.

Nothing interesting could happen in so thinly spread a world".

"On the other hand, if gravity dominated, the world would collapse in on itself again before there was time for the processes of life to get going. For us to be possible requires a balance between the effects of expansion and contraction(....) For the non-numerate I will borrow an illustration from Paul Davies of what that accuracy means. He points out that it is the same as aiming at a target an inch wide on the other side of the observable universe, twenty thousand million light years away, and hitting the mark!'[2]

Apparently, some scientists and others still think that the world came into existence via 'the Big Bang', but this theory seems to be at odds with our known scientific knowledge that there is not a single piece of evidence to support the idea that something can be caused to exist from nothing. Other scientific theories of the origin of the universe are also offered including the Steady State Universe; Eternal Inflation – Multiverse, the Oscillating Universe and the String theory, all of which are based on differing theories.

Professor Stephen Hawking was seen on television during a series of seminars in a Scientific Institute in Canada where a large group of scientists gathered to discuss their theories on the creation of the universe.

The BBC filmed some of the key proceedings in a program entitled, "What Happened before the Big Bang". Seven of the Cosmologists presented their ideas on the origin of the universe. They all had different theories on how the universe might have come into being but three of them interestingly raised the question of the 'Time' problem.

The problem they had found in their research was exposed in their mathematical equations which indicated that there was no such thing as 'time' before the beginning of the universe. My understanding of their conclusions was that since time did not exist before our universe came into being, either a state of infinity must have existed or the possibility that our universe was created out of another existing universe.

It is interesting that they had reasoned that 'time' did not exist before creation of our universe.

Although none of the seven selected Cosmologists were able to provide an acceptable answer for the origin of the universe to the whole group, a clear majority of those attending the course concluded that the 'Big Bang' could not be the first cause. Something else must be the answer, and interestingly one theory promoted was that our whole universe had been created out of nothing. This flies in the face of the basic fact that there are no examples of anything being created out of nothing in the world unless, of course, you believe the world was created by God.

Whatever we see, feel, use or produce is always caused by another source - someone or something. There has to be a first cause for the existence of everything in the world and for the world itself.

For example, reproduction of the species is common to all life forms – humans, animals, birds, insects, fish, etc. A huge 200 year old oak tree began life from a small seed in the ground. There has to be a 'first cause' for everything created, whether animate or inanimate. As the late Dallas Willard, past Professor in the School of Philosophy at the University of Southern California, put it:

> "The "rebutters," with almost no exceptions, quite conveniently manage to forget that evolution, whether cosmic or biological, cannot - logically cannot - be a theory of ultimate origins of existence or order(....) Let us say quite generally that any sort of evolution of order of any kind will always presuppose pre-existing order and pre-existing entities governed by it. It follows as a simple matter of logic that not all order evolved. Given the physical world—however much of evolution it may or may not contain - there is or was some order in it which did not evolve".[3]

This statement is so important to children and young adults growing up in our secular culture. From the time we are born we are subject to the influence, teaching and support of our parents, our families, our educators, our peer group at every age and the behavioural standards of the community we grow up in. The young naturally copy the behaviour of those around them.

In our time they are also subject to the extensive influence of the internet, magazines and films, in particular, showing explicit examples of violence, bad language, sexual promiscuity and immorality of every kind. These problems are not new. How dangerous the results of living without God are, particularly for the young, were expressed in America two decades ago:

> "To what lies have we been subjected? On every side I see the glare of billboards promising that happiness lies in the next car or the next house. Educators promise that if we only tell our children about sex we will reduce the rate of teen pregnancy and the threat of venereal disease. Social workers promise that drug education will remove this scourge from our continent if we will 'just say no.' Politicians promise that technology and communication will lead to a better understanding and to peace. Lawmakers promise that new laws will eradicate racial tensions.
>
> Now we are promised that if we would only get God out of education and get the Creator

out of the scheme of things we will all be better for it. But the duplicity that has emerged from political leaders, legal tacticians, and, for that matter, even from some purveyors of religion has left a generation of young people apathetic, cynical, and even fearful. To the question 'What do you wish for most in your life?' asked of Canadian teens during a survey conducted a few years ago, the number-one answer, revealing our cultural tragedy, was 'Somebody we can trust'. [4]

It is interesting to note how the younger members of most societies are so quick to recognise not only the failures of their elders, but in some cases, their regrettable standards of behaviour. All around them they observe the exploitation of people by those who are looking for personal gain, particularly in the economic and sexual areas of life. They are constantly informed by the media of misdemeanors by people who it seems do not subscribe to any particular moral code of conduct. Many of our young adults have high ideals, but when they leave school or university, they come face to face with the fact that unless a moral code has some ultimate authority, it will be ignored or, at best, be subject to personal interpretation leading, inevitably, to abuse by some.

How sad! At the outset of their adult lives we have many teenagers and young adults who often have no faith in anything or anyone. Millions of youngsters have grown up with little or no knowledge of any spiritual life because it seems many secular 'teachers' and parents have little or no knowledge themselves. Whether God exists or not does not appear to matter too much, for life is busy enough with its own problems to even ask the question.

Love and care for others is not exclusive to 'believers', of course, and there are millions of people in the world who do not acknowledge 'God', but give of their love and service to those they love and those in need. But, there are also those people who appear to have little or no particular love or care for anyone else and who pursue evil means - even the exploitation of their own people - to secure their ambitions. Atheist leaders like Hitler, Stalin, and Mao, were responsible for the deaths and suffering of countless millions of people, including their own citizens.

But, they are not alone. Other rulers, whether despotic, political or religious, who have claimed belief in a God, have also perpetrated substantial crimes against humanity. They are still doing so and now, they are indiscriminately killing more women and children than ever before.

What about the bad things ordinary 'believers' do - sometimes terrible offences? Any decent person would be right to condemn such acts. The dilemma is that every individual has the choice of good or evil in their thoughts, words and deeds whatever their beliefs.

The fact is that everyone is capable of evil – difficult to accept, but demonstrably true.

Evil is a terrible fact of life, but not a valid reason for rejecting God who gave us the free will to choose to love Him or not, and the free will to choose whether we love other people or, at worst, to hate or even want to kill some of them. Those who believe in God need to acknowledge that there have been terrible crimes against humanity committed by people who claimed not only to believe in their 'God', but to be acting in His name.

The variety of communication facilities in this age are so advanced that we can spend a great deal of our time trying to absorb the implications of instant news from around the world, much of which we, personally, can do nothing about. The news which, apparently, captures most of our attention is usually related to disasters, however caused; wars; political or sexual misdemeanors, corruption issues and abuse of any and every kind in State, church or commerce.

Of course, we need information of every kind, but what a relief it would be for good news to be the first order of the day for the media, but, as the saying goes, 'bad news is what sells'. Individuals should be actively concerned with some of that news, but the daily dose of bad news often seems to create a feeling of hopelessness to deal with one tragedy after another. Gladly, we also know there are notable exceptions to this pessimism as, for example, the thousands of people who gave practical support to those who suffered so much in the UK floods and there have been many other acts of kindness and generosity towards those whose lives have been afflicted in the UK and many other countries.

Our world today is 'richer' in knowledge, wealth, food production, medical treatments, technical advancement and so on, than it has ever been. Yet there are still millions of people starving, homeless, persecuted, victims of war, violence – and the list goes on. Why? It is a result of man's inhumanity to man, whether by self-styled believers or non-believers in God expressed in greed, the abuse of power, selfish ambition, corruption and pursuit of wealth, to name but some causes of evil in the world.

Most ordinary people who believe in God, what-ever their faith tradition, hope and expect to find goodness expressed both by themselves and by other people. I write, 'ordinary people', meaning those without substantial power or wealth, but also fully acknowledge that many wealthy, influential individuals and other 'bodies' have been great benefactors to those in need. Wealth, of itself, is not the issue – it is the misuse of wealth and lack of proportionate charitable giving towards the needy which is so appalling by some of those who have so much. The shocking and shameful 'gap' between the richest and poorest people in the world was exposed by Oxfam in a press release issued in January 2016:

> "Runaway inequality has created a world where 62 people own as much as the poorest half of the world's population, according to an Oxfam report published today ahead of the annual gathering of the world's financial and political elites in Davos. This number has fallen dramatically from 388 as recently as 2010 and 80 last year. An Economy for the 1%, shows that the wealth of the poorest half of the world's population - that's 3.6 billion people - has fallen by a trillion dollars since 2010. This 38 per cent drop has occurred despite the global population increasing by around 400 million people during that period. Meanwhile the wealth of the richest 62 has increased by more than half a trillion dollars to $1.76tr. Just nine of the '62' are women."[5]

A few years ago, I worked with a group of University post-graduates in a Christian charity helping some of these poorest people in the world. I asked them what objections their peer group expressed to believing in God. Their response some weeks later read as follows:

> *"We discussed the main issues of belief in God for our generation with our 'non-believing' friends. Here are some of their classic lines":-*

*'If God allows all the suffering in the world
how can he possibly be a loving God?'*

*'Religion causes all the wars in the world;
why would I follow that type of belief?'*

*'Every religion points to the same God,
I'm perfectly happy to live on my terms.'*

*'My life is fine, I don't need God,
I'm perfectly happy.'*

*'It's just a coping mechanism for life's
problems or picked up from your parents.'*

*'Man made God in his image.'*

*'I'm open to a higher power, stuff like
destiny and fate but not God.'*

*'I might consider God when I'm older - now
I'm young - I just want to have fun.'*

Why would these young people be so disinterested in finding evidence as to whether God exists or not? It is probable that this is a response to the secular culture they are living in and, as the last of their answers indicates, they think they have many more years to live before worrying about whether God exists or not. That is not always the case.

Our own dear son died when he was just 27 from heart failure with no prior indications he had a heart problem. Martin had decided not to come to church anymore in his teens, but he came to full faith in his first year at Cambridge University where he gained a 'First' in all three undergraduate years. Emmanuel College wrote of him:

'He will be remembered not only for his immense intelligence, but also for his humility and generosity(...) He was a strong Christian and contributed a great deal to the College Christian Union'. Martin is the finest man I have ever known, full of love, kindness and goodness.

One difficulty for atheism was expressed by one of the best known atheists of the last century in the UK - Bertrand Russell. He was a formidable character who enjoyed considerable public attention. Yet, even this atheist had some doubts, apparently, about his unbelief. He admitted that sometimes he would classify himself as an agnostic in some circumstances, rather than an atheist. He was a highly intelligent man, but he seems to indicate that the prime reason for this quandary was the impossibility of proving that God did not exist. Indeed, he expressed the view that he was 'haunted' by the idea that life might hold something more than death and extinction at the end, but he could not accept that there was a 'God', nor any future beyond death.

It is impossible, of course, to prove beyond any doubt

that either God does, or does not exist, but we need to look at the evidence supporting either conviction which includes the effect these opposing beliefs have on people's lives at every level. We need to acknowledge that no matter which level of intelligence or which arena of life of people are living and working in, we will find people with faith in God's existence and those who do not.

However, there are millions of people who are persuaded neither one way or the other about the existence of God. Peter Kreeft, Professor of philosophy at Boston College and The King's College, considers this other option:

> "But, what about agnosticism? Is that not a third possibility in addition to atheism and theism? Why not refuse to wager either way until the evidence is clearer? That would seem to be the more scientific attitude. The answer is, in Pascal's words, 'You must wager. You are embarked.' The ship of self is moving along the waters of time past the port of God. If it is not our true port, we should turn away; if it is our true home, we should turn to it. But why not stay anchored out at sea until the fog clears, and we can see better whether this is our true port or not. Because, the fog will only clear when it is too late - after death. The ship has a finite amount of fuel. There is a point of no return (....) To every question there are three possible answers:

'Yes,' 'No,' and 'Wait.' Death eliminates the third answer!" (6)

He goes on to suggest that if an honest person sincerely seeks the truth about God's existence they might find the following suggestion helpful:

"The simplest way to test the religious hypothesis is to pray. Go out into the country some night, or into your back yard, where no one can hear you, and say something like this:

'God, I don't know if You exist or not. I suspect I'm only talking to a myth or to my own fantasies. But I'm not sure. So if You do exist, You must hear me now and know me and know my heart. So You know that I'm honestly seeking the truth, whatever it is. You supposedly promised that all who seek You, will find You'.

If You are the truth, I'm seeking You now, because I am seeking the truth. So please let me know that You're real, somehow, in Your own way and Your own time. Presumably, You know best how that's to be done. I'm open and ready if You are.

Who could quarrel with that experiment? It's like fairly testing the hypothesis that someone is in the closet, tied up, by knocking on the door. If the hypothesis is true, you may hear a reply. Why hesitate to knock? The analogy is not perfect because in the case of the closet you can open the door and look with your eyes, while in the case of an invisible God you cannot.

But you can still speak and listen with your mind and heart, and this constitutes a fair test, because the hypothesis maintains not only that God exists but also that this God wants to reveal Himself to you, to set up a relationship of love and faith for a lifetime and beyond. The hypothesis claims that 'all who seek, find.' So test it. Seek. I can think of only two reasons for hesitating: the fear that you will find nothing, and the fear that you will find something. Honesty, like love, casts out fear."[7]

Only worth the experiment, no doubt, if one is being entirely honest in their desire to engage with God, if He exists. I think it is clear that no 'absolute' proof can be offered for God's existence and, certainly, that is also true of the atheist claim that he does not exist.

When I die, if my belief in God is unfounded, I will never know. But, though I have failed many times, I have tried to uphold a moral code provided by Christ which has no equal because it is founded on love. What better foundation for life could there be? If my faith in God and an after-life proves to be well-founded, then I will know and experience God's promise for those who believe and trust in him. Either way, if I could live another life on earth, I would want to choose the same foundation.

As this chapter closes, you may be asking why God has not given us absolute proof of His existence, if He wants the best for us and our love in return. The answer may well be provided by another question: "If we had 'absolute proof', what would our love for God be worth for any other choice would be completely senseless?"

We know the great majority of parents do not want the love of their sons and daughters as a 'right', or an obligation for them to fulfill.

If their children's love is not a 'free' choice and response to the love they have been given, it really has little value, does it?

Loving God is also a free choice for each one of us. God made His choice to love us, His own creation, whatever the cost was going to be to Him. And He knew the eventual cost was going to be the highest sacrifice He could suffer - the excruciating death of His only son nailed to a wooden cross to redeem each one of us from our sins and enable us to be with Him.

*"For God so loved the world*

*that He gave*

## His one and only son,

*that whoever believes in Him*

*shall not perish*

*but have* **eternal life.**" [8]

"It is a mistake to suppose
that God is only, or even chiefly
concerned with religion."

WILLIAM TEMPLE, ARCHBISHOP OF CANTERBURY 1942-1944

# 6. A Door to the Secret of the Universe?

"To abound in wealth, to have fine houses, and rich clothes, to be attended with splendour and equipage, to be beautiful in our persons, to have titles of dignity, to be above our fellow creatures, to command the bows and obedience of other people, to be looked on with admiration, to overcome our enemies with power, to subdue all that oppose us, to set out ourselves in as much splendour as we can, to live highly and magnificently, to eat, and drink, and delight ourselves in the most costly manner, these are the great, the honourable, the desirable things, to which the spirit of the world turns the eyes of all people." [1]

This extract does not come from an article or book by a current philosopher or sociologist, however much you might have agreed it was a justified criticism of our modern society. It was written by William Law, elected a fellow of Emmanuel College, Cambridge in 1711, and in those days there were very substantial differences between the rich and the vast majority of poor people, most of whom could not read or write. The UK was also called a Christian country led by the nation's monarch. In this age, we still have a much loved Christian Queen, but few would now describe the UK as a Christian country if measured by church attendance.

Indeed, most European countries in the 18th Century and beyond were regarded as nominally, if not essentially, Christian in character. However, over recent centuries they have become progressively secular. There are many reasons for this transition in the minds of people, including two horrific world wars which did nothing to persuade them that the Christian message of the abiding love of God for all people and for each other was possible.

The positive and dramatic increases in growth and prosperity in developed countries in the last 50 years may have persuaded many people they have no further need of God. The changes in all areas of life brought about for people during the last century have been monumental and resulted in multi-class, multi-culture, multi-racial communities within nations. In effect, there is no 'big society' to which everyone can belong.

Add to this the failures of too many churches to spread the good news of Christianity to their own communities and we can begin to understand why and how the UK and so many former Christian-based countries have witnessed a secular culture take hold. You may agree that it would be a good idea to carefully analyse what is happening in our modern society and why. There is plenty of adverse criticism available every day on what is going wrong in our world, but very few ideas on what we need to do to bring back the reality of justice, reconciliation, ethics and high standards of morality.

It is necessary to recognise that those in power in the whole of society in its various areas are often concentrating their minds on the immediate problems and challenges they are facing. This is often self-evident in politics and business. The 'leaders' in all fields of human activity are the very people whom we might reasonably expect to take responsibility to ensure they are operating and promoting an acceptable moral framework. This has particular regard to all the people who work for them and buy their goods and services. This is fundamental to the important long-term objectives and success of any organisation. As one senior manager put it, 'Are our people proud to work for us?'

The greater part of our lives is controlled by laws and regulations in every area of human activity and rightly so. That is one important way in which society hopes to protect everyone from harm and evil. Secondly, to provide encouragement and opportunity for every person to achieve a life of fulfillment and promise. Those objectives are both honourable and the rightful expectation of all citizens. Who would disagree with those objectives as one element for a fair and equal society? But where in the world would you find such a society? There are, it seems, countless people who are more interested in achieving their personal ambitions, wealth and status than playing their full part in building a just and caring society.

The first place we should look for good, strong leadership in building such a society is a democratic government where all members on all sides of Parliament in the UK should act honourably, ethically and without self-interest. But, I think we run into one immediate difficulty for what do most of us know about the real qualities, character and standing of the individuals we are electing to govern.

Some may say that is not the important issue. 'It is the party and its policies I am voting for, not the individual!' But it is the individual members of Parliament who, collectively, pass or deny legislation for the government of the day.

Why should we think that the personal moral standards of individual MPs are irrelevant to their responsibilities to pass or reject legislation, particularly those provisions concerned with the well-being and moral conduct of the nation's people at every level and in every sphere of their lives. The scandal of irregular expense claims by some MPs a few years ago and further revelations of other misdemeanours is a disgrace. No wonder there is limited confidence that every Parliamentary Member will act with the population's best interests at heart.

The British public have been subject to the political ambitions of people opposing each other in the Referendum on Europe. It seems the Politicians hardly improved their image in the process with accusations of misleading the electorate on both sides and failing to give accurate facts and substantiated forecasts of the possible future outcomes, whichever way the people voted.

This self-interest and examples of the immoral acts evident at high levels in the public sector are also reflected in the like behaviour evident in other important areas of our national life. It then, so easily, becomes a spreading 'disease' in our so-called society.

Which leads us on to ask what should we expect of business ethics? There has been much criticism, of some major companies and banks over the years who have shown a lack of integrity in the conduct of their businesses and treatment of their customers for whom they have a responsibility of care. The primary business objective of making more and more profit is shared by many firms and often demanded by some investors. Consumers are offered 'bargains' and 'sales' thoughout the year to the point of confusion for many, not least vulnerable poor people, in trying to determine what is really good value. This is nothing new, of course, but the business practice encouraged by some, that firms can charge as much as they can get for a product or service, whether reasonable or not is clearly unfair.

I remember our son, Martin, who worked for one of the major London Accountancy firms in 1990, telling me that his firm had received a number of complaints from clients about the high fees they were being charged.

When those complaints were brought to the attention of a senior partner, apparently, he expressed the notion that if they were not receiving some complaints about the fees that would simply indicate they were not charging enough! Our son was fairly horrified by that expression of professional business practice and the unfair treatment of clients.

I read, with interest, Archbishop Justin Welby's past views on the business world, with particular application to very large companies which he wrote in 1996 in an article in "Third Way" magazine:

> "Evil and sin permeate all human structures, from the monastery to the multinational(...) if we put them in the dock, the charge sheet is long. Political interference, (especially in the Sixties), and non-interference (especially today). The debt crisis caused, or abetted, by the major banks. The exploitation of non-renewable resources, with little or no return to the countries they come from. The sophisticated marketing of harmful products. (....)in the end, the global economy is hardwired to greed, and greed to idolatry."[2]

These are not the only serious problems we face. Sexuality problems are all around us including the terrible abuse of children which has been exposed at many levels in society. Young men, women and even children, are constantly subjected to advertising and articles in the media which convey the theme that the most important thing in life is your body and how it looks with emphasis on sexual attraction. C.S. Lewis, the Cambridge academic and author, considered by many as one of the most important theological writers of the last century, wrote :

> "Our warped natures, the devils who tempt us, and all the contemporary propaganda for lust, combine to make us feel that the desires we are resisting are so 'natural', so 'healthy', and so reasonable, that it is almost perverse and abnormal to resist them".

> Poster after poster, film after film, novel after novel, associate the idea of sexual indulgence with the ideas of health, normality, youth, frankness, and good humour. Now this association is a lie. Like all powerful lies, it is based on a truth - the truth(....) that sex in itself, (apart from the excesses and obsessions that have grown round it) is 'normal' and 'healthy', and all the rest of it.

> The lie consists in the suggestion that any sexual act to which you are tempted at the moment is also

healthy and normal. Now this, on any conceivable view, and quite apart from Christianity, must be nonsense."[3]

One wonders what Lewis would be writing in this century when even more 'sexual indulgence' is not only practised but promoted as quite normal and acceptable, not least to young people.

One tragic result of this 'indulgence' was listed in the official figures of abortions carried out in England and Wales over the years since the Abortion Act of 1967. The NHS reported there were 6,100 abortions in England and Wales in 1966. In the years following the 1967 Abortion Act that number had increased to 49,829 by 1969. In 2013, 185,331 abortions were carried out in England and Wales, compared with 185,122 in 2012. The abortion rate was highest for women aged 22 years, and the majority of abortions (98%) were funded by the NHS. Reporting the statistics for 2013, "The Telegraph" (20/10/2014) read:

"The vast majority of abortions were taken under Ground C of the Abortion Act 1967, of which 99.84 per cent were due to a risk to the mother's mental health. Such a risk is, of course, notoriously hard to define and allegedly flexible in meaning. Opponents of legalised abortion claim that it usually is tantamount to abortion on demand. Maurice Baring told the story of one doctor who asked another: 'About the termination of a pregnancy, I want your opinion. The father was a syphilitic(....) of the four children born, the first was blind, the second died, the third was deaf and dumb, and the fourth had tuberculosis. What would you have done?' The other doctor replied, 'I would have ended the pregnancy', to which he received the response: "Then you would have murdered Beethoven."[4]

The uncertainties and dangers in life have a cumulative, negative effect on the young who, in addition to the difficulty of finding people they can trust, are constantly being persuaded to accept and to 'buy into' the standards and behaviour of older men and women around them.

They are sometimes exploited for gain, many face the future in terms of jobs and security with little confidence and some often have little or no faith in anything or anyone. Numbers of young people in the UK and, apparently, many other countries with a Christian heritage, have little knowledge about matters of faith and morals because they have never been taught.

This is not a new problem, it has simply become worse since C.S. Lewis indicated the same problem some decades ago when he wrote:

"If the younger generation have never been

told what the Christians say and never heard any arguments in defence of it, then their agnosticism or indifference is fully explained. There is no need to look any further: no need to talk about the general intellectual climate of the age, the influence of mechanistic civilization on the character of urban life.

And having discovered that the cause of their ignorance is lack of instruction, we have also discovered the remedy. There is nothing in the nature of the younger generation which incapacitates them from receiving Christianity. If anyone is prepared to tell them, they are apparently ready to hear (......). The young people today are un-Christian because their teachers have been either unwilling or unable to transmit Christianity to them.(...) No one can give to another what he does not possess himself."[5]

In the current UK political climate, attacks are now being made on schools who offer teaching about belief in God. The Christian Institute reported (Oct 2014), the way girls in a Jewish school were dealt with by Ofsted inspectors:

"We are extremely concerned that they are interfering with traditional religious beliefs in education under the guise of promoting 'British values'.

"Shocking news has now emerged of girls at Jewish schools being 'traumatised' by Ofsted inspectors using the new standards. The National Association of Jewish Orthodox Schools (NAJOS) says it is 'appalled' by questions asked during recent surprise inspections and that girls felt 'bullied' by the experience. The pupils were asked whether or not they had a boyfriend, how babies are made and whether they knew that two men could marry."[6]

This is regrettably one consequence of the secular agenda in current legislation and there is much concern about it. If pupils are being subjected to interrogation of this kind by Ofsted inspectors for the purpose of persuading children to adopt a secular philosophy and morality, it constitutes approved government policy to interfere with parent's rights to have their children educated to the standards of morality expressed by their faith.

In a democracy, how do a small minority of people in power frame important new laws and regulations which were never specified in their election manifestos and to which, therefore, the people have not even given their tacit approval. The answer is invariably the same - the majority remain silent unless they feel they are personally going to suffer from whatever changes are being proposed.

Democracy does not prescribe solutions for problems.

It simply allows ordinary people to have some element of control over who governs them at election times which is essential because no man, woman or political party can be trusted with lasting power. Power corrupts as history confirms.

Mankind in every century has experienced the appalling results of 'leaders' policies and actions resulting in death and devastation being suffered by millions of people. And still the lesson has not been heeded. Only true love for our fellow men, women and children can ensure that everyone can be cared for and protected and that all encompassing love flows from God's love for each one of us. If people do not believe in God and his love, what hope have we of change?

What about the objection made by those who do not believe that science and a belief in God are compatible?

> "Scientific or philosophical pursuits, and a belief in God, ought not to be seen as contradictory approaches to reality. That assumption misunderstands their nature. It is not accidental that it has generally been in the milieu of Christian belief that investigation in science and thought have flourished. A love for God prompts a love for knowing the world that He has created. The quest for knowledge and truth, therefore, is not hindered, but guided by the very purposes of God."[7]

This statement is backed by a number of scientists who have made significant contributions to their particular fields of scientific discovery with no difficulty in expressing their belief in God, both in past centuries and up to the present time. Kepler, Newton and Boyle are former examples. More recently, scientists such as Francis Collins, born in 1950, who is an American physician-geneticist noted for his discoveries of disease genes came to faith after reading C.S. Lewis. Lewis pulls no punches in his challenge to all of us:

"If Christianity is untrue, then no honest man will want to believe it, however helpful it might be: if it is true, every honest man will want to believe it, even if it gives him no help at all. As soon as we have realized this, we realize something else. If Christianity should happen to be true, then it is quite impossible that those who know this truth and those who don't should be equally well equipped for leading a good life(.....) a Christian and a non-Christian may both wish to do good to their fellow men. The one believes that men are going to live for ever, that they were created by God and so built that they can find their true and lasting happiness only by being united to God(...) The other believes that men are an accidental result of the blind workings of matter, that they started as mere animals and have more or less steadily improved.(...) Here is a door behind which, according to some people, the secret of the universe is waiting for you. Either that's true, or it isn't. And if it isn't, then what the door really conceals is simply the greatest fraud, the most colossal 'sell' on record.

Isn't it obviously the job of every man (that is a man and not a rabbit) to try to find out which, and then to devote his full energies either to serving this tremendous secret or to exposing and destroying this gigantic humbug?"[8]

The Bible's last book, "Revelation", has these words from Jesus: "Here I am! I stand at the door and knock. If anyone hears my voice and opens the door, I will come in(...)"[9]

Where is this 'door'? How do you find it? Is it locked? Where does it lead? You will find the answer in your heart, mind and soul – your whole person. No key is needed to open it – just belief and trust in the God who loves you.

Holman Hunt's famous painting, '*The Light of the World*', shows Jesus Christ knocking at that 'door'. It might be your door. There is no handle on Christ's side of the door – only we can open it to let Him enter – it is, or was, your personal decision, as it was mine.

John Stott, the late much loved Christian evangelist,

told of his own challenge and experience with this 'door' when he was a younger man:

> "Here, then, is the crucial question which we have been leading up to. Have we ever opened our door to Christ? Have we ever invited Him in? This was exactly the question which I needed to have put to me. For, intellectually speaking, I had believed in Jesus all my life, on the other side of the door. I had regularly struggled to say my prayers through the key-hole. I had even pushed pennies under the door in a vain attempt to pacify him. I had been baptised, yes and confirmed as well. I went to church, read my Bible, had high ideals, and tried to be good and do good. But all the time, often without realising it, I was holding Christ at arm's length, and keeping him outside. I knew that to open the door might have momentous consequences. I am profoundly grateful to him for enabling me to open the door. Looking back now over more than fifty years, I realise that that simple step has changed the entire direction, course and quality of my life."[10]

"More things

are wrought by prayer

than this world dreams of."

# 7. What do we Expect if we Pray?

We all have questions during life which are very important in relation to those areas where the decisions we make are critical to our future happiness and well-being: Should I marry? Would it be best to finish our relationship? Is this the right work for me? How am I going to cope with this illness? Which friends can I count on in times of trouble? Who really loves me?

The answers are not going to be decided by some intellectual assessment, but on how we feel about the particular situations, backed by reasons to support those feelings. That is one reason why we all make some mistakes with our decisions in life. If, when you get home with your new purchase, you decide it was a mistake to buy it, you can take it back. But few of the most important decisions we make can be so easily reversed.

Nowhere is this decision process more vital than in the spiritual sphere. Choosing between a belief in an after life or oblivion following death will have consequences for all the other main decisions in life's journey and a direct effect on the lives of other people, especially those we love.

People who believe in God, generally pray about life's issues both for themselves and for others, although relatively few people, if any, regard themselves as experts in praying!

It is a curious fact that when we humans are faced with extreme danger, many people do not hesitate to pray, whether they have believed in God or not. My wife and I were once flying to Hong Kong and our Jumbo Jet was being bounced up and down by a very deep head-wind of more than 100 mph for a long time. It was quite scary and some of the passengers were clearly praying. Even people who are undecided about the existence of God still turn to prayer, particularly when faced with terrible danger or life threatening circumstances. As, apparently, one army officer indicated, "There are no atheists in a fox-hole". But for anyone who has seldom or never prayed before, this is not always easy to do.

This may be, in part, because so many of the prayers said in church, on the radio or television are very formal and have been handed down from one generation to the next.

Many of them are beautifully composed and loved, but difficult to copy in private prayer by those who are not experienced in personal prayer. But, does God want us to copy these prayers?

I do not think so. He surely wants us to speak to Him

from our own hearts regardless of how fluent our language is. When Jesus gave us the Lord's Prayer He told us we should keep our prayers simple:

> "And when you pray, do not keep on babbling like pagans, for they think they will be heard because of their many words. Do not be like them, for your Father knows what you need before you ask Him".[1]

Two gifted writers, (Philip Yancey & John Stott), make valuable points on prayer:

> "Prayer is not a comparison contest. The least educated and least notable soul has as much opportunity - and sometimes more - to become a master at prayer as do church professionals. Martin Luther, who averaged two hours a day in prayer, counselled others, 'the fewer the words, the better the prayer.' Indeed, two of the Bible's shortest prayers, from a tax collector and a crucified thief, proved most effective. Luther reacted against the formal, showy prayers of his time, which tended to produce hypocrites. Pray from the heart, he said. Think of the God you are addressing and not of others who may be listening". [2]

> "There is no doubt that our prayers are transformed when we remember that the God we are coming

to is 'Abba, Father, and infinitely good and kind.' What could be simpler than this concept of prayer? If we belong to Christ, God is our Father, we are His children(....) The trouble is that for many of us it seems too simple, even simplistic. In our sophistication we say we cannot believe it, and in any case it does not altogether tally with our experience. So we turn from Christ's prayer promises to our prayer problems".[3]

The last points are right. There is a prayer negative, namely, that in people's experience, many prayers go unanswered and few would disagree. However, what is the purpose of these particular prayers? They are not prayers of praise or thanksgiving because that is the way of expressing our love for God without asking for anything ourselves. They are requests for someone or something which God, in His wisdom and love, may or may not grant. In many of these situations it may be preferable to ask for guidance. Some misunderstanding about answers to prayer may also have arisen because of this statement made by Jesus:

"Again, truly I tell you that if two of you on earth agree about anything they ask for, it will be done for them by my Father in heaven. For where two or three gather in my name, there am I with them".[4]

It was Jesus who told His disciples to pray directly to

God, the Father, 'in His name', recorded in John's gospel. But how? Archbishop William Temple asked and answered that question:

> "How can I, in practice, ask in Christ's name or as His representative? Only if I am abiding in Him and His sayings abide in me. It is through His sayings that this mutual indwelling is effected. (...)all that we can ask in His name is that we really do His will and bear fruit for the vineyard.(...)Here we have a searching test of our prayer-life. Is it fruitful - in the effectiveness of our intercessions or our own growth in grace? If not, it is because we are not praying in His name; and that, again, is because we are not abiding in Him, nor His sayings in us."[5]

The granting of our prayers in Jesus Christ's name depends on whether we are led by the Spirit and praying for God's will to be fulfilled, not on our own wishes or desires. We pray, 'Your Will be done', not 'My will be done'! But we know that God has healed many people, not least when Christians have gathered to pray for a sick or disabled person. But why not all such requests? It is possible we misunderstand the primary purpose of miracles. The Bible tells us that Jesus healed more than 30 specific individuals during His ministry and many others who needed healing as, for example, Luke's gospel reveals.

But, clearly, He did not heal every sick person He met. It seems that Jesus is telling us the first purpose of His miracles was to demonstrate He was God's Son with His power as indicated, for example, when He was confronting the unbelief of some hostile Jews:

"Why then do you accuse me of blasphemy because I said, 'I am God's Son'? Do not believe me unless I do the works of my Father. But if I do them, even though you do not believe me, believe the works, that you may know and understand that the Father is in me, and I in the Father".[6]

His 'miracles' were demonstrable proof of God's power in and through His Son, Jesus Christ. It is also important to remember that Jesus, Himself, experienced unanswered prayer before His arrest in the garden at Gethsemane when He prayed:

"My Father, if it is possible, may this cup (Ed. His crucifixion), be taken from me. Yet not as I will, but as you will".[7] and the Apostle Luke, a doctor, writes, "And being in anguish, He prayed more earnestly, and His sweat was like drops of blood falling to the ground".[8]

We now know this was probably a medical condition known as hematidrosis which is a very rare condition which can occur when people faced with extreme physical or mental agony suffer capillary ruptures resulting in blood entering their sweat glands.

Prayer is the act of drawing close to God and being willing to carry out His will even if that means a cost to us. That cost is not always measured by money. There are times when we pray for people in difficulties of one kind or another and we may become aware that we are the very people who could help them. Giving time, support and love to those who are suffering is often 'costly', but often more valuable than money to them. Giving money is essential but, in one sense, the easiest support we can give, if we have it.

One difficulty I have when praying is to listen to what God may want to say to me.

I am quite happy to bring Him my concerns and requests but usually I allow little time to wait in silence, ready to listen to Him. No matter how often I apologise to God for failing to listen for what He may want to say to me, I still have that problem.

My second problem is distractions whilst praying. Sometimes these deviations in my mind arise without me noticing their presence for more than a moment or two. When I realise what has happened and to whom I am praying there is really no excuse I can make for my lack of concentration.

In his remarkable book on "Prayer", Philip Yancey, freely admits he has had his own problems with praying which is of some comfort to many others, like me. We can fill our lives with so much 'busy-ness' of one description or another that finding time to pray becomes either difficult or even impossible on a daily basis.

Not so, when we have a major illness, accident or a substantial problem on our hands and there seems to be no answer coming from any other available human resource. Then people who believe in God will make the time to pray because they desperately need help.

Jesus was quite clear that we need to pray always, everywhere and with persistence. We should not give up because we do not receive immediate answers and He gave us more than one example of the value and necessity of persistence in our prayers.

My personal problem of keeping silent before God to wait on any thoughts He may want to give me is one which some people may share. There are probably a variety of reasons for this. Do we really believe God is listening to us or just hoping He is? If we are not certain He is, it follows we would not be expecting to hear from Him, would we? Many people are also very busy and have difficulty in giving even enough time to make their own prayer requests without waiting in concentrated silence for the Spirit to speak to them or not, as the case may be. Many of us are happier when we are either doing things or engaging in dialogue with other people. Even then, some people find listening attentively to what others are saying quite difficult, often because they cannot wait to speak their thoughts on the subject.

If we have this problem when visible people are speaking to each other, it is little wonder we may find carefully listening to an unseen God more difficult. But I do find praying on a daily basis is very helpful and does make a difference. We can mostly set aside time to pray each day if we think it important enough.

I have been writing about personal prayer, but what of corporate prayer? Is this more, or less, important than individual prayer? Are numbers of believers giving their 'Amen' to church prayers more likely to be heard by God? Jesus, himself, gave His disciples 'The Lord's Prayer' when they asked Him how to pray, but we read that He was continually going off alone to pray to His Father in heaven. Clearly, then, God wants both individuals and communities of Christians to pray to Him.

I think Dietrich Bonheoffer, the German Pastor, who was hanged by the Nazis only a short time before the end of World War 2, wrote with a clearer understanding about prayer:

"True prayer is done in secret, but this does not

rule out the fellowship of prayer altogether, however clearly we may be aware of its dangers. In the last resort it is immaterial whether we pray in the open street or in the secrecy of our chambers, whether briefly or lengthily, in the Litany of the Church, or with the sigh of one who knows not what he should pray for. True prayer does not depend either on the individual or the whole body of the faithful, but solely upon the knowledge that our heavenly Father knows our needs. That makes God the sole object of our prayers, and frees us from a false confidence in our own prayerful efforts."[9]

He speaks about 'True prayer' and that can only come from the love in our hearts for God. The Father will always respond to those who truly love Him because He loves each one of us so much. There is, however, a real danger with corporate prayer that our minds can all too easily wander off, not least because 'set prayers' may become a habit rather than a heart's cry.

But there are also wonderful examples of church fellowships praying for God's Spirit to lead them in revivals down the centuries and to face other challenges and the Spirit has done just that!

In some churches I have attended, prayers during a morning service have often been restricted to a few minutes, particularly when prayers have been led by an ordinary member of the church. Not so, the 'three point' sermon, which may occupy 20-25 minutes or more with important points to make. But, most of the preacher's message may be forgotten by many people within a relatively short time on just one hearing, because information is now flowing into our minds from so many sources. One Bishop I knew some years ago thought 'one valuable point or issue' made in 10 minutes was more likely to be remembered and put into action than 'three'. We learn and remember mostly through experiences; teaching; discussion; observation; reading and, importantly, repetition.

We also need to recognise that repetition of certain prayers whether daily or at Sunday services can be said quite easily whilst our minds are thinking about something else. God surely wants each one of us to pray from our hearts, whether we are alone with Him or praying together. Jesus made all this clear as Matthew's gospel indicates in his report on the instructions Christ gave to His disciples in the Sermon on the Mount. It is not easy to understand how the priority of corporate prayer in our church services can be subjected to time restraints in preference to the time sometimes allowed for long sermons, hymns and other matters. A point made by John Stott with this question:

"I sometimes wonder if the slow progress towards world peace and world evangelisation is

due to the prayerlessness of the people of God(...)
If local churches were to bow down before God
every Sunday for ten or twenty or even thirty
minutes, what might God be free to do?"[10]

What indeed? But individual churches in many
denominations seem to set up their own priorities, rules and
practices within, of course, an approved denominational
format as far as services are concerned, including those
using outdated language foreign to younger people.

As for the latter, this problem was non-existent for the
early disciples, (or more correctly translated - 'students')
who prayed and spoke in their common Aramaic language
of the day. Why do some Christians think that young people
today might be encouraged to attend church services
where the English language relevant to 1662 is being used?

In the latter part of that same 17th century, a renowned
French lady, Jeanne Guyon, wrote a book, "Experiencing
the Depths of Jesus Christ", which had, and continues to
have, a considerable influence on many people:

"The simple, undisguised emotions of love express
infinitely more to God than the words of any
language. For some reason men try to love God by
forms and rules. Can you not see it is by these very
forms and rules that you have lost so much of that
love? How unnecessary it is to teach the art of loving!

The language of love is strange and unnatural to that man who does not love. Oh, but it is perfectly natural to the one who loves. And how shall you love Him? It is amazing and delightful to see that it is the simplest Christians who often progress farthest in an inner relationship with Jesus Christ! Why? Because the Spirit of God simply does not need our tapestry! The simplest can know Him, and in the deepest way, with no help from rituals or forms or theological instruction!"[11]

There were no church buildings, as such, until the 4th Century, as far as we know, and followers of Jesus Christ gathered in people's homes and outside in e.g. the Temple Courts. The Greek word 'ekklesia' in the bible New Testament is correctly translated as 'an assembly or congregation called out', - not a 'church' meaning a building or organisation. William Tyndale, fluent in eight languages and proficient in ancient Hebrew and Greek, produced the first English 'New Testament' bible in 1526 translating 'ekklesia' correctly from the dialect of Greek and, possibly, Aramaic. King James had it changed to 'Church' for the bible named after him.

For nearly 300 years after Jesus was crucified and rose from the dead, the early Christian communities were very different from the churches men have established since the 4th century. The major reason for the rapid growth in Christianity over the first three centuries was that believers were full of love for God and each other; followed Christ, and were inspired by the Spirit to share and to express their faith in words and deeds. The earliest followers of Jesus Christ met frequently in their homes each week to learn from each other and their elders, to pray and support each other in their determination to go out and spread the 'good news', led by the Spirit.

They had no church buildings, no clergy, very little money in relative terms and no positions of power as the 'Acts of the Apostles' in the New Testament makes clear. 'Elders' were appointed from within their small groups, because they had demonstrated their commitment to follow Christ over many years and acknowledged for their experience in life and the love of their neighbours. Groups were not free of troubles within and persecution without, but they were full of motivation to take the message of salvation through Christ to as many people as would listen. Countless people did listen and believed. The significant growth of what later became known as Christianity happened because of their unity of purpose and their hearts of love and fire inspired and led by the Spirit. What do we have to learn from their example?

My own experience suggests small groups encouraged by their churches, meeting each week, have the best opportunity of replicating the early Christian meetings. Providing they are free and encouraged to discuss issues agreed within their own group, showing their love for each other with practical help for those in need and praying for the Spirit to guide them in ways to spread the gospel.

Little enough time is often given over to prayer in many church services whereas small groups have no such constraints. I know from personal experience in the groups I have attended over many years, how valuable that time of prayer has been for group members.

Small groups meeting in their homes are places where true Christian fellowship and love for one another can be built up which is no surprise for in the early church that is exactly what they practiced. And, clearly, prayer was a priority for all the early followers of Christ when they met – not just for one or two believers to undertake on behalf of everyone else who would say 'Amen' at the end!

One result of this common commitment to meet and pray 'constantly' was expressed in their care, concern and action to help those who were in need – practicing what they preached. Many Christians over the years have shown equal concern for the needy as well as supporting their established churches. However, getting the balance right between the needs of the corporate 'church' and those who suffer is often difficult. Using our time and talents to help and support those in our own communities who are in real need and giving money and goods for others worldwide, mainly through charities, including millions of suffering children who do not have even the basic requirements for life is also a priority for Christians. We know that God not only expects, but commands us to 'love our neighbour as ourselves'.

Prayer in church, in small groups and by individuals is fundamental to Christian life. It is our expression of love and trust in God, our Father. We are His children and He wants a loving relationship with each one of us. Sometimes we can forget to praise Him, to thank Him for His infinite love, and His past blessings before making yet more requests to Him. Surely, the former are the first priorities. God knows all that we need as Jesus told us, so the length of our prayer requests is not an issue. Nor are the words we use if they are sincere.

The Lord's Prayer emphasises our first priorities are to pray His name will be hallowed, 'honoured as holy', for His kingdom to come and His will to be done in our lives. Only then are we to make our requests. How short the Lord's Prayer is, giving us the space within the prayer to express our love for God, our praise, our thanks and then, our requests. Brevity and simplicity were hallmarks of Jesus teaching on the really important commands He gave.

When asked by a Pharisee an expert in the law, "Teacher, which is the greatest commandment in the law?", Jesus replied, "Love the Lord your God with all your heart and with all your soul and with all your mind(...)Love your neighbour as yourself. All the law and the prophets hang on these two commandments".[12] Jesus did not give us dozens of rules or regulations to follow – just two simple commands. True love covers everybody and everything.

Many people for centuries after Jesus died could neither read nor write, but they truly believed in the love of God, the Father, His son Jesus Christ and the Holy Spirit. They continually prayed and in doing so were filled by the Spirit. They had no doubts about spreading the gospel even when they were being persecuted and killed for their faith and true believers have continued to do so in every century since then, right up to the present time. That commitment by ordinary people, since Christ's resurrection, to pray and to follow Jesus in spreading the 'Good News' are the principle reasons why it is estimated that more than 30% of the world's population now claim to be Christians.

May I thank you for reading this book.
I hope and pray it has been of some value to you.
Much more can be gained by reading any of the books
relevant to each chapter listed in the Bibliography which
follows. I am deeply indebted to all these authors who
have given me so much understanding and many answers
to these 'Questions' in my own journey of faith.

As I approach the end of my long life,
I know more clearly than ever that Paul, the Apostle, was
so right when he wrote in his letter to the Corinthians:

> "Now I know in part; then I shall know fully, even
> as I am fully known. And now these three remain:
> faith, hope and love. But the greatest of these is
> love."[13]

As I close this book,
may I offer you this lovely prayer of blessing:

'Go, and know that the Lord goes with you:

let him lead you each day

into the quiet place of your heart,

where he will speak with you;

know that he **loves** you

and watches over you -

that he **listens** to you in gentle understanding,

that he is with you always

wherever you are and however you may feel:

and may the blessing of God –

Father, Son and Holy Spirit

be yours for ever.' (14)

# 8. Group Questions

**CHAPTER ONE**
WHICH LOVE MAKES THE
REAL DIFFERENCE TO LIFE?

**1.** Who are our 'neighbours' in this 21st Century? How can we express our love for them? What limits do we put on our love? Do we expect a return of our love in some form?

**2.** How do we respond to Christ's instructions in Matthew's Gospel? (Ch. 25 v.31-46) (p.26-27)

**3.** Is John Stott right in his description of how we should express God's love for our 'neighbours'? (p.33)

**CHAPTER TWO**
DO WE NEED TO FORGIVE?

**1.** How did you re-act to Corrie ten Boom's experience in facing one of her SS Guards? (p.36-37)

**2.** Is it difficult to distinguish the difference between 'forgiving' and 'forgetting' the harm we may have received from others?

**3.** Are we generally good in confessing our wrongs or do we, sometimes, try to give reasons why they were really caused by something or someone else?

**4.** What is our attitude towards people who will not forgive our wrongs or mistakes?

**CHAPTER THREE**
WHY WOULD YOU BELIEVE
IN JESUS CHRIST?

**1.** What was your re-action to Alison Morgan's partial profile of Jesus Christ? (p.52-54)

**2.** Do we try to go the 'extra mile' to help people whether we think they deserve our support or not?

**3.** Do we know and are we prepared to give the evidence for Christ's resurrection to anyone who questions its validity?

**CHAPTER FOUR**
HOW ON EARTH DOES A
LOVING GOD ALLOW PAIN
AND SUFFERING?

**1.** In what ways could we influence Governments in rich nations to take more action to meet the basic needs of the poorest people in the world?

**2.** What were your feelings when reading Philip Yancey's experience of visiting Green Pastures Hospital with his wife and meeting Danmaya? (p. 83-84)

**3.** How do we explain healing miracles for only a few, when prayers for healing are offered for so many?

**CHAPTER FIVE**
LIVING WITH HOPE
OR JUST SURVIVING?

**I.** What credibility does the Atheist conviction have? Can we answer their claims?

2. Do you think Ravi Zacharias was right in his views on the dangers for young people living in an increasingly secular society? (p. 99) What could be done to help them?

**3.** In what ways, and when, can we help and support Agnostics who may be seeking the truth about God's existence?

**CHAPTER SIX**
A DOOR TO THE SECRET
OF THE UNIVERSE?

**I.** Was C.S. Lewis right in his analysis of why so many young people were indifferent to Christianity last century? (p.121-122) Is it the same today and, if so, who is to blame?

**2.** What is your opinion on the standards of morality which our society projects to the young? What are the ways in which we might show them how a Christian life would make a real difference to themselves and the people they know and love?

**3.** How do we, as individuals, protest about new changes in the law or business practices which we view as wrong with good reasons from a Christian perspective ?

**CHAPTER SEVEN**
WHAT DO WE EXPECT
IF WE PRAY?

**I.** What difficulties, if any, do we find in praying each day?

**2.** How do we deal with unanswered prayer?

**3.** What is your response to John Stott's view on the time allowed for Church prayers? (p. 139-140)

**4.** Do you think Jeanne Guyon's advice on individual prayer, centuries ago, would help more people today to pray simply from their hearts? (p. 140-141)

## Notes

**CHAPTER ONE**
WHICH LOVE MAKES THE REAL DIFFERENCE TO LIFE?

(1) GIVING ALL — www.websites-host.com/insp/istories.html
(2) DEPT. OF HEALTH — Abortion Statistics, England and Wales: 2013/2014
(3) THE TELEGRAPH — 09.03.2015
(4) PRISON FELLOWSHIP WEBSITE 2015
(5) BIBLE — Matthew's Gospel — Ch.22 v.37-39
(6) BIBLE - I John — Ch.5 v.19
(7) LAW, WILLIAM — 'A Serious Call to a devout and Holy Life' (2009) - p206
(8) BIBLE - Matthew's Gospel - Ch. 25 v.31-46
(9) FRANK VIOLA & GEORGE BARNA - 'Pagan Christianity?'
(10) DALLAS WILLARD — 'Personal Religion, Public Morality?' (2009) — p209-210
(11) THE MESSAGE BIBLE — I Corinthians: Ch13 v 3
(12) JOHN SCOTT — 'The Contemporary Christian' (1992) — p256

**CHAPTER TWO**
DO WE NEED FORGIVE?

(1) CORRIE TEN BOOM (2003) — 'No Hiding Place' — p215
(2) BIBLE - Matthew's Gospel — Ch.18 v 32-35
(3) BIBLE - Matthew's Gospel — Ch.5 v 23-24
(4) BIBLE - Matthew's Gospel — Ch.5 v 44-47
(5) BIBLE - Matthew's Gospel — Ch.7 v 1-2

(6)  BIBLE - Luke's Gospel – Ch.15 v 25-32

(7)  BIBLE - John's Gospel – Ch.8 v 3-11
     'The earliest manuscripts do not have John 7:53-8:11'

(8)  BIBLE - Paul's Letter to the Colossians – Ch3 v.12-13

## CHAPTER THREE

WHY WOULD YOU BELIEVE IN JESUS CHRIST?

(1)  MATTHEW PARRIS – 'The Spectator' – 12.02.2012

(2)  ALISON MORGAN – 'The Wild Gospel'(2005) - p62 & p82

(3)  MICHAEL GREEN – 'But don't all Religions'(2003) - p31/32

(4)  PHILIP YANCEY – 'What's so Amazing about Grace'
     (1997) – p242

(5)  BIBLE – Matthew's Gospel Ch.5 v 33-37

(6)  BIBLE – Matthew's Gospel Ch.5 v 39-42

(7)  PROF. J. POLKINGHORNE – 'Quantum Physics &
     Theology'(2007) - p38/39

(8)  BIBLE – Matthew's Gospel Ch.20 v 18-19

(9)  BIBLE – Luke's Gospel Ch.24 v 39

(10) PETER WALKER – 'The Weekend that Changed the
     World'(1999) - p195

(11) DALLAS WILLARD – 'Personal Religion, Public Morality'
     (2009) - p106

(12) PETER WALKER – 'The Weekend that Changed the World'
     (1999) - p195

(13) STUDDERT KENNEDY, G.A. – Poem "INDIFFERENCE"

## CHAPTER FOUR

HOW ON EARTH DOES A LOVING
GOD ALLOW PAIN AND SUFFERING?

(1)  PHILIP YANCEY – 'The Jesus I never Knew' (1995) – p171

(2)  PETER KREEFT – 'Making Sense out of Suffering'(1987) – p19-21

(3)  PHILIP YANCEY – 'Where is God When it Hurts?'(1990) – p57/58

(4)  PHILIP YANCEY – 'Where is God When it Hurts?'( 1990) – p260

(5)  RAVI ZACHARIAS – 'Cries of the Heart' (1998) – p216

(6)  PHILIP YANCEY – 'Prayer'(2006) – p265/6

(7)  RAVI ZACHARIAS – 'Can Man Live Without God?' (1994) – p52

(8)  BIBLE – I John Ch.3 v17-18

**CHAPTER FIVE**

LIVING WITH HOPE OR JUST SURVIVING?

(I)  MICHEL QUOIST – 'Meeting God'(1989) – p16-17

(2)  PROFESSOR J. POLKINGHORNE – 'One World'(1986) – p68/69

(3)  DALLAS WILLARD – 'Does God Exist?'(1993) – p208/9

(4)  RAVI ZACHARIAS – 'Can Man Live without God'(1994) – p94

(5)  OXFAM – Press release January 2016

(6)  PETER KREEFT – 'Does God Exist?'(1993) – p290

(7)  PETER KREEFT – 'Does God Exist?'(1993) – p291

(8)  BIBLE – John's Gospel – Ch.3 v.16

**CHAPTER SIX**

A DOOR TO THE SECRET OF THE UNIVERSE?

(I)  WILLIAM LAW – 'A Serious Call to a devout and Holy Life' (2009) - p204

(2)  WELBY, ARCHBISHOP JUSTIN – 'Third Way Magazine'(2013)

(3)  C.S. LEWIS – 'The Business of Heaven' (1984) edited by Walter Hooper –p88

(4)  THE TELEGRAPH – 20.10.2014

(5)  C.S. LEWIS – 'The Business of Heaven' (1984) edited by Walter Hooper –p88

(6) THE CHRISTIAN INSTITUTE REPORT – (October 2014)

(7) RAVI ZACHARIAS – A Shattered Visage – The Real Face of Atheism(1995) - p122

(8) C.S. LEWIS – God in the Dock(1986) – p68

(9) BIBLE – Revelation – Ch.3 v.20

(10) JOHN SCOTT – 'Your Confirmation' – (1991) – p23/24

## CHAPTER SEVEN

WHAT DO WE EXPECT IF WE PRAY?

(1) BIBLE – Matthew's Gospel – Ch.6 v.7-8

(2) PHILIP YANCEY – Prayer(2006) - p182

(3) JOHN STOTT – The Sermon on the Mount - p185

(4) BIBLE – Matthew's Gospel – Ch.18 v.20

(5) WILLIAM TEMPLE – Readings in St John's Gospel (1950) - p262-263

(6) BIBLE – John's Gospel – Ch. 10 v. 36-39

(7) BIBLE – Matthew's Gospel - Ch.26 v 39

(8) BIBLE – Luke's Gospel – Ch.22 v.44

(9) DIETRICH BONHEOFFER – The Cost of Discipleship (1978) – p147

(10) JOHN STOTT – The Living Church(2007) - p145

(11) JEANNE GUYON – Experiencing the Depths of Jesus Christ (1975) - p123

(12) BIBLE – Matthew's Gospel - Ch.22 v.36-40

(13) BIBLE – Paul's 1st Letter to the Corinthians – Ch.13 v.12&13

(14) AUTHOR ANONYMOUS – quoted in Best Loved Prayers & Words of Wisdom - p (2009) - p154

# Bibliography

Copyrite permissions have been given in respect of quotations or extracts included in each chapter, where required. Apologies are made for any omissions or inaccuracies that have been made by mistake. If notified of any, these will be corrected in future printings.

**CHAPTER ONE** WHICH LOVE MAKES THE REAL DIFFERENCE TO LIFE?

GIVING ALL — www.websites-host.com/insp/istories.html - with permission

DEPT. OF HEALTH — Abortion Statistics, England and Wales: 2013/2014

THE TELEGRAPH — 09.03.2015 - © Telegraph Media Group Limited 2014/2015 - with permission

PRISON FELLOWSHIP WEBSITE 2015 - with permission

LAW, WILLIAM (1686-1761) — Extract from 'A Serious Call to a Devout and Holy Life'(2009) published by Hendrickson Publishers

VIOLA, FRANK & GEORGE BARNA — Source: 'Pagan Christianity?: Exploring the Roots of Our Church Practices'(2008) Copyright © 2002, 2008 by Frank Viola and George Barna. Tyndale House Publishers, Inc

WILLARD, DALLAS — Personal Religion, Public Reality?(2009) Copyrite © 2009 Dallas Willard. Reproduced by permission of Hodder and Stoughton Limited

STOTT, REV'D JOHN — The Contemporary Christian(1992) published by Inter-Varsity Press. Copyrite © John R. W. Stott 1992 granted within 'fair dealing' limits by SPCK/IVP

**CHAPTER TWO** DO WE NEED FORGIVE?

TEN BOOM, CORRIE — 'No Hiding Place' (2003)
published by 'Chosen Books', a division of Baker Publishing
Group © 2003. 'Used by permission'


**CHAPTER THREE** WHY WOULD YOU BELIEVE IN JESUS CHRIST?

PARRIS, MATTHEW — The Spectator (12.02.2012)
with permission from The Spectator and Matthew Parris

MORGAN, REV'D DR. ALISON — Extracts from The Wild Gospel
(2005) byAlisonMorgan,copyrite©2004Alison Morgan.
Used with permission of Lion Hudson plc.

GREEN, REV'D MICHAEL — 'But don't all Religions Lead to God'
(2003) published by SPCK/IVP granted within 'fair-dealing' limits.

YANCEY, PHILIP — Taken from 'What's so Amazing about Grace'
(1997) by Philip Clancey. Copyrite © 1997 by Philip D.Yancey. Use
by permission of Zondervan www.zondervan.com

POLKINGHORNE, PROF. JOHN — 'Quantum Physics & Theology'
(2007) published by SPCK. Copyrite © 2007 by John Polkinghorne
granted within 'fair dealing' limits by SPCK

WALKER, PETER — taken from 'The Weekend that Changed the
World'(1999) by Peter Walker. Copyright © 1999 P.W. L. Walker.
Use by permission of Zondervan. www.zondervan.com

WILLARD, DALLAS — Personal Religion, Public Morality?(2009)
first published as 'Knowing Christ Today: Why We Can Trust
Spiritual Knowledge Today' by Dallas Willard, Copyrite © 2009
by Dallas Willard. Reprinted by kind permission of Harper Collins
Publishers.

STUDDERT KENNEDY, G.A. (1883-1929) – "Indifference"
poem - quoted in 'Best Loved Prayers and Words of Wisdom'
compiled by Martin H. Manser © 2009 by Martin Manser.

**CHAPTER FOUR**

HOW ON EARTH DOES A LOVING GOD ALLOW PAIN AND SUFFERING?

YANCEY, PHILIP – Taken from 'The Jesus I never Knew'(1995)
by Philip Yancey. Copyrite © 1995 by Philip Yancey. Used by
permission of Zondervan www.zondervan.com

KREEFT, PETER – 'Making Sense out of Suffering'(1987)
published by Hodder with permission for the UK and in the USA
permission granted by Franciscan Media under 'fair use'

YANCEY, PHILIP – Taken from 'Where is God When it Hurts?'
(1990) by Philip Yancey. Copyrite © 1990, 1977 by Philip Yancey.
Used by permission of Zondervan www.zondervan.com

ZACHARIAS, RAVI – Taken from 'Cries of the Heart'(1998)
by Ravi Zacharias. Copyrite © 1998 by Ravi Zacharias.
Used by permission of Thomas Nelson

YANCEY, PHILIP – Taken from 'Prayer: Does it Make any
Difference' by Philip Yancey. Copyrite © (2006) by Philip Yancey.
Used by permission of Zondervan. www.zondervan.com

ZACHARIAS, RAVI – Taken from 'Can Man Live Without
God'(1994) by Ravi Zacharias Copyright © 1994 by Ravi Zacharias.
Used by permission of Thomas Nelson. www.thomasnelson.com

**CHAPTER FIVE** LIVING WITH HOPE OR JUST SURVIVING?

QUOIST, MICHEL – 'Meeting God'(1989) published by
Gill Books with permission

POLKINGHORNE, PROF. JOHN — 'One World'(1986)
published by SPCK. Copyrite © 1986 by John Polkinghorne
granted within 'fair dealing' limits from SPCK

WILLARD, DALLAS — quoted in 'Does God Exist?(1993)
by J.P. Moreland & Kai Nielson published by Prometheus Books.
Permission granted under 'fair use' policy

ZACHARIAS, RAVI — Taken from 'Can Man Live Without God'
(1994) by Ravi Zacharias Copyright © 1994 by Ravi Zacharias.
Used by permission of Thomas Nelson. www.thomasnelson.com

OXFAM — The material on page 90, from '62 people own same
as half world', 2016 is reproduced with permission of Oxfam,
Oxfam House, John Smith Drive, Cowley, Oxford OX4 2JY, UK
www.oxfam.org.uk Oxfam does not necessarily endorse any text
or activities that accompany the materials.

KREEFT, PETER — quoted in 'Does God Exist?(1993)
by J.P. Moreland & Kai Nielson published by Prometheus Books
Permission granted under 'fair use' policy

**CHAPTER SIX** A DOOR TO THE SECRET OF THE UNIVERSE?

LAW, WILLIAM (1686-1761) — Extract from 'A Serious Call to a
Devout and Holy Life'(2009) published by Hendrickson Publishers

WELBY, ARCHBISHOP JUSTIN — 'Third Way Magazine'(2013)
Permission granted by the Church Times. Also quoted in
'Archbishop Justin: The Road to Canterbury'(2009) by Andrew
Atherstone, published by Darton, Longman and Todd Ltd.

LEWIS, C.S. — quoted in 'The Business of Heaven'(1984)
C.S. Lewis © C.S. Lewis Pte.Ltd. 1984. Edited by Walter Hooper.
Extract reprinted by permission

THE TELEGRAPH — (20.10.2014) - © Telegraph Media Group Limited 2014/2015 - with permission

THE CHRISTIAN INSTITUTE REPORT — (October 2014) - with permission

ZACHARIAS, RAVI — 'The Shattered Visage – The Real Face of Atheism' (1995) by Ravi Zacharias published by Baker Books. Copyrite © 1990 by Ravi Zacharias. Used by permission of Baker Books

LEWIS, C.S. — 'God in the Dock'(1986) by C.S. Lewis copyrite © C.S. Lewis Pte. Ltd. 1970. Extract reprinted by permission

STOTT, REV'D JOHN — 'Your Confirmation'(1991) Copyright © 1991 John R.W. Stott. Reproduced by permission of Hodder and Stoughton Ltd. Also quoted in 'Best Loved Prayers & Words of Wisdom'(2009)

**CHAPTER SEVEN** WHAT DO WE EXPECT IF WE PRAY?

YANCEY, PHILIP — Taken from 'Prayer: Does it Make any Difference' by Philip Yancey. Copyrite © (2006) by Philip Yancey. Used by permission of Zondervan. www.zondervan.com

STOTT, REV'D JOHN — The Sermon on the Mount (1984) published by Inter Varsity Press. Copyright © John R.W. Stott 1978 granted within 'fair dealing' limits by SPCK/IVP

TEMPLE, ARCHBISHOP WILLIAM — Readings in St. John's Gospel (1950) published by McMillan & Co

BONHEOFFER, DIETRICH (1906-1945) — The Cost of Discipleship (1978) published by SCM Press Ltd

STOTT, REV'D JOHN — The Living Church(2007) published
by Inter-Varsity Press. Copyrite © John R. W. Stott 2007
granted within 'fair dealing' limits by SPCK/IVP

GUYON, JEANNE (1648-1717) — quoted in 'Experiencing the
Depths of Jesus Christ' published by Seed Sowers,
© P.O.Box3317 Jacksonville, FL32206
Email:books@seedsowers.com Gene Edwards MCMLXXV

ANONYMOUS - quoted on p154 in 'Best Loved Prayers & Words
of Wisdom'(2009) —published by Collins (highly recommended),
edited by Martin Manser. Copyright © 2009 Martin Manser.
Author unknown.

## JHS Books
P.O. Box 613, Dorking RH4 9JT
www.jhsbooks.com
(Further copies can ordered from
the above address or website)

## About the Author

John, married to his loving
wife Margaret, lives in Surrey.
They share the joy of having
had two precious children - Martin and Deborah.

He enjoyed a very long career in Financial Services,
holding various senior management positions in
his first 17 years,  However, at the age of 50, John
decided  to leave corporate life and concentrate on
providing personal financial advice to families, private
individuals and small companies.

At the heart of his life, has been a passion to
care for others with integrity and a quiet generosity.
John's Christian faith and experience has led to his
involvement and commitment to numerous charitable
organisations working to meet the needs of those who
are marginalised and suffering.

John retired from work in his mid-seventies.
He continues on his faith journey. He is a man
who treasures contemplation and time spent with
God. He is also a man who speaks and writes about
the Christian faith with an informed mind and a
compassionate heart.

BROKEN CONSORT

Will Eaves is a novelist and poet. *Murmur,* his most recent novel, won the 2019 Wellcome Prize and was co-winner of the Republic of Consciousness Prize. *The Absent Therapist* (CBe, 2014) was shortlisted for the Goldsmiths Prize; *The Inevitable Gift Shop* (CBe, 2016) was shortlisted for the Ted Hughes Award. He has worked as Arts Editor at the *TLS* and Associate Professor at the University of Warwick. He is a columnist for the *Brixton Review of Books* and co-host with Professor Sophie Scott of *The Neuromantics,* a podcast on science and literature.

also by Will Eaves

*The Oversight*
*Nothing to Be Afraid Of*
*This Is Paradise*
*The Absent Therapist*
*Murmur*

*Sound Houses*
*The Inevitable Gift Shop*

# Broken Consort

*Essays, reviews, and other writings*

WILL EAVES

First published in the UK in 2020
by CB editions
146 Percy Road London W12 9QL
www.cbeditions.com

The right of Will Eaves to be identified as author
of this work has been asserted in accordance
with the Copyright, Designs and Patents Act, 1988

Printed in England by Blissetts, London W3 8DH

ISBN 978-1-909585-35-5

For Michael S. Caines

# Contents

# Notebooks

Last week I lost a notebook and found it again at the weekend, my relief tempered by disappointment when I turned the pages and saw how little I'd used it. Notebooks are a writer's workshop, says Somerset Maugham in the preface to his own published selection of sketches and impressions, but if so mine was deserted. Where were the great ideas and suggestive phrases? All I could see were offcuts and shavings, odd memos to an absent creator ('put the pterodactyl *after* A comes round'). And, of course, the gaps in the record, the stories that stopped or weren't written at all: 'He was everywhere, his head poking out of the fireplace, those wide eyes bobbing about in the soup.'

Entries in notebooks aren't dated (a dated notebook is a diary), but omissions and changes in direction often signify a break in activity – illness, death, work – from which the writer returns in a different hand, re-inked by experience. What was I thinking all that time? What was I reading? Perhaps I was writing properly. 'You should have been an actor', the long gaps say, like friends at an awkward reunion when they are reminded of something funny from the past, when the things they have done with their lives (like proper writing) seem for a moment to be the things they ought not to have done, when the path not taken shines particularly brightly.

I was an actor briefly, in the late 1980s after university, when I joined a small ensemble called The Irish Company and found myself cast as James Joyce in a dramatic anthology by Gemma O'Connor of extracts from Irish literature called *Ferocious Chastity*. It was a good selection, the title phrase of which was borrowed from Sean O'Casey (who may have borrowed it from Karl Marx), and used to describe the sexual temperament of Irish women. We toured. The last venue was the Irish Centre in London, on St Patrick's Day. My Irish accent border-hopped very freely. Joyce wore little round spectacles, too, but there the resemblance between us ended. I took mine off because the audience was so silent and frightening. I got my Equity card and went to a remote part of Norway to catalogue a private library.

It was a relief to stop acting, but the relief wore off. I didn't know how to catalogue anything and spent three dark winter weeks looking at copies of Dickens's magazines, *Household Words* and *All the Year Round*, originally collected by a Victorian minister, Charles Lillingston, who'd left England in protest at the rise of the Oxford Movement. I sorted the magazines chronologically and the books alphabetically. That took a few days. For the remaining two and a half weeks I stared out of the window or drifted from room to room, pursued by a Lillingston-shaped conscience, afraid the phone would ring and the house's kindly owners, away visiting family in Scotland, would announce their return. One day it did ring. 'How are you getting on?' they enquired. 'Oh, you know,' I replied. 'Still making notes.' I read *Peer Gynt*, and looked out of the window again. The view was of a glaciated inlet, a sharp tooth at the back of Dalsfjord's jaw. Across its black water, walls of snow-flecked granite rose hundreds of feet into the air.

I did write a catalogue, of sorts, but I can't imagine it was of any use. It was a list, that's all. I made notes in abundance, too, though I have not re-read them; writers often don't, Maugham says, pointing out that, if you write fiction, it is easy to be seduced by your note-taking into using 'research' that does not belong, imaginatively, to the work in hand. Behind that distinction, though, is something less benign: the idea that there is provisional work and proper work; and then the fear that the provisional will distract you from more important work, the real book you're meant to be writing; and then again the delusion, common to many, that one is always being distracted.

But making stuff up *is* a distraction. Novels aim to divert. And sometimes, too, a necessary diversion from writing brings you to your senses. Three years ago I felt very trapped and a bit sorry for myself, what with family difficulties and a back problem that got steadily worse until I found myself in hospital watching a surgeon on a monitor put a needle into my spine. I'd wanted to be a runner! I'd joined the Herne Hill Harriers! I'd bought some cross-country trainers with big spikes in them! The two years after that are greyed-out. I managed fine with painkillers, but I was taking too many. The notes became medical notes. I spent £5,000 on a new chair, a desk, drugs, physiotherapy, more drugs, all the usual fixes, and I fretted about the novel I was supposed to be writing. In the end, I decided to stop worrying and, remembering that view in Norway, heeded the call of the Boyg in *Peer Gynt*: 'Go Round!' I signed up for a course in Geology at Birkbeck.

Being Walter Mitty will take you so far. I really enjoyed that course, and will go back to it at some point, I hope. It was hard, though, especially for someone whose last exposure to science was at school, watching Mr Stevens being taken away in an ambulance after vividly demonstrating the difference between a flask of water and one of thirst-quenching mercury chloride. I took many notes. Science writing is ideally notational, as were the tutors' comments on my answers: 'Not a real compound.' 'Not really.' 'No.'

The best part was a field trip to Aust, a small town on the River Severn, right next to the first suspension bridge over the estuary into Wales. As a family we used to stop at the motorway services there and I found them excitingly busy – with their carousels of I-Spy books and travel sweets, the bridge outside the café window disappearing into the mist – but how much smaller, how much quieter, they are now. Today, most of the traffic flows over the bigger bridge downstream, built in 1996, and the road to Aust is the ghost road to childhood. Or, for us students, the road to Severn beach and the rocks of Aust Cliff, where the geological strata and their succession are exemplarily exposed.

At the top are shelly limestones and clays from the Jurassic Period, then come the shales, the green marls, red marls and gypsum of the Triassic; and then, before the Carboniferous limestone on which the bridge is built, there is a bit missing: the Permian. No deposits, a gap in the record of about 45 million years. This is what geologists call an unconformity. And that break in the weather (not much rain in the Permian) put matters into perspective for me. My lost-and-found notebook has almost nothing in it from 2009, but I have files of equations and palaeontological diagrams from the same year. They diverted me and I learnt something in the process: gaps in the record aren't always absences. Paths not taken may still lead somewhere. An important part of writing is throwing everybody, oneself included, off the scent. It keeps your work, your thoughts, private. On the coach back to Birkbeck, our tutor caught me adding to an already too-long homework answer. 'That's too much,' she said. 'Notes will do. You're not writing a novel.'

## GoldenEye

Admirers of Ian Fleming's James Bond novels have always taken a dim view of the films. After *Thunderball* (1965), they certainly had little to do with the books in terms of plot, but then plotting, as his editor E. L. Doctorow observed, was never Fleming's strong suit. More importantly, Anthony Burgess complained that Bond had become 'gimmicky' on screen; that the cinema's obsession with devices, rather than desires, misrepresented the hero. This isn't altogether true. In fact, because Bond is a Cold War warrior, the distinction between different kinds of devices, or gadgets, is germane to both books and films. Good gadgets are life-enhancing (Rolex Oyster Perpetual Chronometers, Lotus sports-car submersibles), whereas bad ones (deadly weapons) usually serve the needs of a bloated state such as the Soviet Union or a crime syndicate (SPECTRE).

In *GoldenEye*, the seventeenth Bond film and the first since the collapse of Communism, the Cold War is no more, political loyalty is cheap (the arch-villain Janus, as his duplicitous name suggests, is a renegade MI5 agent), but the gadgets, good and bad, remain. GoldenEye itself, spuriously named after Fleming's Jamaican home, is an old Cold War 'rumour' that turns out to be real – a satellite that fires an electro-magnetic pulse capable of wiping out whole communications infrastructures. Smaller utensils for the hero, now played by Pierce Brosnan, are supplied by the octogenarian Q (Desmond Llewellyn), and include an exploding Biro and a wrist-watch detonating device. One of the catches is that Janus, who has filched GoldenEye from the Russians, remembers how to deactivate the watch. 'Is Q still up to his old tricks?' he smirks, before pressing a button. The director, Martin Campbell, places the emphasis on know-how, not fire-power; the technology is unmysterious. We even hear GoldenEye referred to, prosaically, as 'the world's greatest cashcard', which implies that anyone could use it.

The film opens with an extraordinary mocked-up stunt: an unpiloted plane drops off a mountain edge into the abyss. Bond rides a bike after it, free falls a thousand feet and catches it. But this, we are soon informed, is a stunt set in the past – part of MI5's photo album. The rest of the film, set in the present, is largely concerned with 007's ambiguous status as a modern man of action. In one long sequence, Bond carves up most of St Petersburg in a tank and skewers a bronze pegasus on his gun turret. For an encore, he rescues the beautiful Russian computer programmer Natalya Simonova (Izabella Scorupco) from Janus (Sean Bean), but Natalya isn't much of a hard-action fan. 'Boys with toys,' she sniffs, and quietly sets about hacking into GoldenEye's nerve centre in the virtual world, while Bond drums his fists on the wall in the real one.

The suggestion is not so much that Bond has been emasculated by the political and technological transformations of the past six years, but that the link between sex and heroic endeavour is no longer an automatic reflex of the plot. There is, if you like, no clubbable spur to his philandering. Fleming's readers will not fear this approach. We are told often enough in the novels that Bond's womanising offends M's 'Victorian soul'; it even offends a puritanical strand in Bond himself. Aptly, then, M is now a woman – Judi Dench in a severe suit with a budget to balance. She calls Bond 'a sexist, misogynist dinosaur'; the boys at MI5 dub her 'the evil queen of numbers'; Brosnan keeps his counsel. This is shrewd characterisation, for Fleming's 007 is as incompatible with sexual partners, in the long term, as he is wary of his boss. All girls leave him in the end, apart from his housekeeper, and who is M if not the national housekeeper?

Solitariness should be essential for the film hero, as it is for the hero of the books. The trouble with the gags and gadgets in the films was never their improbability – the Soviet double agent Oleg Gordievsky recently revealed that the missile-firing cigarettes and jet-propelled back-packs were taken perfectly seriously by the KGB – but the fact that they were wielded, for the most part, by a chatty, sociable animal. And Bond, like most snobs – like Fleming, one suspects – loathes the lack of distinction that conviviality implies. This is not true, say, of John Buchan's Richard Hannay, an obvious source in other respects, in whom national and personal grace are combined. There is, instead, something 'alien and un-English' about 007. As we discover in *Moonraker* (1954), Bond is 'not the sort of chap one usually sees in [the club] Blades'; he is 'a difficult man to cover up. Particularly in England.' One explanation for this is simply that Bond is not English at all, but half-Scots and half-Swiss. Another is that his un-Englishness brands him a knight errant out of place at home, mentally scarred because the violence of his moral code disqualifies him from enjoying its social benefits. He is St George on self-thwarting repeat.

*GoldenEye* gets to the heart of this when Janus taunts 007 with a vision of his funeral – 'nothing but some doormen and a few tearful restaurateurs'. The bitchiness, far from being a waste of time, shows how nearly alike the two men are: to every snob commander, his inverted lieutenant. It also reminds us that James Bond is, above all, a spy, and that spies work under cover, condemned to anonymity. A well-known, or iconic, spy is therefore a ludicrous idea, and one that Fleming satirises in *From Russia with Love* (1955), in which the Soviet organisation of terror, SMERSH, identifies Bond's celebrity as the weak point of the Secret Service.

This truth has always presented problems for the films, which necessarily make stars of the actors who play 007, but it also gives a fresh face a natural advantage. In this respect, Brosnan is ideal: distinctive but not yet famous, assertive but never brash or cocky. He acts well, too, though not with the thespian scowl that troubled Timothy Dalton's interpretation of the role. Rather, Brosnan makes the right moves, perfecting a walk with the leisurely swing of a nine-iron, and a swerving run for the action sequences that suggests something of the art of *wedeln* (hip-waggling) on the piste. He is handsome without being a dandy; tough, but not invincible; wry, but not, as Roger Moore seemed, an aspiring comic. All three qualities are put to good use in his flirtation with Janus's fellow conspirator, Xenia Onatopp (Famke Janssen), who kills her lovers by crushing them between her thighs. Bond and Onatopp meet first in evening dress and enjoy a vodka martini. They spar again, less amicably, in a St Petersburg sauna. She comes to a nasty end, finally, half-way up a tree. Her name is the one amusing thing about her.

Onatopp is also a lot smarter than Bond. Like Natalya and Janus; like M; like Samantha Bond's theatre-going Miss Moneypenny, even. The whole cast, in fact, is a step ahead. On one level, this is true to the Fleming blueprint: Bond is not a great thinker. He has read Edgar Allan Poe, Bram Stoker and Ambrose Bierce, and he has heard of Wagner, but too much thinking or cultivated introspection is 'the death-watch beetle in the soul'. At the same time, we should not have to remind ourselves that 007 works for military intelligence. He takes pleasure in his craft and in his craftiness. He relishes the wit that sets him apart from villains who may possess superior intellects but who, like Ernst Stavro Blofeld, have no curiosity, no inner resource.

Much of his learning, in other words, is a device, not a desire, designed to force the enemy's hand. It is in this spirit that 007 saves Britain in *Moonraker*, when his 'half-remembered lessons from a card-sharper' help him spot a fascist cheating at bridge. Sean Connery draws on similar reserves of cunning in the film *Diamonds Are Forever* (1971), when Bond quizzes an assassin, posing as a wine waiter, about claret. There is little comparable craft in *GoldenEye* – once only we see Bond break Onatopp's winning streak at baccarat (it's his game, after all) – and so no sense of Bond's delight in benign gimmickry, the eccentricities of taste and learning that give his character depth. The lesson of the books, if any, is that power without the power to detect the value of useless information is a thing to be feared. It should be so, once again, in the films.

## Titanic

'In a way,' admitted the oceanographer Robert Ballard, after his 1985 expedition to photograph the wreck of RMS *Titanic*, 'I'm sad we found her.' A little late in the day perhaps – the search had taken him thirteen years – Ballard was forced to acknowledge something unfathomable about the 'Ship of Dreams', which foundered in the early hours of April 15, 1912, with the loss of 1,503 lives. The hulk retained a solid dignity, and so the technical achievement of making the two-and-a-half-mile dive possibly seemed hollow by comparison. James Cameron's *Titanic* is a completely different affair, flaunting its huge scale and expense with vulgar panache. But even in this, the latest most expensive film ever made (at a cost of $200 million), an extraordinary sophistication of design is ultimately overcast by the same pall of regret.

In pre-production for *Titanic*, Cameron hired two Russian submersibles and made a series of deep dives with a remotely operated camera unit, capable of penetrating the wreck's interior. The astonishing footage he brought back has now been edited to provide the framing story, in which a winsome centenarian explains to a group of marine scientists the romantic origins of a charcoal portrait hauled up from the depths. 'Wasn't I a dish?' she coaxes, to polite silence – perhaps because it is a terrible drawing, but more probably because our eyes still swim with images of the real drowned ship, her decks and corridors like furred arteries, the dead fireplaces tended by tentacular afterlife. Like Ballard, the fictional experts grope towards a respectful melancholy ('it gets me every time . . . to see her sad ruin after that long fall from the world above'), and, for a moment, we are permitted to feel aptly diminished.

Not for long, though. The whole purpose of a wide-screen epic is sensual glut, and its director is contract-bound not to disappoint. Ballard prodded the wreck and tactfully withdrew, leaving a bronze memorial plaque. Cameron, by contrast, landed his subs on top of the officers' quarters and modestly decided to rebuild everything, to scale, in a 17 million-gallon tank off the coast of Mexico, using Harland and Wolff's blueprints and the original manufacturers of, among other things, the lifeboat davits (Wellan Davit Company) and 'D' Deck's saloon carpets (BMK Stoddard). This kind of precision reconstruction is, of course, imperceptible to the viewer, and, in the context of a disaster movie like this, comically redundant, since we can guess how useful it was the first time. It is quite typical, though, of James Cameron, whose science-fiction thrillers to date (particularly *The Terminator*, 1984, and *Terminator 2*, 1992) have been concerned with how over-precise technology may, subtly or not, change the course of history. One wonders briefly what substance there may be to the rumour that 20th-Century Fox at one point considered a happy ending, minus the iceberg?

Bereft of this possibility, *Titanic* seeks narrative reassurance in an intermittently affecting love-story between seventeen-year-old Rose DeWitt Brukater (Kate Winslet) and the happy-go-lucky Jack Dawson (Leonardo DiCaprio). Rose is a first-class Philadelphian, suffering under the yoke of her betrothal to the grisly plutocrat, Cal Hockley (Billy Zane). Their interests differ: he makes new money; she collects modern art, and has daringly, if illogically, acquired Picasso's 'Desmoiselles d'Avignon', along with some waterlilies by Monet and a Degas. 'Picasso? He'll never amount to anything,' says Cal, whose equally daring use of eyeliner has already marked him out as a cad. In the course of a half-hearted bid to throw herself from the bow railings, Rose is saved by Jack, a starving artist from steerage who won his passage in a game of poker. Society is scandalised by what ensues. The couple court and dance Irish jigs at midnight; Jack draws Rose with no clothes on and makes love to her in the hold. Their antics even attract the attention of the crow's-nest officers on ice watch – a bad idea.

The text of this romance is laughable, swiftly undermining whatever other claims the picture may have had to histori-cal veracity (Jack's middle-finger salute to another passenger is only the most glaring anachronism). But DiCaprio and Winslett rise above their material; the carelessness of their passion is a surprisingly touching metaphor – not for per-fection of spirit, but for negligence in design. As the grand central staircase curdles with watery wreckage, the master shipbuilder and chief architect, Thomas Andrews (Victor Garber), makes a gracious apology – 'I'm sorry I couldn't have built you a stronger ship, Rose' – which is not inconsistent with portraits of the man drawn by Colonel Archibald Gracie (in *Titanic: A survivor's story*, Far Thrupp: Sutton, reprinted 1997) and Violet Jessop (in *Titanic Survivor: The memoirs of Violet Jessop, stewardess*).

The upstairs-downstairs love story also gives Cameron a chance to map the ship's baffling interior. In flight from Cal's eerie manservant, Spicer (David Warner – luckless survivor of another dramatisation, *SOS Titanic*, in 1977), Rose and Jack dash through hellish boiler rooms, where pistons rear and strike like industrial hydras, and along endless corridors. The latter are a Cameron staple (most of *Aliens*, 1986, is set in a slimy maze), because they enforce a convenient moral sche-maticism: there is a right way to go down them (to escape, to rescue someone) and a wrong way (to die). In addition, the swilling corridors of this *Titanic* seem to prophesy and deliver a folkloric judgment; 'Jack will find his own level', the nau-tical saying goes, alluding to the weight of a drowned man's sins, and so, collectively, it proves. Back on the boat-deck, there is film-set chaos. Contrary to witness evidence, Second Officer Lightoller ('for what he did he is entitled to honour from his countrymen,' wrote Colonel Gracie) is portrayed as a gun-waving hysteric. A steerage passenger is shot, and Officer Murdoch commits suicide. The musicians play 'Nearer, My God to Thee' as the ocean floods the bridge, although historians mostly agree that what they in fact played was a French waltz, 'Songe d'Automne'. Some guilt is pre-emptively assuaged and some blame attached. Aghast to see half-empty lifeboats leaving the ship, Andrews protests that 'they were tested, in Belfast, for seventy!' We sense that he would like to add, 'by 15,000 honest Irishmen', but cannot, because it has already been said in an earlier scene.

One instance of cowardice is well handled; as he takes his unearned place in the last boat lowered to starboard, the President of the White Star Line, Bruce Ismay (a nervous Jonathan Hyde), shields his face with a shaking hand to avoid his officers' silent reproach. There is more to be said, here (Gracie says it unequivocally), and more to be dramatised in extraordinary scenes attested by survivors before both the American and British Courts of Inquiry. Rescue, in this version of events, is almost instant; no one appears to have rowed very far or for very long, although in reality it took the lifeboats four hours and more in steadily worsening seas to reach the rescue ship, the *Carpathia*. People died in the boats, or rolled off them; in her memoirs, Violet Jessop recalls being thrown a 'forgotten baby'; Colonel Gracie, clinging to an overturned Englehardt collapsible, had to listen to those he could no longer assist wishing him well.

Alongside the documentary restraint of Eric Ambler's admirable black-and-white reconstruction, *A Night To Remember* (1958), Cameron's antagonistic blend of period detail and heroic agency in *Titanic* often seems cavalier. In padding out the fictional bravery, he passes up opportunities to assess factual incompetence. There is no whisper of a collision with the *New York* narrowly avoided by RMS *Titanic* as she left Southampton docks, nor yet of the *Californian*, which may have been as little as five miles away when disaster struck. In her novel *Every Man For Himself*, Beryl Bainbridge recounts the substantial rumour of a fire in the coal stacks, already raging before embarcation, which could have weakened the hull. In Cameron's film, it does not rate a mention.

Yet it would be perverse to deny that the last hour of *Titanic* has an imaginative sympathy which sets it apart from other accounts. Waves ripple gently beneath steerage bunks as an abandoned woman tells her sons a bedtime story; a cupboard sheds layer upon layer of pristine crockery into the salt. Everyday objects are transformed: the bed on which an old couple embrace, blinking, turns slowly in the current as though brought to life. The power of these images derives in part from the fact that the director's only rivals, when it comes to filming water, are John Boorman (in *Deliverance*), Andrei Tarkovsky (especially in *The Mirror*) and Sergei Eisenstein (the Battle on the Ice in *Alexander Nevsky*), but it springs, too, from something Ballard glimpsed in his expedition to film the wreck in 1985. In *Titanic*, fear is writ large, though it is difficult to say what the object of that fear might be. It is certainly personal, yet not quite amenable to characterisation, especially by two leads as chipper as Winslet and DiCaprio.

To a heartstopping soundtrack, the stricken vessel – after all, the most important character in the whole drama – gulps and groans before breaking in two. She is the symbol, as all ships are symbols, of a universal leave-taking. But, to the viewer's surprise, the legacy of her departure is something much smaller, less grandiose – as domestic and commonplace as those saucers falling slowly out of memory: a simple regret.

# Being and Doing

Alan Sinfield, *The Wilde Century: Oscar Wilde, effeminacy and the queer moment* (Cassell); Guy Hocquenghem, *Homosexual Desire*, trans. Daniella Dangoor (Duke University Press); Mark Simpson, *Male Impersonators: Men performing masculinity* (Cassell)

'Personality is a very mysterious thing,' avowed Oscar Wilde in 1891. 'A man cannot always be estimated by what he does.' The indecent irony in this is easy to spot, coming four years before his celebrated conviction for doing what came naturally. But in this muted moment from 'The Soul of Man Under Socialism' (Wilde's otherwise trenchant plea for Emersonian individualism underpinned by public ownership), one also detects the old contest between essential and contingent identities – being and doing – that continues to hold sway in constructionist theory and queer studies. On the face of it, there is no real contest: essentialism, even from Oscar's lips ('the important thing is to be'), is regarded as so much baloney; constructionism, which declares sexual identity to be a social formation, a tethering of true sexual variety, is more convincing.

Wilde is nevertheless crucial to the constructionist case, as Alan Sinfield shows, for his queer 'typicality' in fact comprises 'elements that (only) came together at the (1895) trials: effeminacy, leisure, idleness, immorality, luxury, insouciance, decadence and aestheticism'. *The Wilde Century* is Sinfield's attempt to unravel that typicality; to trace the origins of the Wildean dandy and to observe his residual, though marked, influence on modern gay culture. More precisely, the book is a social and literary history of effeminacy that spars deftly with Freud and begins, a little incongruously, by defending Michel Foucault, arch-constructionist, against the charge that sexual and political dissent, in the French philosopher's terms, are reactive, and therefore self-thwarting, offering no hope of political change. Wilde the playwright, or perhaps Lady Hunstanton (in *A Woman of No Importance*), would be amused by this first theoretical tussle ('How clever you are, my dear! You never mean a single word you say') but it would irk Wilde the essayist and ex-con, whose (uncited) letters to the *Daily Chronicle* on abuses of the prison system adduce the cruelties of institutional dogma rather more tellingly.

Sinfield's historical and textual analysis begins in earnest with the early 17th century. Effeminacy in England at this point, and for the next 300 years, meant 'being emotional and spending too much time with women. Often it involved excessive cross-sexual attachment . . . at the expense of heroic responsibility.' Samson, Romeo and Antony are the literary archetypes. At the same time, the absence of distinct social categories, pre-1700, for 'masculine' and 'feminine' permitted adult males 'to have sexual relations with women and with male adolescents' so long as property and family remained intact. Fops, mollies and rakes were all, in other words, 'feminine', but effeminacy, per se, did not clearly denote same-sex passion. 'Social behaviour was defining and sexual practice was secondary,' Sinfield observes; although if the two are mutually constitutive, as any constructionist ought to maintain, much the same could surely be said of any era. Pope's *Epistle to Arbuthnot* demonstrates how effeminacy was 'a general sign of (powerful but dissolute) aristocracy', and the argument begins to solidify.

Sinfield also shows, briefly, how the 18th-century cult of sensibility yoked feminine, domestic consumption to masculine wealth-production – a civilising trend which threatened to impugn masculine integrity by exposing it to the affectations of a life of leisure. Manliness was subsequently reclaimed in the literature of Victorian English public schools as an imperial marker of fitness to rule and ethical purity. Thomas Hughes's *Tom Brown's Schooldays* (1857), for example, reconciled 'rebellious-masculine and religious-feminine' tendencies in the hero by removing his weaker companion, Arthur, to erase any hint of 'disreputable sensuality' from the story.

Within the public-school stories themselves, the eradication of such sensuality is worked out according to a sort of Darwinian 'narrative' selection. Thus, in *Tom Brown's Schooldays*, the pale-limbed Arthur catches the fever and is sent home (Sinfield is under the misapprehension that Arthur dies), allowing the 'brown-fisted' hero to complete his term at Rugby, untroubled by 'feminine' intimacies. It is a manoeuvre that Charlotte Brontë, it might be argued, had already reversed in *Jane Eyre*. Arthur is a failed male and leaves Rugby, returning briefly to play a rather inexpert innings in the Marylebone cricket match. Whereas at Brontë's Lowood, Jane's consumptive friend Helen Burns dies, not because she is feeble, but because she is too genuine, both as a model of self-abnegating femininity and as an educated female. Her tormentor, the canting school-owner Mr Brocklehurst, is the real failed gender type: unmanly not because he is accompanied everywhere by his daughters, but because his loud evangelicalism is a doctrinal sham.

Not only are these novels important witnesses, but literature itself, throughout the 19th century, was subtly invested with the potential to un-man the reader. Its influence, Sinfield argues, was found to be at odds with the prevailing political economy and therefore 'intrinsically effeminate'. Literature's perceived lack of function made it a liability, too easily associated in the aesthetic (Walter Pater) and decadent (J. K. Huysmans) traditions with the good-for-nothing rich. Wilde's place in this debate is assured. In *The Picture of Dorian Gray*, Basil Hallward is a sincere artist and Lord Wotton a dandy, but Dorian 'merges art and leisured accomplishment'.

This is true, although Dorian hardly represents the first instance of such a convergence. Certainly his non-productive personality opposes 'philistine, masculine practicality', but Wilde's insistence that the forms of art and society might be perfected in an individual such as Dorian also resolves, at one level, the old problems of patronage, and of how to sponsor (useless) art. His vision of the artist-citizen is of a self-sufficient intellect that subsumes the roles of patron and pupil, critic and artist. W. S. Landor was chasing something similar, sixty-six years before Wilde's novel appeared, in the first volume of his *Imaginary Conversations*. In it, he addresses both the (perceived) effeminacy of poetry and the critic-artist's intellectual claim to underwrite the whole history of patronage. To a suspicious court, Landor's Queen Elizabeth defends poetry's right to celebrate her reign and the threat it poses to rebellious masculinity by invoking the sexually contentious figure of Alexander the Great, and his contemplative tutor. 'I desire in future to hear no more contempt of penmen,' Gloriana pronounces. 'If Alexander was the Great, what was Aristoteles who made him so?' Sinfield goes on to stress that effeminacy in Dorian Grey, unlike Alexander's cultivated and studious Greatness, signals queerness as soon as 'Wilde enters the dock and his relations with Alfred Douglas are invoked', but, again, this is not quite the revelation its author intends it to be.

How much of a surprise is it to find that a court verdict constitutes a defining moment? Literature, as the 1794 treason trials proved a century earlier, is often asked to declare itself under oath. The Wilde trials can justifiably lay claim to producing the 'category' of the homosexual, and bringing to birth one model of gay presence in society. They are also, as Sinfield demonstrates, the point of departure for a particular species of cross-class gay relationship in Britain, founded on issues of ownership and economic dependency. But in helping to turn homosexual practice into deviant personality (the shift from doing to being), the 1895 indecency trials stand only at the point of conversion. They are not the whole, or even the bulk, of the story, as the Freudian emphasis of Sinfield's last two chapters tacitly acknowledges.

The bulk of Sinfield's post-Wildean commentary concentrates instead on showing how the marriage of psychological culpability to legal guilt has dominated (and continues to inhibit) gay self-awareness. To the category of 'pervert' created at the indecency trials, he argues, psychoanalysis has added a sophisticated but ultimately incriminating myth about the origins of homosexuality. Guy Hocquenghem's brilliant, if dated, repudiation of that myth, *Homosexual Desire*, is a major influence here, and Sinfield follows Hocquenghem in suggesting that Freud's detachment of sexual practice from gender, and of instinct from object choice, though provocative, is not forceful enough to dispense with the categories of masculine and feminine. These are, both critics agree, the powerful, biological principles which 'keep finding their way back'.

Hocquenghem is explicit in his condemnation of the extent to which this 'competitive rule', which knows the price of every desire and the value of none, shores up a familiar economic model: not only is the 'law of the Father . . . vital to the fulfilment of institutional laws' by ensuring 'there is no real justice until the accused (homosexual) has a guilty conscience', but, like a mature market economy, it is endlessly absorbent. Psychoanalysis has an answer for everything, including resistance and repudiation ('denial'), just as capitalism has a knack for commodifying counter-cultures to give birth to the next generation of consumers.

The problem is that the opportunism that characterises both psychoanalytic method and capitalism – they make use of everything – also defines the kind of Foucauldian constructionism where 'attempts to challenge the system help the dominant to assert and police the boundaries of the deviant and the permissible'. Sinfield resists, or rather rephrases, this authoritarian language trap, and comes up with the hopeful notion that an opportunistic system cannot help but give voice to the dissenting groups it (barely) tolerates. 'Even to misrepresent, one must present,' he writes, 'and once that has happened, there can be no guarantee that the subordinate will stay safely in its place.' Sinfield is pleased enough with this idea in his first chapter to repeat it word for word 200 pages later. But reiteration cannot disguise the fact that, for all its radical sophistry, this is a theory of intervention, not a vision of change.

The irony is that the terms by which such theory is expressed are too often evasive, and the jargon smacks of conformity, to whose claims, as Wilde reminds us, 'no man may yield and remain free at all'. In his introduction to Mark Simpson's *Male Impersonators*, an examination of the 'crisis of masculinity as a crisis of looking and looked-at-ness', Sinfield says that 'the erotic sex-gender jumbles of our time ... may be reinscribing the system that, at first sight, they seem to undermine. They may be producing unanticipated modes of oppression.' What he seems to mean is that the 'freeing up of sexual identities' is currently sold to us on the understanding that we let the market-place dictate terms. In other words, some images of gay freedom are permissible, sellable (camp chic), but others (buggery) are not. Homogenising sexuality to sell Calvin Klein underpants is one thing; real diversity (heterogeneity) is another. The unpalatable truth, as Sinfield well knows, is that popular culture is consumer culture, and consumerism affords no common ground that is not paid for by political quiescence.

Simpson is an assimilationist, where Sinfield and Hocquenghem would wish to preserve the gay community's political difference. In one important sense, however, they are after the same thing: an understanding of all sexuality as a continuum of desires rather than an axis offering one thing or the other. (Freud, too, conceded that the highs and the lows of normalcy and perversion were, in truth, behavioural neighbours – 'Himmel durch die Welt zur Hoelle' – even if he had to rely on Goethe to find the right words.) Hocquenghem and, to a lesser degree, Sinfield, both see the potential of this continuum. Where we are sexually various, they intimate, we are liberated by that contentiousness. For Hocquenghem, writing in 1970, this feral eroticism aspired to a socialist utopia that Wilde might have appreciated: 'Civilization', he said, 'is the trap into which desire keeps falling', but, in the post-AIDS world, Hocquenghem's poetic and frankly sexual politics have been tamed, perhaps inevitably, by political concern.

Safety in conduct has found its less laudable corollary in theoretical propriety. Sinfield is so obviously a kind and responsible critic that it hurts to suggest that the whole point of fiction and of cultural criticism is to supply the vision and adventurousness that life and society commonly lack. But while AIDS and 'doing' – that is, having sex – have led to intimate protocols to ensure the care of the self, theory has provided no equivalent care of the personality. It makes a series of conventional appeals for tolerance within the gay subculture: 'We need to be heterogeneous, contentious without falling into blaming each other for the situation in which we find ourselves.' No complaints there. But must we also accept that the simplest constituent of such non-conformism, 'individual self-consciousness', is 'an unpromising source of dissident identity and action'?

How various can 'we' afford to be? How many subdivisions can a subculture stand? How many contradictions can an argument support? Sinfield makes the constructionist case for there being nothing ineluctable or constitutive about gayness. He does so because those (medical) theories that do view homosexuality as a fixed, essential quantity rather than a behavioural possibility have always sought to categorise queers, keeping them at arm's length or on the psychoanalyst's couch. On the other hand, if our identity is merely 'performative', diffuse and paradoxical, how do we make it stick, in the wider political sense? In life as in art, the struggle to preserve argumentative integrity – the ability to disagree with oneself, to change one's mind – is tempered by the need to be intelligible to others; to assert the author's rights in public; to communicate one's desire.

Constructionism disparages 'individual self-consciousness', because in the face of political oppression it is helpless. And a collective identity is important. AIDS, as the great leveller of the 1980s, demanded an explanation and a coherent, collective response. The AIDS activist lobby insisted, rightly, that epidemiological research and sex education would have happened sooner, faster, had the disease broken out among the heterosexual majority. But, as David Kirp has pointed out (*The Nation*, July 4, 1994), we cannot go on being outraged in the same vein. The enduring problem is not so much institutional prejudice and obstruction but the fact that science has been unable to come up with a cure. AIDS goes on being perversely, polymorphously intractable; it cannot yet be fully described at a collective level.

Literature, as Edmund White has correctly observed, remains one of the gay community's most effective responses to the epidemic, because the sheer contrariness of its constituent voices from the elegiac and erotic (White, Alan Hollinghurst) to the quizzical and surreal (Armistead Maupin, Patrick Gale) helps to remind us that we are individually, ineradicably gay, while coping with a disease which, famously, does not discriminate. And because cultural theory, by contrast, is saying nothing new. Far from engaging with real life, it dithers in the margins of assertiveness, producing a desperately civilised radicalism that states the obvious. Hence Simpson's 'the secret of (the rapper) Marky Mark's gay success is that he is a straight boy who plays the queers'. Some secret. What is the matter with theory that it has become so intellectually docile? No wonder Oscar scorned it for having debased perceptive criticism. No wonder that, in witnessing the wretched fate of an insane inmate at the hands of Reading Gaol's doctor, Wilde cast their confrontation as a fight between theory and being. 'The doctor is fighting for a theory. The man is fighting for his life,' he wrote. 'I am anxious that the man should win.'

# Laura Riding

Laura Riding, *First Awakenings: The early poems*, ed. Robert Nye (Carcanet);
Deborah Baker, *In Extremis: The life of Laura Riding* (Grove Press)

'All I know of her,' wrote William Carlos Williams to a curious *Time* magazine correspondent in 1938, 'is that, personally, she's a prize bitch.' His pride had been pricked. According to a *Time* book review, Rainer Maria Rilke and Laura Riding, then approaching the end of a fourteen-year affair with Robert Graves, were the two indispensable voices of 20th-century poetry. Williams came third. The fact that the review of Riding's *Collected Poems* was largely a put-up job – commissioned by a close friend and awkwardly written by Riding's future husband – only emerged later. Ironically, however, the bronze medallist's barb hit home about the strained relationship between Riding's work and the poet herself. For the 'bladed mind' which produced what is perhaps modernism's most philosophical poetry also gave rise to a frenetic literary and moral idealism (she would say 'spiritual realism') whose 'play with the possibilities of extreme statement' was deeply, divisively personal. Other poets have broken up marriages; not many have stood by while the ousted wife is carried away in a straitjacket.

In most accounts of her life, therefore, Laura Riding, champion of truth in poetry ('literally, literally, literally, without gloss, without gloss, without gloss') and scourge of adulterated meaning, emerges as both prize and bitch. There are polite testimonials from friends and acquaintances; Julian Symons characterises her struggle to affirm the personal truth of her work as 'the tendency towards extreme individualism and poetic isolation'; Martin Seymour Smith, in his biography of Robert Graves, Riding's partner from 1926 to

1940, is less kind, calling her semantic protectiveness a delusion of 'infallibility'. Yet the life itself, its ethnic-intellectual origins and education, remains obscure. In part, this is the price one pays for pronouncing history 'nothing more than the bad dreams of poets' – hardly an inducement to attempt a balanced biography – but it is also the inevitable result of spending most of one's life trying to get the life to fit the work; of being one's own worst enemy. At Riding's insistence, the early years, during which she produced some of her finest verse, have been ignored. The consequence, sadly, has been that the twenty-year-old Cornell radical and poetic apologist for Voltaire is now chiefly remembered as the 'baleful' muse who wrecked Graves's first marriage to Nancy Nicholson, held court in Majorca from 1929 to 1936, abandoned poetry in 1938, sent a Pennsylvanian farmer's wife mad, and dwindled into shrill obscurity on a citrus plantation in Florida.

As Deborah Baker's informative and sympathetic new biography points out, this is a travesty of poetic justice. Riding's self-defeating ambition and insecurity were not infantile responses to Graves's greater success, though they may have had their origins in her own intellectual infancy. In her eighties, she was reportedly delighted to hear that a Soviet anthology of American and English poetry gave her five more lines than Graves, whom the editors denounced as 'decadent'. The entry also approved her father's 'tailoring and working-class background'. Here, if anywhere, are the roots of Riding's irascibility and obsession with setting the record straight. Graves came from a wealthy background; so, too, did most of the Fugitives, the American modernist movement of the early 1920s which awarded Riding her first poetry prize in 1924. Riding, by contrast, was poor, and schooled in the many calibrations of class, language and economic advantage by which her Brooklyn immigrant community organised itself. Her aesthetics were more essential than those of her privileged contemporaries: poetry, as she described it at Brooklyn Girls High, offered the second-generation immigrant a refuge 'where the fear of speaking in strange ways could be left behind'.

Her father, Nathan Reichenthal, a Polish-Jewish emigré worn down by his years in Manhattan's garment sweatshops, was her tutor in political idealism. Born to his second wife, Sadie, but named after his first, Laura Reichenthal was weaned on the peculiar, oxymoronic veneration for self-improvement and the ideals of organised labour that constituted Jewish socialism at the turn of the century. Its voluble adherents, gathering in Lower East Side teashops to pit faith against ideology, developed a strand of Marxism that promised spiritual reward as well as material revolution. Taking this heady dialectic with her to Cornell in 1918, Riding, as she had begun to call herself, wasted no time in establishing herself in the front ranks of a Jewish intellectual clique with dazzling exegeses of *Das Kapital*, before surprising everyone by dropping out to marry her history lecturer, Louis Gottschalk, in 1920, and moving to Urbana, Illinois. Higher education, she had decided, would be of no intrinsic value to a confirmed autodidact; and poetic, not political, idealism was her natural philosophical currency – a realisation summed up by the long narrative poem, *The Vain Life of Voltaire*, in which the hero of reason and justice is plagued by an insatiable intellect:

> What reconciles the garden
> Does not reconcile the mind,
> Which demands instruction
> The more it is blind,
> Sets little store by speeches,
> Can understand only what it knows,
> Knows only what is secret.

*Voltaire* made it into the 1938 *Collected Poems*. The bulk of her early work, written before Riding left for England in 1926, and abandoned inside a folder marked 'Ancient History', did not. Instructions to destroy the folder's contents were nevertheless ignored, and their availability now in *First Awakenings* (with a contorted disclaimer from Riding written just before she died), confirms *Voltaire*'s promise. The 'tendency towards poetic isolation' – toward personal truth – is everywhere the dominant impulse.

It is not difficult to see how the popular conception of her as Graves's cruel White Goddess, demanding constant propitiation, at once satisfies and sensationalises this antisocial aspect. It is more accurate to turn Eliot's dictum about the 'extinction of personality' in poetry on its head and say that, given her background and sensitivity to accent, origin and class, Riding craved an *intinction*, or confirmation of selfhood, in verse.

In this, the odds were against her. Responding to a letter Riding wrote in 1935 recommending James Reeves's inclusion in the *Oxford Book of Modern Verse*, the editor, W. B. Yeats, shocked Riding by rejecting Reeves on the grounds that he was 'too reasonable, too truthful'. Poets, maintained Yeats, 'should be good liars'. His devilment was pertinent. He meant to remind her that a poet's shaping experience should infuse the world, not be confused in it. Riding's renunciation of poetry (made public in a BBC radio broadcast in 1962) bore witness to such a confusion: the last fifty years of her life, most of which she spent cultivating lemons in Wabasso, Florida, with Schuyler Jackson (who wrote that book review for *Time*) were intermittently dedicated to expounding a doctrine of literalism – in *A Dictionary of Related Meanings* – intended to fix word meanings for good and all. It was never published, or even finished.

The political equivalent was equally ambitious. Returning

to England from Majorca with Graves in 1936 at the outbreak of the Spanish Civil War, Riding sought to reintegrate her poetic ideals of truthfulness with political activism. 'A Personal Letter with a Request for a Reply' was duly dispatched to 400 influential politicians and intellectuals asking what might be done to secure 'a peaceful, civilized existence, in a world which has steadily become more and more disordered'. In compiling the responses – many of which were bemused by the letter's lofty tone – Riding conceived the notion of an intellectual oligarchy, to be called the Council of the Inside People, which would combine her father's high-minded radicalism with her own militantly reactionary feminism. Beneath the Council, Riding proposed a system of central distribution run by 'women of grace with no ulterior motives' – the Order of Love.

At a distance, both projects inspire disbelief. I. A. Richards ('you can't put words into straitjackets') declared the dictionary intellectually bankrupt from the outset; but some publishers (Little, Brown), poets (Norman Cameron, Graves) and friends (Jacob Bronowski) took it quite seriously; and it is easy to forget that the idea of obtaining an original – or foundational – meaning for words, which necessarily has to look first at the range of meanings in use, is itself a New Critical process familiar to both Richards and William Empson (and one that Riding's *Survey of Modernist Poetry*, in 1927, helped establish). Politically, however, Riding would have been wise to heed her own 1925 caution that 'a poet outside his poem is messianic'.

Bound by a 'Covenant of Literal Morality' (1938), drawn up with Graves, the poet Alan Hodge, his wife Beryl (later Beryl Graves) and others in late 1937, Laura Riding's Council of the Inside People convened on March 28, 1938. Its aim was to stop the war by deciding on 'moral action to be taken by inside people for outside disorders', and it admonished its adherents to have 'no seclusion with self in place or mind, to which we could not admit others without guilty immodesty'. More ingenuous than the totalising tone suggests (one tier of government was to consist entirely of 'men of power who are also men of goodwill'), 'literal morality' outstripped the poetic struggle to get words to conform to intention by proposing a logocracy whose verities would teach everyone 'How To Speak Purely In A Way To Avoid Fallacies Of Language And Mediocrity Of Thought'. It was a utopian vision, not a Hobbesian contract, concerned with perfecting power rather than maintaining it – Riding even had a blueprint for a better railway system – but it was also a confusion of idea and fact. Life, as Northrop Frye once said, 'imitates literature up to a point, but hardly up to *that* point'.

*In Extremis* considers the origins of this failure to keep life and work apart in terms set out by Al Alvarez's study of poetry and suicide, *The Savage God*. At the epicentre of this confusion Baker locates Riding's suicide attempt – the leap from a Hammersmith flat in 1929 which broke up a ménage with Robert Graves and his wife, Nancy Nicholson, that had lasted since Riding's arrival in England three years before. It was typical, Baker says, of the epoch's violent self-destructiveness: 'When Laura Riding's imaginative self exhausted its self-generating resources, her own body became the new medium of the nihilistic expression.' Somehow this doesn't quite convey the drama of Riding guzzling a bottle of household detergent in front of an astonished Graves and Nicholson – and the Irish poet Geoffrey Phibbs – before jumping out of a fourth-storey window yelling 'Goodbye, Chaps!' More importantly, it suggests 'exhaustion' and sagging desperation where there was, and continued to be, death-defying energy. A high proportion of the unpublished *First Awakenings* joust with Death to prove the young author's mettle: 'Listen for the voices to cry *danger!/* Then you may go . . . Fly to the monster/ Lean to its fierce heart low'.

Riding wanted to be confused in the world; and like an uncommonly vigorous Lady of Shalott, turned from her tapestry to take the plunge. Written in Urbana, Illinois, where Riding strained – and failed – to fulfil the duties of a polite young professor's wife, 'The City of Cold Women' rails against the deadly primness of Midwestern life, while the thwarted poet longs for some kind of reviving defenestration:

> The roofs of the city are a bleak mist
> Brooding over the sharpness beneath them:
> Walls stroked to corner by the hands of the cold women,
> Fireplaces for irony,
> We shall not wonder at rimed mirrors –
> Windows give up their secrets,
> Not mirrors.

The sublime quality in this passage is not its suicidal drive, but its sensuous violence – 'Somewhat frolic, somewhat fierceness' – and the creeping sensation that Riding is daring metaphor on the window-ledge with one hand on the reader's neck. Like other American poets and writers of the Twenties – Hart Crane, Thornton Wilder – she looks over an edge, or a bridge, and sees frustration and ferment. In common with Eliot, whom she writes off in an early essay for his intellectual 'debauchery', she observes a wasteland in which the present continuous is a vision of hell: 'Death dropped me by mistake . . . / Into the lost isle of the living. / What have we done to Death, / Inventing dying?' This may be callow poetry, but its confident inversions command our attention. Riding could match her Poe-influenced peers, Allen Tate and Robert Penn Warren, phantasm for phantasm when it suited her, marking in one poem 'the swift clairvoyance / Of flesh translated into death / Before it dies'. The key note sounded through most of her work, however, is not this kind of suffering suspension but, rather, a brute wager between poetic witness and the moment of injury, or insight.

In 'The Defense', a man sets out to prove he can reach a higher intellectual plane by climbing houses and scaling steeples: 'Bet you I can bring me nearer / To that star than [you] could ever/ Come to canniness if God were / To make you ten times as canny / As you are.' On one of his ascents, he falls and breaks every bone in his body. This is pure Marlowe; *homo fuge* seeps out of the verse as the spell of higher knowledge breaks man in two. It is also euphoric in pursuit of self-transcendence – the aim of every intellectual myth – and the 'possibilities of extreme statement'. Yet Riding does not always hurtle at us from the fourth storey. Many of the most telling verses in this collection, cleanly edited by Robert Nye, are lyric quatrains which fulfil the Poundian injunction '*ut doceat, ut moveat, ut delectet*; to teach, to move or to delight':

> If at noon it may be found
> Like a scarf upon your shoulder
> Be at dusk a little bolder
> Trail your shadow on the ground.

To be 'burned down to a fact' by breaking the body, or to be 'a little bolder', and parade one's self-awareness: these are the imperatives of sacrifice and renunciation that govern Riding's work. The canvas is impossibly large; of the moderns, Riding alone dares to be Brunnhilde, pledged to resolve her own contrariness by knowing and obliterating simultaneously: 'Forgive me, giver, if I destroy the gift! / It is so nearly what would please me, / I cannot but perfect it.'

Deborah Baker's biographical treatment of this urge to overdress poetic faith is often serenely witty. It is, she discovers, a literal overdressing. After her miracle recovery from the suicide attempt, Riding takes to wearing a shawl with a 'representation of her damson-coloured surgical scar on it', and referring to herself as 'Finality'. Later, in a compelling discussion of her reign at Canellun (the house she built and shared with Graves in Deia, Majorca), the wars of intellectual attrition waged with Graves, Bronowski, Cameron and John Aldridge are similarly enlivened with a spot-check on her wardrobe. Having given up sex in 1933 ('I like men to be men, and women to be women, but I think bodies have had their day'), Finality starts wearing an 1830s all-in-one – with a bustle – to remove any vestiges of 'art school allure'.

These are prize moments. But Baker is no critic. Assessing *The Quids*, the satire on modernist quips and quiddities which first drew Riding to Graves's attention in 1924, Baker applauds 'Riding's ability to treat words with more than their dictionary definition in mind'. The point surely, is that, to Riding's mind, the provincial moderns (Penn Warren, et al) are using the wrong dictionaries – 'resolved to predicate,/ to dissipate themselves in a little grammar' – in which dissipation has forestalled definition.

Other opportunities to open up the biography's critical remit are also missed. In a potentially lively discussion of *The Life of the Dead* (1932), Riding's bilingual collaboration with the painter John Aldridge, the extraordinary resemblances between Aldridge's shamanic illustrations and the collage novels of Max Ernst, particularly *La Femme 100 Têtes*, are ignored. Bird-headed daemons – close kin to Ernst's familiar Lop-lop – cavort on the clifftops; mountainous women (Venus/Vesuvius) swallow fallen angels, but the commentary remains conservatively biographical and Baker substitutes speculative comparison for reliable research. All of life in Deia is inscribed in these verbal comedies: Graves, Aldridge and *Time* magazine's future Managing Editor, Tom Matthews, turn up as the Three Men-Spirits of the Dead. Here, too, is Graves's botched courtship of Julie Matthews,

Laura's fondness for playing cards, and most poignantly, the lilt of the gramophone: 'the voice of all those races that time has not admitted / Into the lavish happenings and courses / That make life so full of interest and death so foul.'

'I think you got away just in time,' remarked Edmund Wilson to Matthews, at the end of his exhausting six-month stay in Majorca. The congratulations were premature. Riding repatriated to Pennsylvania in 1939 with Graves, Alan Hodge and Beryl Pritchard (collaborators on the Covenant, or First Protocol) and James Reeves' son, David. Lodging at first with the Matthews' in Princeton (while Schuyler Jackson undertook the conversion of a cottage on his farm), Riding's 'special authority' and 'celebrated power' soon made themselves felt. Within three months of her instalment on the Jackson farm, Riding had renounced her vows of abstinence ('Schuyler and I do'), convinced Julie Matthews she was Christ, and pronounced Katherine Jackson 'evil' after Schuyler's wife was found strangling their nine-year-old daughter. As proof, Baker notes, Riding uncovered a 'maleficent' arrangement of tampons in the Jackson bedroom. Meanwhile, Riding presided over daily meetings of the Second Protocol in which the Inside People were interrogated about their love for her.

Baker finds her narrative feet and generic niche in the ghoulish unravelling of events on New Hope farm. It is, inescapably, *In Cold Blood* territory, plotted as a series of gripping stalk-and-chase sequences. There is nothing malicious about this: the facts really are too extraordinary, the charismatic pungency too remeniscent of Salem for the story not to radiate a certain lurid fascination. But the after-chill is not manufactured, and the considerable merit of Baker's book is that we never cease to read Riding's excesses as an index of poetry's greater loss.

The hard truth is that Riding's final doctrines of literalism and spiritual realism were, and must remain, hopelessly void.

Poetry is prophecy, at least in part, and it has an unprovable claim to some kind of truth. She was right about that. But in order to tell us something we do not already know, the language must be fresh – *unrecognisable* – each time we wish to know something. By standardising received meaning, Riding denied herself the possibility of perception; by being confused in and with the world, she became a solipsist; by claiming self-sufficiency she lost that sense of history-without-me which frees a poem for its readers. The following sestet got out just in time:

> But this strange present world is not of me.
> If I could find somewhere a secret sign,
> That one might say: In this an Ancient sings,
> I should acknowledge then my legacy
> And love to call this modern fabric mine.
> Perhaps, once, in my sleep, I dreamed such things?

# Beginnings

The sellers pull up at the gate from around 9 a.m., every Saturday and Sunday, and the buyers are already there, in packs. Drive in too slowly and your car will be mobbed. People bang on the windows anyway, yelling 'Watches? Any watches? Jewellery? Any clothes?' It's mudlarking crossed with *Mad Max*, the engines gunning, Tina Turner's 'Simply The Best' curdling the air, huge men wandering around with burgers and plastic bags full of, well, crap. And tools.

Why are there so many tools, in among the discarded children's toys and damp-fattened books and boxes of armless sunglasses and remote controls for screens so remote they no longer exist and terrifyingly stained overalls? A part of the answer must be that car-boot sales have an obvious kinship with travellers and the idea of trade as a way of handing on useful skills; with ironmongery and agriculture. Here are boxes of files, knives, spanners, pitchforks, angle-grinders, claw-hammers, rotavators and chisels. These heavy goods are by no means the only desirable objects. Everything goes. 'This is insane,' says my friend Stuart, who has a carful of stuff from his garage to offload.

The woman next to us, on the touchline, is cross because someone has nicked her shoes. She looks round, outraged. 'You, thief!' she says, pointing at a young girl with a pram. 'I never,' the girl replies. Someone reminds the woman that the shoes weren't nicked: she sold them a minute ago and has forgotten. 'Oh.' The young mother rolls her eyes, pushes on and stops at our mat. 'How much for the lamp?' It's an orange metal standard lamp, with a fitting hanging out. 'Five quid. It's vintage,' says Stuart. His honesty gets the better of him: 'It needs rewiring.' The girl nods, unperturbed. 'My boyfriend's an electrician, but I'm on a budget.' She smiles. She comes back later. Four quid is still too much, and so, later still, is three.

Euphemisms for 'broken' are part of the sale's inventive dialect. 'It's still in its box' (because it doesn't work) is a popular one. Along with 'They're Adidas/Nike' (with the tread worn away) and the occasional bespoke understatement. My first typewriter, which I loved, was a Silver Reed Silverette. Mum bought it for me in 1983, when I finished my O-levels. In Fisher Athletic FC's goalmouth, a part-time psychic – I know this because she has a card – is selling an identical model and I'm tempted to buy it. The carriage goes one way; the release catch won't release. The back of the typewriter is staved in. It has been hit or bashed with a tool, or perhaps thrown across a room. Maybe the psychic knows. 'What happened, here?' I ask. But she's having none of it. 'You can write nicely with that,' she says, flatly. 'It's just . . . unclipped.'

The whole place is unclipped. It's not the objects so much as the silent relationships between them and their sellers that gets me going. When Stuart invited me along, I thought 'Great! Material!', as you do if, like me, you're pondering a new story. Not that I expect to be writing a novel set in SE16 about a car boot sale; but I do expect to overhear suggestive remarks and glimpse predicaments. The mats and trestle tables are laden with the no-longer wanted – an attractive idea in itself and one that raises the question 'Why?' or 'Who says?' As I walk away from the woman with the typewriter, I turn a 'different quality of attention' (Hilary Mantel's guarded phrase) on the chaos of the sale, and find myself considering not simply what is being said or done, but how the adrenaline and suspicion driving it might animate a trial, a fight, an opening scene. Paying this kind of attention is important, and rather heartless. It is a form of staring.

The buyers are poor. When they knock on the car window, shouting 'Have you got any clothes?', it's because they need clothes, not because they're some sort of scenic metaphor for the end of the world. Who do I think I am, wandering about looking for the links between things? What kind of twisted self-indulgence is that? Feeling good about feeling this bad – I've really nailed my own class guilt – I'm suddenly free to spot a dartboard next to an unrolled sight-test, with its big letters dwindling to small ant-like characters, and a man sitting alongside both with several sets of spare legs, manikin's legs. I can't quite piece this lot back together. He's also selling some tubs of aqueous cream and a book: *Dancing in the Light*, 'another' #1 memoir by Shirley MacLaine.

Perhaps these things aren't connected and there isn't a story. Stuart has brought along two golf clubs, which don't belong to him. They are the casual bequests of his flat's previous owner. Of course, some stories do appear to suggest themselves, like objects at a sale. Daphne du Maurier's 'The Birds' 'began' after the author saw a flock of seagulls circling, menacing, a farmer in his field. *Anna Karenina* 'began' with a newspaper clipping about a suicide. Most are not startled into life, however; their authors may see or overhear things, but those things await a context, which tends not to be a product of excited invention but of patient stitching-together.

It is an uncertain, dreamlike process, starting a novel, and one which, like the sale, has no official beginning. I know that what I'm waiting for is an emotion from the past, echoed in the present. A moment of joy or bewilderment, and exposure, often allied to feelings of culpability: What have I done? What will I do next? How can I put it all right? I'm not particularly interested in the origins of that feeling. What I care about is the quality of the emotion, its electrical sensation as I make the memory circuits come alive. When that happens, I might be on to something.

The craziness of the sale recedes, like a swift tide. People and objects disperse. Tina Turner is on the Jubilee Line back to Nutbush. Before it is quite over, the girl with the baby, who eventually bought the orange standard lamp for £2, taps me on the shoulder as I'm packing up. 'That lamp is fucked. My boyfriend can't do anything with it,' she says and for a second I'm speechless with remorse. It isn't even my lamp. Stuart has made himself scarce: so much for his honesty. I manage a kind of cough, and dig into my pockets for a refund. She laughs – and she's gone. With the pram and no boyfriend that I can see. I feel apologetic, with no one to apologise to.

When I was about six I fought with my brother in the kitchen and we broke a Mexican dish. My father is an even-tempered man, but on this occasion he went beserk – eyes bulging, spittle flying, the works. I never found out why. Was it valuable? Perhaps in more ways than one. What came back to me was how sorry I felt. And now I'm left with this feeling, in a new setting, about broken things and the effort of others' lives: what they can't say, because they're protecting you, because it runs too deep or because the gulf between you is too wide. Fisher Athletic FC, 'The Fish', was wound up in 2009. Supporters formed a new football club, Fisher FC, which still plays in Dulwich. The old grounds hold a car-boot sale and ragwort curls in from all four corners at once. Over the water is Canary Wharf, which looks unbreakable, but isn't.

# Titles

Some writers can't get started on a novel until they have a title, a kind of promissory note to self that the unwritten book will happen, is real. I have the opposite problem: a finished book still waiting for its title, which is beginning to feel unreal, like the set text in your dream you read at school but which you're about to be examined on all over again. The work is done but the harder I trawl the typescript for key ideas and phrases the more it all unravels, like a Chandler plot.

My publisher is a patient man. He received my first suggestion – *The Visitors' Book* – in diplomatic silence. It was a 'quiet' title, he said quietly. It is a quiet title, I agreed, thinking: but then it's a quiet book (family story with one death and no animals). 'And it's not a quiet book,' he went on. 'We need to bring the reader in.' This was something I felt I ought to have known after years of writing headlines for articles by other people. But a headline is different. It's a précis of the story it introduces, as in 'Chinese Farmer's Melons Explode' (*The Guardian*, May 17). A headline announces the point of what follows, whereas a title tries to intrigue rather than explain outright, although it may do that, too: like *Our Man in Havana* or *The Time Machine*. The other difficulty with *The Visitors' Book* is that it invites readers to do what they normally do with such books, i.e. visit them, look at the contents, say 'a quiet affair', then wander off.

'Tell me what you come up with for possible titles,' my publisher said, 'and I will be delighted to give you my shamelessly commercial response.' After which I began to come up with dud after dud, in a sort of frenzy of self-misdirection. *The Nest* (too James Herbert), *A Lovely Part of the World* (too Bainbridge), *Vigilance* (too Rushdie), *The Individuals* (too

Franzen). Or, my ideas seemed OK, but elliptical and not to do with the story I'd written. *Kin Limbo* I quite liked until a friend said: 'Kin Limbo? Sounds like "Relatives in Space".' Which I also considered.

The enemy is bathos of one kind or another. A one-word title can seem stagey, the echo of another title too effortful, the formula – 'The This of That', 'On This', 'All About Who-ever', 'Whoever' – too easy. (Though formulae have form, and 'Ludlum' is a great parlour game. To play, take one definite article and decorate with two nouns of which the first must be proper, e.g., *The Bourne Identity* or *The Jane Calamity*.) And puns, of which I've made occasional use in headlines, are out.

Grabbing the reader is a good start, as long as what fol-lows makes sense of the title or, ideally, unsettles its meaning without betraying it. Bathos can also be your friend. Readers, not writers, are the people who count, and they don't mind a dose of the dull. What the search for the 'grab' leaves out is the fact that some writers, deliberately or not, come up with unremarkable titles all the time and it doesn't matter. Edward St. Aubyn does this deliberately (*Never Mind*, *Some Hope*, *At Last*), and writes very well, though perhaps the attractive, Henry Green-ish blankness of the titles also carries with it a small risk of seeming uninformative and knowing at the same time. Alice Munro does not do it deliberately, and a lot of her collection titles are surprisingly soporific. *Hateship, Friendship, Courtship, Loveship, Marriage. Open Secrets. Too Much Happiness.* Who cares? The stories are wonderful.

You can't predict, either, what people will do to titles – how they will misremember them. Last year I was browsing in Alice's Bookshop, an excellent second-hand store in Mel-bourne, when a lady came in and asked for *The Jew in the Crowd* by Paul Scott. This has since led to a better game than 'Ludlum', in which players on one side have to enquire after a misunderstood title or author while the other side unmasks the original. Marks are given for 'grabability' and likelihood. 'Do you have *The Day Was Terrific* by John Wyndham, I wonder? Or *The Folding Chair* by Alan Hollinghurst?' Being led astray and finding a title that way is a common experience in poetry, too. You have to write the verse in order to see what it's about or what kind of metaphor it's elaborating; whereas novelists tend to aim at a subject from the outset, even if they're unsure of where exactly the story is going.

Plato said that writing was forgetting, taking something out of your head and putting it on the page, leaving a gap behind. The written word weakens the retentive facility. I bet he was a terrible shopper. ('Have you got a list?' 'I don't need one.' 'Soap, pumice, olive oil.' 'Soap and pumice, I heard you.') Still, it makes sense to me. While you are working on your characters you're always remembering them; when it's over, the remembering stops – but without a title I can't afford to forget them yet.

I'm worrying about all this while I'm in Kent, staying with my partner. He listens, nods, sends me out for a walk. Everything in the real world suddenly has a brilliant title. I'm in Chatham, to be precise, where Fort Amherst and its associated defences once enclosed the naval dockyards. Collectively, the redoubt, its rising embankment and thistly plateau, home to skylarks and goldfinches, are known as 'The Great Lines'. Coming down the hill, I walk back to Sturla Road and past a series of unimprovably well-named shops. First comes an Afro-Caribbean chemist-cum-grocer, with hair extensions and coconut milk beside each other in the window, called 'Choose Your Choice'. Next along is the Chinese restaurant, 'Confucius'. And last, my favourite, the poetically downbeat 'Modern News', which sells the *Times Literary Supplement*.

Things grow into their names, or titles, which may be lightly given, and other names or titles arise out of long association. Memorability is not a magical essence, aptness can only be achieved with hindsight. It takes time. And the titles that seem to come in a flash arguably do not. Some other activity has prepared the ground. Writing is the work you do, whatever it is, to invite that happy accident.

I get back from my walk and talk to my partner about his impending move. He's been in Chatham seven years now, has great neighbours, but knows it is time to go. It's the way, isn't it – you make the jump when you're quite happy somewhere. Sally and Brian will miss him and he'll miss them. They wouldn't mind the garden bench, if he's not going to need it in Crystal Palace. And the worms. And some of those pots. After dinner, I get out my typescript, shut my eyes and stab a page at random. It's a scene in France, in which an English father is shouting back at his misbehaving son. 'We didn't have holidays like this when I was young', he says. 'You've no bloody conception. *This is paradise.*' Larkin, I later realise. ('High Windows'). And my title.

# Speed

My new job at Warwick university, teaching English and creative writing, involves a weekly commute from London and a lot of running around between tutorials in my office and classes in a large studio called the Writers' Room, with padded chairs and desks on wheels you can slide into position across doorways, thereby cutting off any means of escape. Though if the students are trapped, so am I. Seminars are repeated back to back. I half-expect to hear my Head of Department in the corridor, saying cheerily 'And don't come out until you've finished', as a key turns in the lock.

The walls are covered with helpful hints of the kind which instil fear in anyone who has published a book and then thought 'better luck next time'. Perhaps the most alarming is Elmore Leonard's 'I try to leave out the bits readers skip'. Which bits are those, then? Another one of Leonard's famous rules is 'Never use the word "suddenly"', which is fine until you try to put it into practice or apply it to anyone who isn't Elmore Leonard. I have my own rules, which are 1) start, and 2) keep going. But of course Leonard's prints are all over the second, because keeping going is about avoiding undue haste.

I am a slow writer and therefore attracted to slow methods of composition (writing in longhand, typing up, rewriting as I go) in the belief that the laborious grind, though it will not produce many books, will be adequate in the long run. I suspect, too, that haste, quite apart from inviting error or any dilution of intensity, can be itself a sort of subconscious delaying tactic. It's eagerness as opposed to enthusiasm. Students doing the Long Project – ideal for a long stay in the Writers' Room – dash off 8,000 words and then say 'I'm stuck. I want to start again.' The trouble is that they want to have written a book. And that is not the same thing as writing one, a process which, however fast you spill the ink, also involves cultivating a sort of existential languor as well as the habit of putting stuff off – other work, friends, partners; the desire to be a 'proper' writer, even.

'I'm sorry, it's a cop-out,' said a student last week. I like Rachel. She was apologising for having written a 'fluffy sketch' about her housemates' ambitious attempts to cook a rack of lamb. The story was mostly in dialogue ('Ah, but our fridge has many varieties of mould') and very well heard, and I disputed that it was a cop-out, because it was about learning to fend for oneself. Behind her characters' ribbing was, as she later admitted, a real anxiety: that some in her house would get to eat while others would not. I'm glad she didn't think about that possibility as she wrote her piece; glad that she didn't, in this case, ask herself 'What am I trying to say?', as George Orwell recommends, and glad that she unconsciously sided instead with Gay Talese, a different kind of essayist, who learned early on, while working in his mother's dress store in Ocean City, Maryland, to 'listen with patience and care'. Writing can be the art, Talese says, of Hanging Out, and Rachel is an instinctive writer.

My own instincts are telling me to take a leaf out of her book, put my notes on Orwell and Talese to one side, and take a more relaxed approach to the next few classes. But as I walk slowly across the campus I spot a rat in the roadside ditch among the take-out cups and marsh marigolds. It bustles unpleasantly, I hurry up, and Orwell is at my shoulder again. Why the great rush? What does Room H515 contain that am I so afraid of? Is it peer pressure? The fact that I have to talk about my 'research' at a departmental meeting next week? (I'm in the William Golding and J. G. Ballard camp, where fiction research is concerned: think hard and make it up.) Or is it something simpler? Students are coming towards me. Some of them are laughing, in groups. Others are like ghosts, floating along on their own, tilting out of the perpendicular, heading for the Physics block.

I wouldn't want to go to university again, but apparently that's what I'm doing. I'm in a rush because I'm worried time has stopped. The world is full of echoes: my room is as bare as the room I had in Garden Hostel, Cambridge, in 1986. This summer, I took a blue trunk of books to Warwick. I took the same blue trunk (and some of the same books) to King's twenty-five years ago. My Head of Department welcomed me when I arrived, and said, 'You could do with some green in here.' On my second day at Cambridge, I bought a maidenhair fern in a pot and the must-have Eighties species, a spider-plant.

I want to have settled into my new life the way I wanted to be grown up. That's the trouble with second chances and new lives: they are usually only mildly variant copies of first chances and old lives, and it's the mildness of the variation that induces vertigo, the small change heading for the large consequence, like the time I had a fish supper on a Eurostar train to Paris, looked idly out of the window, saw the mackerel's doubled-edged reflection as we plunged into the Channel tunnel and found myself wondering what it would mean, given our location, if there really were a mackerel on the other side of the glass. This is Jorge Luis Borges's fictional territory, I suppose – I have to teach him, too – and that of the counterfactual tales of Philip K. Dick, Christopher Priest, Robert Harris, Ballard and others, where settings that are only minimally off-key to begin with, different by a degree, turn out to be big, scary alternate realities.

But variations can be benign, too, and a way out of, rather than into, trouble. Life famously isn't a dress rehearsal, except that it is, in the realm of art, and where writing and teaching are concerned. The second seminar of two is never the same as the first. I'm tired, an hour and a half older, less sure that my insights into Orwell's four motives for writing (they boil down to two: egotism and the search for the truth) are pertinent, and annoyed with Elmore Leonard, whom I like a lot, but whose presence on the wall is like my mother's baiting suggestion that I water an obviously dead fern.

I am trying to explain to the group why a non-fiction piece about religion and the New Age in America, which I began writing seventeen years ago, never worked out. (This is research-led teaching: where students get to see your first drafts, in the interests of parity and honesty, and end up losing all respect for you.) Briefly, the tone was wrong, I didn't trust what I'd gleaned in interviews, and I lost patience with the project. A student tiredly suggests that I junk the commentary, retain the quotes and expand them. 'Just do it in the first person, like a piece of oral history.' But what if that turns it into a work of fiction? 'If you have to make it up, it'll be fiction. If you don't, it'll be non-fiction.' Suddenly, the Writers' Room regains its appeal. I stay late and write a longish piece subtitled 'Forty Days Among the Faithful', which has been waiting patiently for the call. I should have made that small but significant change in voice a long time ago, but I was a different person then, and as it turns out there was no rush.

# Music and Painting

Richard Leppert, *The Sight of Sound: Music, representation and the history of the body* (University of California Press)

A thousand twangling concepts inform Richard Leppert's cultural-materialist account of music and visual art. Its subject – how images of the human body at musical play underscore or undermine clauses in the social contract, particularly the role of women at home and the British abroad – is too various to yield much in the way of a consistent theory; its chronological and geographical embrace (England, the Netherlands and India from 1600 to 1900) too 'scopic' (his word) to develop a proper historical argument. In individual instances, the analysis of music as a sight/site is eccentrically brilliant – he is good on the didactic allegories of fidelity and wifely duty in 18th-century harpsichord marquetry, for example – but the more strenuous his efforts to 'argue for music's ubiquitous presence [as a sight, as something seen] in people's readings of reality', the more suspect his categorisations become.

The sight of music being made gives it meaning, and the link between sight and sound in public performance (opera, masque, etc) is well documented, and theatrically obvious, unlike the 'untheorised' link in other genres of art music (say, the music of a Renaissance parley, or a Victorian parlour); but the links in all cases are still, as *events*, simultaneous productions: you would really have to be in the room to see and hear them. Or would you? As a record of those events, visual art, Leppert argues, is capable of '"translating" the three-dimensional and sonoric world into a two-dimensional and silent 'argument' for and about the world'. But something inevitably is lost, and it is surely that loss – the untranslatable actuality of sound – that 'musical' painting laments.

Leppert admits as much in a fascinating account of the distance between sound and painting – and the social tension it describes – in 'Spring' (1607) by the Dutch artist Abel Grimmer. An idealised declaration of social order in the middle of the Eighty Years War with Spain, it shows peasants cultivating a chateau herb-garden in the foreground while musicians entertain the feudal landowners in a distant bower. Life at all levels of the hierarchy is on display, the nobility's power denoted by the fact they can afford to spend time cultivating something as intangible as music. The question is: how much time? Hearing, Leppert says, envelops human beings temporally. Sight separates them spatially. And, 'to the extent that sight distances us from the world . . . painting becomes politically problematic to the self-representation of feudal society'. It shows how far apart the classes are. The further loss of sound, of an unfolding present, implies there is very little holding the world together. What will happen? Oddly, Leppert reads the visual 'trace' of music as an 'argument that the spring idealized in Grimmer's painting is still possible'. How, though? Spain has yet to accept the Northern Provinces' secession, and it is forty years before the Treaty of Munster. 'Music is there because it must be; it cannot be done without,' claims Leppert. Its inaudibility presumably suggests otherwise.

To the related question – what kind of music cannot be heard? – there are some informative answers. In England, Leppert shows us how music theory was rationalised during the Enlightenment as a science, and valued as a masculine, mathematical principle. Once heard or realised, however, music abandoned the high ground of cognitive abstraction and became embodied, a domesticated accomplishment rather than an intellectual discipline, suitable for women. In conversation-piece genre paintings of the period, women are deployed around harpsichords and clavichords in patently unmusical poses to suggest the expendable luxury of their artistic endeavour. Yet the whole issue of music made by women also nourished, as Leppert enjoyably demonstrates, a complementary set of masculine anxieties about 'performing' wives and the threat to spousal virtue their activities posed. Writing in 1722, John Essex itemises the musical instruments suitable for women, recommending the harpsichord, spinet, lute and bass violin. Flutes and oboes are considered less appropriate, 'the last of which is too Manlike, and would look indecent in a Woman's Mouth'. (What does it look like in a Man's?) Domestic music-making was tolerable, in other words, so long as it preserved women in a captive state, 'consuming' passively, 'unheard of' and behind the scenes. The suggestion that there might be private, bodily pleasure involved in musical practice and tuition could only find expression in small-scale (comic) drawings which, for all the above reasons, lacked the official sanction of oil on canvas.

The sophisticated part of this construction of music as a domestic, feminised pursuit comes in the historical bridge Leppert builds between the harmonic theory of the period and the social order its system of classification imitated. We learn that rationalist music theory, as characterised by the French Cartesian Jean-Philippe Rameau (*Traité de l'harmonie réduite à ses principes naturels*, 1722) and his English imitators, regarded harmony as a conceptual proof of the 'natural' stratification of society. To each note and every social body its place on the cultural stave. Played music, by contrast, attested the instability of experience (or the waywardness of individuals) and, in a domestic setting, continually threatened to disturb the peace. Leppert also shows how these arguments for a naturally pre-eminent tonality reflected British concerns for cultural supremacy abroad. John Keeble's *Theory of Harmonics* (1784) thus 'proved' the natural superiority of

Western musical modality in so far as it articulated principles and laws to keep notes (and people) in line. Against this theoretical backdrop, the women figured in a number of contemporaneous portraits of the British in India by Johann Zoffany 'stand in' for the domestication of another culture; their silent harpsichords mark what Macaulay later called 'the pacific triumphs of reason over barbarism'.

Macaulay's speech to the Commons in 1833, defending a draft penal code for the subcontinent, predicated on 'the imperishable empire of our arts and our morals, our literature and our laws', gives Leppert an opportunity to sum up. 'Political empire', he writes, 'is mirrored by the empire of culture [which provides] the rationalization – hence justification – for imperialism.' The difficulty here is that this tells us nothing new about the proportions of the mirror. Why, from the beginning, should a culture be so keen to export its domesticity, lock, stock and barrel? There is no development of the idea that 'empire' somehow concedes the instability of life at 'home'; that the desire for a universal motherland goes hand in hand with the fear of a specific or single locality. The use made of music theory is also too selective. One understands how Rameau's mechanistic aesthetic is 'congruent with eighteenth and nineteenth century theories of political economy', but not with all of them, and not all of the time. There is no mention of Jean-Jacques Rousseau, for instance, who replied specifically to Rameau's 1722 treatise in his *Essay on the Origins of Language*. 'In the harmonic system,' he wrote, 'no sound is anything by nature. It is neither tonic, nor dominant, nor harmonic, nor fundamental, because all these properties are only relational.' Leppert is probably on Rousseau's side, not least when the philosopher tries to capture the excess of meaning in melody – 'its language, though inarticulate, is passionate; and it has a hundred times the vigour of speech itself. This is what gives music the power of representation and song its power over sensitive hearts' – but he should declare the debt he owes.

Leppert is on firmer ground in the last four chapters, in which he works hard to connect semantic excess in music with the sexuality it often implied in 19th-century art. A series of adroit analytical maneouvres shows how women and the music allotted to them were viewed with libidinous suspsicion by a culture increasingly interested in the psychopathology of sex and the 'affective', effeminising power of sound. A first-rate discussion of Tolstoy's long short story 'The Kreutzer Sonata', in which a husband murders his wife after her performance of the eponymous Beethoven duet with a hired accompanist, fleshes out the idea that the sonata's effect on the jealous husband is 'produced by what he sees . . . as well as by the music he hears'. Another lengthy consideration of Holman Hunt's painting *The Awakening Conscience* (1853), in which a mistress disengages from her lover in front of an upright piano, ties together two apparently contradictory definitions of music – as the lure of sex and the promise of salvation (in this instance, a turning away from adultery). Behind both studies Leppert perceives a fear of music as an embodied, visible practice; a fear of the pleasure of private musical performance 'in which the separation of mind from body momentarily disappears'. The very parlour music supposed to domesticate its female interpreters thus stimulates a physical (sexual) response; the 'inarticulacy' to which Rousseau referred, and from which Mendelssohn drew inspiration in *Lieder Ohner Worte*, is found to supersede speech – the language of men.

Invoking the shade of Roland Barthes, Leppert addresses a last portrait, *En écoutant du Schumann*, by Fernand Khnopff (1833). In it, a woman listens to a hidden pianist – only the right hand and the end of a keyboard are visible – with her head in her hands. Her body is embarrassed by music. (Either that or he is a lousy player.) The flinching pose surrenders 'the erotics of doing, for Barthes the sensual, sensate, tactile effort to do' – and this, Leppert claims, is the price one pays for rendering music as theory and thought. What we need instead, he concludes, is to reclaim a 'sensate and historical materiality, which aesthetics [Schopenhauer's urge to instate music as the universal language] has worked hard to erase'. His point is that visual art in the West has conventionally sanctioned the latter, theoretical bias. Of the two musics that Barthes identifies – 'the one you listen to, the one you play' – Khnopff's painting underwrites the former.

But looking at a picture of someone listening to music is not the same as listening to that music, or even looking at someone listening to it in the same room. The two-dimensional representation of a three-dimensional artistic world is, in the end, *nothing like* a translation of it. The issue of whether we are passive (watchers, listeners) or active (doers) musical subjects is not 'inscribed' in the act of looking at a painting – although it certainly is when we sit down to play at an instrument that has been engraved or decorated, where sight and sound perform simultaneously. As a registration of the loss of sound (and hence, the loss of time), painting on its own will never be able to tell us anything about the muscular pleasure of 'being there'. However joyous the depiction, however near we get in real life to relishing music's 'sensate and historical materiality', our experience of the musical image on canvas will always be elegiac, 'aesthetic'. Finally, it is the paint that silences the woman in Khnopff's portrait; were she to beam radiantly and wave her arms in the air, the 'totality of music', like the totality of Leppert's argument, would remain 'an unrealized aspiration'.

# The New Age

Melanie McGrath, *Motel Nirvana: Dreaming of the New Age in the American desert* (HarperCollins); Ian Cotton, *The Hallelujah Revolution: The rise of the new Christians* (Little, Brown)

Melanie McGrath's first book, *Motel Nirvana*, is a half-serious attempt to understand the origins and objectives of America's New Age culture, now flourishing in alternative bookstores across the continent but spiritually rooted in the South-West, and particularly in New Mexico and Arizona. The half-seriousness is inevitable. One of the frustrations of talking to alien abductees and immortal beings is that their conversation is not consistently of this world. Higher beings, such as Lady Athena Ashtar-Athena of the Ashtar Command Ascension Activation and Christ Healing Center in Sedona, Arizona, struggle with the limits of language and with a familiar biblical paradox: since God is ineffable, how should we describe Him?

> In the midst of confusion there is light.
> Focus on the white light, my Eagle.
> Soar above the third dimension and you shall see.
> Oh, once all was clouds, now all is clear. Ashtar has spoken.

As McGrath discovers, the problem with the majority of New Age rites and creeds is that they are therapeutic before they are religious. This means that the attempted description of the transcendental signified (God, Ashtar) is less important than the miracles he can work for his supplicants. The result, typically, is a mix of metaphor (eagles and clouds) and self-help demotic ('Focus on . . .'), which cannot decide whether it should venerate the Most High or demand a prescription.

The other significant feature of New Ageism, attendant on this therapeutic self-consciousness, is its incapacity to tolerate criticism. At the Annual Convergence of the Flame Foundation for immortals – former mortals, that is, who have experienced a 'cellular awakening' – McGrath records a memorable loss of poise on the part of the real-estate agent, James Russell Strole: 'We don't tell you what to do with your money, no-one should fucking tell us what to do with ours,' he rages, before adding, intriguingly, 'People try to label us a cult, but they are in death cult, which is the biggest fucking cult of all.'

What does Strole mean by cult, and why is he so offended by the term? A cult may be broadly characterised as the socially unacceptable expression of a particular set of strongly held beliefs in rites which are often inseparable from the person and presence of a charismatic leader. This distinguishes it from, say, mainstream Christianity, which may have started out as a cult, but has since evolved acceptable, poetic metaphors to address the separation of God and mankind, heaven and earth. More crudely, a cult denotes something defiantly post-rational, which New Ageists are happy to think themselves, and weird, which *pace* Strole, they are not.

The trouble is that they are neither. When the immortal clerics of the Flame Foundation (Chuck, Bernie and Jim) appear at the Annual Convergence, they are rapturously received. But religion requires submission of one sort or another, and cults may demand even greater sacrifice; for most of the convergence delegates, the notion of either is simply too undemocratic, too offensive to their sense of personal development, to entertain. Consequently, money is not offered to Chuck, Bernie and Jim in divine propitiation, but as a tithe paid to keep the spirit world indefinitely at bay.

McGrath is an excellent guide to this self-deceiving interior landscape. Her conclusions are predictable – that 'the narratives of our prosperous, materialist society . . . do not describe mythological archetypes, but psychological truths' – yet she finds her way to them along byways strewn with mischievous, toe-curling incident: a prayer-wheel ceremony with music by John Lennon and Michael Jackson, authenticated by the presence of a bored Indian; a tour of the Mesa Verde, in which the guide likens the Anasazi to Robin Hood and his merry men; a visit to Biosphere 2, the closed environment in Arizona, where, ominously, the 'human habitation tower' has been roped off. Her half-seriousness is also offset by the intensity of the New Age cultural ignorance she encounters, and by her realisation that, at least where Native American spirituality is concerned, what the fashionable holism of here-and-now conceals is a history of division and rule. The singular achievement of the Anasazi was, she realises, 'to disappear centuries before Manifest Destiny would have rendered it necessary to exterminate them'.

Ian Cotton's discussion of charismatic Christianity in Britain, *The Hallelujah Revolution*, tries to achieve the same ironic lightness of touch, but his thesis – that the left-leaning, community-church fundamentalism of organisations such as March for Jesus and Dawn 2000 springs from a deep-rooted disenchantment with science and reductionist economics – is too cumbersome and confusing. It is also contradictory. On the one hand, Cotton argues that the New Church's irrationalism and 'supernaturalism' (talking in tongues, raising the dead, interpreting signs) is socially and pyschologically contingent (work-related stress, marriage failure and childhood trauma predispose certain people to convert). On the other hand, it is apparently intrinsic: Cotton visits a neuroscientist's laboratory and is soon convinced that quantum philosophy, post-industrialism and new-wave religiosity are somehow encoded in the right parietal lobe.

His simpler point, borrowed from Norman Cohn's classic study of medieval fanaticism, *The Pursuit of the Millennium*, that social flux prepares the ground for certain kinds of religious revival, holds good as it would for McGrath's soul-searchers. What Cotton's book lacks is an awareness of how political structures shape that revival. Evangelical Christianity wants to enter the mainstream, but that will mean different things on either side of the Atlantic. In the United States, the (primarily right-wing) evangelical constituency is larger and better placed to affect policy-making at a local and national level. The quietism of British charismatics may be, by contrast, an admission that nobody in power is much interested in them.

# *Macbeth*

*Macbeth,* dir. Tim Albery, Royal Shakespeare Theatre, Stratford-upon-Avon

The dramatic virtue of *Macbeth* is usually thought to be its pace. As a usurper fleeing his crimes, the tragic hero has no leisure for courtliness ('measure, time and place' – that's Malcolm's domain), nor does he enjoy the kind of self-examination that we associate with inveterate villains (Richard III, say, or Iago). He fights hard, in fact, to avoid thinking too much about anything, and says that matters 'must be acted ere they may be scanned'. The chain of murders, the swift rebellion, his wife's precipitate decline, the charnel-house of the fifth act – in *Macbeth*, as in no other Shakespeare play except, perhaps, *Titus Andronicus*, Fortune's wheel appears to be powered by a dynamo. Why, then, is Tim Albery's intelligent new production for the Royal Shakespeare Company so slow?

Part of the answer seems to be that, in Albery's reading, the world of active change and retribution is not, dramatically speaking, the only interesting one. Rather, guilt is long, but political life is short. Roger Allam makes Macbeth a burly depressive, his every action 'smothered in surmise', who pauses to read the future, after Duncan's murder, in hands dripping with blood. When we next see him pondering the same hands, the blood is his own. For a moment, it feels as though he has spent the whole play repeating the same wordless gesture. The despairing look that passes across Allam's face acknowledges the turn of events, and is mingled with relief. But it also admits a deeper concern of the play: that we may be destroyed, as well as preserved, by what we believe in, and that belief, as distinct from knowledge, is slow and hard to change.

Macbeth falls apart because he believes so much in the witches (and, indeed, in what anyone tells him), not because the witches, or any objective forces of evil, are actually doing him in. (By the same token, the rebels really do believe in Malcolm as a magical-healing king, though they know that his ability to move trees about is simple military trickery.) Conceived as grim governesses straight out of Lowood, these witches (Janet Whiteside, Susan Elliott-Knight, Jan Chappell) are the sort of creatures that might inhabit a child's subconscious, and there survive into adulthood as credible demons of authority. Together, they move with painful, corseted precision, apparently turning to stone at the end of Act One, Scene Three, when a silhouette petrifies them atop Dunsinane Castle.

Bríd Brennan's Lady Macbeth totters around the interior with the same schooled nervousness. If the witches are governesses, Brennan is surely their scrawny charge – undernourished, credulous and pop-eyed; greedy for power as a child might be greedy for attention, and maddened by it. Words come slowly to her, as they do to her husband, and her invocation to the spirits is a splendid struggle. Exhausted after the banquet scene, the gap between what she has made herself believe (that power is intrinsically desirable) and what she now knows (that, like her, it is barren) reduces them both to silence. Allam tips a bottle of whisky into a glass and watches the contents spill over the table and across the raked floor. The boxy set which, until now, might have passed for the Expressionist interior of *Bluebeard's Castle*, begins to look more like a dosshouse.

On other occasions, Stewart Laing's operatic, ahistorical design is less atmospheric. The cast's many forestage entrances along narrow ramparts are tricky enough. With an added rake, they can seem under-rehearsed. Arthur Cox's Duncan does well to make it inside the castle in one piece, and Griffith Jones's Old Man sticks wisely to a bench. Adrian Schiller's magnificent Porter – a sozzled variety turn in 1930s pinstripe – has a shape-changer's immunity to physical obstacles, and can stumble around as he chooses, but the physical self-consciousness of the other parts sometimes risks bringing an already slow production to a halt. In an interminable England scene, Macduff (Colum Convey), Malcolm (Sebastian Harcombe) and Ross (Robert Demeger), perched inappropriately on Scottish battlements, are never really at their ease – an awkwardness that is understandable in Ross, bearer of bad tidings, and in Macduff, their recipient, but less so in the crafty Malcolm, who always knows what he is doing.

# Antony Sher

Antony Sher, *Beside Myself* (Hutchinson)

His first entrance was auspicious. Antony Sher was born with a 'cowl' – a membranous veil over his head. He means 'caul', although the mistake feels somehow appropriate: one likes to think of this great actor emerging from the womb got up as St Francis of Assisi. Marge Sher, his loving mother, prophesied greatness and Little Ant, as his family called him, duly excelled in the art classes of Sea Point Boys' High (he is an accomplished painter) and, later, drama lessons with one of Sid James's former co-stars, Esther Caplan. It was a materially privileged – white, South African, Jewish – but not untroubled childhood. In common with many successful performers, Sher records an early awareness of difference and imposture. A schoolboy crush was suppressed by anxious parents; he couldn't sing at his bar mitzvah (he is tone deaf); his boozy father, Mannie, kept his distance. More disturbingly, on the periphery of his vision Sher detected the imposture of apartheid, of 'women fighting and men urinating in the gutter', as his family's limousine barrelled past Cape Town's District Six.

The crisply evoked South African episodes are at the heart of *Beside Myself*, an urgently written if also strangely protracted memoir, and provide the key to a sympathetic reading of the rest. They are a reminder that Sher can write well, and that his gifts as a painter, novelist and actor are those of a caricaturist who is often angry, revealing and acute: 'Rugby was never South Africa's national sport – racism was.' Army service is in the Namib Desert, and Sher is clear-eyed about the warped but respectful relations maintained between Jews and Afrikaners. Thirty years on, he conjures in a single phrase the high-stepping horror of army life when Steven Berkoff, bawling at a poor National Theatre set designer, is likened to a 'drill sergeant danced by Nureyev'.

It's not hard to think of the seventeen-year-old Sher – weedy, artistic, gay – as an outsider, even a reject, in the South African Defence Force. It is a less convincing premiss once he becomes an actor, moving to England in 1968, training at the Webber-Douglas Academy, and landing his first job at the Liverpool Everyman. In the 1970s and early 80s, Sher worked with Max Stafford-Clark, Caryl Churchill and Mike Leigh; then came the lead in the TV series of Malcolm Bradbury's *The History Man*; then the RSC and, in his second season, a landmark Richard III, which won Sher an Olivier Best Actor award and helped launch his literary career, with the publication of *Year of the King* in 1985.

By this point, Sher was doing a lot of cocaine, and allowances should be made for the paranoia that prolonged use of the drug induces. It probably helps to explain the excesses of his 1992 performance as Marlowe's Tamburlaine. But, as Sher writes novels (two of them, *Middlepost* and *The Indoor Boy*, pretty good), paints furiously, greets Nelson Mandela ('better than meeting Olivier'), lands three plum roles at the National and settles down with RSC director Gregory Doran, readers may be forgiven for wondering what he means by his use of the word 'undervalued'.

He has not won as many Oliviers as he would have liked, and there have not been many big movies, apart from John Madden's *Mrs Brown* (1997), in which he played a very funny, eye-rolling Benjamin Disraeli, and for which he won another award. And Richard Attenborough apparently led him up the garden path while casting *Chaplin*. (The role went to Robert Downey Jr, who gave a fine performance.) Really, so what? By any standards, since his early thirties Sher has led a charmed professional life. I know actors who have appeared, recently, in sell-out shows at the Almeida and Young Vic theatres, who could not afford the tube home afterwards.

Nobody who has seen a friend wrestle with an addiction will dispute the misery involved, and Sher's descriptions of his treatment for substance abuse are a grim reminder of it all: the nightmares, the babbling group therapy, the grey-skinned alcoholics. If only his analysis of how he got into such a state (he's in recovery now) made a little more sense: 'I was brought up with two conflicting messages. One parent said you're a genius, the other said you're not even interesting.' Happily, between the lines of *Beside Myself* we find evidence to the contrary. Mannie Sher may have been troubled and awkward, but he travelled the world to see his son on stage, helped him buy a house in Islington, and welcomed both his long-term boyfriends with open arms. And Sir Antony Sher isn't shy – at least not in any self-limiting sense of the word. Rather, he is understandably insecure about his status, and perhaps slightly ashamed of the ambition that has helped secure it. Can it be a coincidence that the recent RSC *Macbeth* contained his most insightful, and chilling, performance to date?

# Gay Photography

F. Holland Day, *Suffering the Ideal* (Twin Palms); Robert Mapplethorpe, *Altars*, ed. Mark Holborn and Dimitri Levas (Cape); *Peter Hujar: A retrospective*, ed. Urs Stahel and Hripsime Visser (Scalo / Stedelijk Museum, Amsterdam)

Fred Holland Day, fin-de-siècle American publisher and Pictorialist photographer, continues to arouse anxiety. Though reviewers of his Boston exhibitions in the 1890s admired Day's technique – the prints were hand-touched, painstakingly well-lit and ornately framed – they balked at the subject-matter (naked youths in forest glades, African Americans, pagan allegory, occultism, an eroticised Crucifixion), which, in the shadow of the Wilde trials, marked Day out as an extravagant personality. 'Strange stories are told about him,' wrote the art critic Sadakichi Hartmann in 1898, 'and he in no way objects to them.' Superseded by the realists, he died, forgotten, in 1933, but has since been reclaimed as the photographic emissary of late 19th-century British literary decadence, sympathetic to the utopian Socialism of Edward Carpenter and responsive to the Hellenism of Walter Pater, John Addington Symonds and Wilde.

It is a welcome rehabilitation, and James Crump's introduction to *F. Holland Day: Suffering the Ideal*, which reproduces a generous selection of his most famous images, makes a fair case for Day as a serious-minded interpreter of male beauty and as a skilful portraitist. Like Hartmann, however, he is significantly unwilling to admit that the mythological and Platonic contexts of Day's photographs of naked young men were *pretexts*, as they were for the work of other photographers and artists of the period, such as Baron Wilhelm von Gloeden and Thomas Eakins. It is surely impossible not to recognise them as such. Little Good Harbor – Day's summer retreat, to which he brought young male guests for the purposes of intellectual and artistic instruction – may have been alive with the ideals of Uranian Love, but the philanthropic drive of his relations with these protégés is hard to discern in the photos themselves.

The boys are clearly objects of desire, discovered in unselfconscious reverie beside pools, behind bushes, playing the lyre or grasping a thyrsus. One possible Uranian gloss has it that they are innocents in need of instruction; in fact, the puerility is on the side of the photographer-mentor, who wishes to be instructed in, and to rediscover by association and witness, the self-delighting pleasure of youth. There is something childish, too – as well as charming – in Day's complementary search for an image of the soul in his portraits. The objective is sensible enough; many other Pictorialists, Julia Margaret Cameron among them, looked for the same effect. What makes Day's quest bizarre is its theatricality. In his dramatisation of the martyrdom of St Sebastian, for example, there are moments when the camera catches a look that has nothing to do with the model's mock-ecstasy. It is, rather, the awkwardness of pretending to be St Sebastian that passes across the young boy's face. Day saw this kind of involuntary disclosure as a spiritual revelation. From our point of view, it says more about the redundancy of the props and the staging.

Day's sexuality makes his case particularly interesting, but his artistic dilemma is a common one: if a photographic subject is posed, how can it be unselfconscious? In much portraiture, supportive critics can be relied on to emphasise co-operation, where it exists, between the model and the photographer as a kind of ethical guarantee against voyeurism. Crump ties himself in knots defending Day's Uranian community against such charges: 'Little Good Harbor housed a rare exchange that ultimately benefited Day and his models.

While it provided the visitors with a chance to develop social, intellectual and artistic skills, it also gave Day the atmosphere for his most ambitious photographs of the male nude.' Robert Mapplethorpe, who had sex with many of his models (usually before taking pictures), needs no such defence, yet Edmund White, who provides the afterword to *Altars*, still cites the intimacy of artist and model as a powerful argument against lingering accusations of racial and sexual exploitation. Not for Mapplethorpe the 'sleeping boys or the dead Christ or the martyred Saint Sebastian' or any of the other 'alibis' for early gay photography. 'What is extraordinary about Mapplethorpe', White argues, 'is his abandonment of all these contexts for, if you will, the naked fact of sexual curiosity and erotic intensity.' Good for him.

Is it true? Explicitness and curiosity don't always get on. Mapplethorpe's work, though exquisitely produced, is phlegmatic and fearless to such a degree that his faces, where they are visible, utterly lack any animating consciousness. No one smiles. Everyone is a little bored. Roland Barthes found himself entranced by Mapplethorpe's portrait of Robert Wilson (with Philip Glass), but it is difficult to see why. The image, of Glass and Wilson on two spindly chairs in front of a divided blank canvas, is as undifferentiated as a two-bar stretch of Glass's calamitously overrated music. You would need the whole contact strip, or opera, to make sense of it. The work collected in *Altars* attempts to furnish itself with a context by reinstating the religious 'alibis', mocked by White, at the level of sacrilegious parody. Where the subject-matter concentrates on still-life composition (the famous lilies, mostly) and sexual organs (pierced, humiliated, devoured), Mapplethorpe's triptychs and cruciform collages – sharply lit, clinically reproduced, framed in bloody symmetry – retain their fetishistic power. But where the angle widens to show an unimpressed youth removing his jeans (two photos: before and after), the insistence on the talismanic properties of these full-length nudes and portraits begins to look like pretentiousness.

Momentary self-consciousness – a startled look, a sense of unpreparedness, of internal resignation or of delight – is the magical ingredient in portrait photography, and in nudes where the subject is named or known. Again, what the friendly testimonials in *Peter Hujar: A retrospective* insist on is the absolute trust and affection inspired by this neglected gay, Ukrainian New Yorker, who died of AIDS in 1987 (two years before Mapplethorpe). What his pictures expose, conversely, is the gap between the model and his or her assumed role – the fleeting acknowledgment that, in the blink of the shutter, no pose is entirely serene.

The best of Peter Hujar's remarkable oeuvre, like Day's, catches men and women catching themselves at play, at rest, or grinning at the impertinence of the lens. His subjects are celebrities, lovers, camp theatrical nudes, drag queens, people in 'splendid isolation', boys, cityscapes, animals and still lifes. The images are uncluttered, singular. Their eroticism is often comical and, like a comic skit, transient. There is no lingering pathos or sentimentality. Mapplethorpe's sex shots begin by startling us and end up inviting us to make the moment last; Hujar's concede his models' impending and softly bruited departure. Here is a lover in narcissistic contortions on the floor, executing a backward roll; here is Cindy Lubar as Queen Victoria, tracked down to a bare tenement room but, so it seems, just on her way out; here absurdly, are two bullocks, rooted to the spot in the farmyard, clearly waiting for Hujar himself to leave.

Hujar worked as a fashion photographer in the 1960s and early 70s, and then unlearned his trade, emotionally speaking. His photos of the gay underworld and the avant-garde art scene lack what Max Kozloff calls fashion photography's 'derogatory instinct'. The effects of exposure are celebratory, even where the subject-matter is melancholy, or where Candy Darling, dressed to impress with one arm folded behind her, the other outflung, stares at us from her deathbed. Hujar's finest still life, of a single, elegant woman's shoe, recognises, too, the irony of the fashion shoot: that clothes can be replaced, whereas models are discarded. In this case, the 'Shoe for Elizabeth' is also a self-conscious reminder. Like the photographer, it is unique where we find it; like these photographs, it is what remains of the wearer, when the wearer has worn out.

# Allan Gurganus

Allan Gurganus, *Plays Well with Others* (Faber)

In a crowded New York subway in the mid-1980s, the aspiring writer Hartley Mims Jnr, the narrator-hero of Allan Gurganus's second novel, makes an artistic vow. Above ground, his friend, the once-beautiful composer Robert Gustafson – probably a stand-in for the pianist Paul Jacobs – is dying of AIDS; below, the adoring Hartley, tormented by his inexplicable exemption from the pandemic and weighed down with two large bags of Gustafson's more personal possessions, swears that he will one day 'find a way to make Comedy of this shuffle towards the crypt'. The bags promptly burst, bouncing thirty dildos with 'hideous rubberized zest' on to the carriage floor. A woman shrieks: 'Do we deserve this?' The question echoes throughout *Plays Well with Others*, by some margin the best novel yet to be written about AIDS, and certainly the funniest.

It opens in familiar territory: Manhattan, 1980, at the height of liberated gay self-regard. The story is winningly simple. Hartley arrives in town ready to be a writer and meets Gustafson in the queue for an editing job neither wants – 'Still unemployed, we adjourned to whine over coffee.' They are soon joined by Angie Byrnes, a five-foot-nothing painter who changes her name to 'Alabama' – 'I come from Georgia but O'Keeffe beat me to it.' Angie is smitten with Gustafson; Hartley idolises both. All three crave sex and fame.

In Ossorios, a dismal West Village café, tiled like a 'mouthful of broken teeth', the trio congratulate themselves on their 'latent immortality'. Why should they not be discovered? Lana Turner was – 'and we each had 60 IQ points on Lana Turner, if not her complete way with a short cashmere sweater.' Youthful ambition is mocked, a mockery that would sound merely derivative – Edmund White's fictional memoirs are full of the same backchat – were it not for the hard note of yearning and jealousy that accompanies it. ('Private effort, not group sex, became the deep dark secret of our circle, and our age.') At the age of thirty-three, Hartley has earned a grand total of $196 from 'actually selling some of my, like, you know, writing', Angie can barely admit to being a waitress, and Robert ('the god, terminally attractive') has yet to complete more than two draft movements of his obsessively reworked First Symphony: The Titanic.

The canvas is small and the subject-matter vulnerable to cliché. Romantic friendship, unrequited love and artistic sensitivity are hardly underexposed topics in fiction (or opera, or art of any sort). By the time the aesthetes gather in a freezing cold uptown concert-hall to hear Gustafson's work in progress, conducted by an ailing Aaron Copland, we may feel over-prepared for the coming crisis. When it comes, the bathos is overwhelming. Seated beside his beloved, Hartley sees a spot 'no bigger than a tuxedo shirt stud' on Robert's wrist. He is perturbed, but the imagined music, wonderfully rendered as 'a large crowd's parting cheers', distracts our attention. Later, Hartley wanders into Gustafson's flat to find his two friends making love on the kitchen floor. He flees, howling with grief. 'Even then, my first concern was for their health,' he explains. We know he's lying, and we also know it's an honest lie: 'Knowing you're just extra and aside, that kind of isolation can do many things to you. Including save your life.'

Perhaps Gurganus wants us to read this sense of isolation as 'survivors' guilt'. If that is so, then it is not without its portion of glee. At the heart of *Plays Well with Others* is an unpalatable truth. We admire Hartley, Angie and Robert for their glamour and vitality. We are moved by their predicaments. But our admiration for them is, at least in part, a narrative sleight of hand. The competitive contract that constitutes their friendship is retrospectively dignified by Gustafson's suffering. The greater malaise absorbs lesser, more personal slights and betrayals. In a fantastic epilogue that recalls the kvetching cherubim of Tony Kushner's *Angels in America*, a heavenly messenger invokes the narrator, noting with approval how 'you chanced loving those that, trying, just could not quite fully love you back'. AIDS is the saving and making of Hartley Mims. It demands his full attention as a carer, while providing scale and a proper perspective by which to measure other woes, including the loss of a father. It gives his life purpose, and his art a subject. It perfects his friendships. In ways that uncomfortably answer the subway passenger's outrage, it is what we, too, require.

## James and the Giant Peach

Ethel L. Heins, writing in the *Boston Library Journal* soon after the publication of *James and the Giant Peach* in 1961, deplored Roald Dahl's 'violent exaggerations of language and almost grotesque characterizations'. To his detractors thirty-five years on, the author is still capricious (nine-year-old James is orphaned on the first page by a rampaging rhinoceros); racist (the Ooompa-Loompas in *Charlie and the Chocolate Factory* were recognisably pygmy slaves, before Dahl gave them long hair and rosy-pink skin in a revised edition); and, most consistently, misogynistic (the aunts, Spiker and Sponge, with whom James is billeted, are referred to as 'ghastly hags').

All these objections have a basis in fact, much of it autobiographical. Dahl's life was a patchwork of cruel incident and insensitivity. His four-month-old son, Theo, was brain-damaged in a traffic accident; his daughter Olivia, one of the dedicatees of *James*, died in 1962 of measles; and his first wife, the actress Patricia Neal, suffered a series of strokes. Dahl could also be a publisher's nightmare – the president of Knopf described his manner as 'unmatched in my experience for overbearingness and utter lack of civility'. In the early 1980s, he refused a request from his editor, Stephen Roxburgh, to tone down *The Witches*, saying he was 'not as frightened of offending women as you are', and, not long before his death, denounced Salman Rushdie to the *Times* as an 'opportunist'.

Dahl was, at the very least, a poor analyst of his prejudices. If that's being too kind, let's call him what he was, a sexist, racist piece of work, and be done with it. Or not, because something else is going on, nearly always, in the books themselves. What is repulsive in real life may be less so in the world of the fairy story, where the teller of tales is also a natural tell-tale, and where the instinct for invention vies with the urge to crow and distort. By this standard, *James and the Giant Peach* has always been an instructive tale, for the hero – who, after fertilising a barren fruit tree with some magic worms, befriends a family of bickering invertebrates inside a fifty-foot peach, and with them crosses the Atlantic – must refine both these instincts if he is to survive and be happy, learning to distinguish between the imaginatively true (the Grasshopper's body is a violin) and the unimaginatively false (grown-ups are always right, peaches can't fly, ladybirds don't marry firemen). He is often tripped up by comic excess – the Centipede falls off the fruit in the middle of his favourite nonsense song – but when the peach, floating far out at sea, is threatened by sharks, James's calm inventiveness (harness some seagulls and lift the ship out of the water) saves the day.

Asking a child actor to play such a wise innocent is probably an unwise thing to do, since all actors are too knowing, even young ones. It also flouts Dahl's first law of child psychology, which stipulates that a gifted child (James, Charlie, Matilda) shall never know he or she is gifted or 'chosen', and that those who do know it shall suffer horribly for their presumption. Thus, James, on a mission to rescue the Centipede, is not allowed to hear the Earthworm sob, 'I really did love that little boy', and the clever Matilda, in Dahl's last book, is quite unable to account for her precocious mathematical genius. (The rich and spoilt Veruca Salt, on the other hand, in *Charlie*, disappears down a rubbish chute.) Henry Selick's enchanting film adaptation of *James and the Giant Peach* gets around this problem by filming the core of the story – the imaginatively true adventures on board the peach – in stop-motion animation. Only while he is in thrall to his two wicked aunts at the beginning of the film, and when he arrives in New York at the end, with the peach impaled on top of the Empire State Building, is James played by a real actor, Paul Terry.

Terry is a credit to these difficult live-action scenes, day-dreaming with his soon-to-be-swallowed parents about New York, cowering in his aunts' attic, and somehow making it all the way through a feeble Randy Newman song, 'My Name is James', without wincing. He is meek, he is mild; as meek and mild as Joanna Lumley and Miriam Margolyes (Spiker and Sponge) are ripe and rank, pitching the villainous, child-beating duo somewhere between pantomime lunacy and the camp horror of Robert Aldrich's *Whatever Happened to Baby Jane?* Lumley, behind a Joan Crawford wig and saffron dentures, has the time of her life as the emaciated Spiker. And so she should; because these 'hags', far from being the products of a misogyny unique to Dahl, are vibrant allegories of Vice – the flip side of the wise grandmothers and resourceful daughters, scattered throughout Nordic and European fairy-tale (Little Red Riding Hood, Gretel, the demon-naming princess in Rumpelstiltskin), who also surface elsewhere in the Dahl canon. (In *The Witches*, the mouse-hero's grandmother helps to defeat the Grand High Witch – a haggardly role much enjoyed by Anjelica Huston in Nicholas Roeg's excellent 1989 film version).

We know that Spiker and Sponge are 'hags', not just because they are ugly and wretched, but because they are delusional. Dahl has a whole Hilaire Belloc-inspired poem in the book, which hymns the absurdity of the witch who does not recognise herself; Selick, though, allows us only the least offensive verse ('"I look and smell", Aunt Sponge declared, "as lovely as a rose. / Just feast your eyes upon my face, observe my shapely nose!"'). This may be an error. As Marina Warner has pointed out, the representation of Vice as a crone is often a mixture of allegory and social context – a vain witch can figure comically as a trollop or an inn-keeping bawd, for example (Doll

Tearsheet in *Henry IV*, Mistress Overdone in *Measure for Measure*). But Dahl sticks to the allegorical archetype, and for a good reason. His aunts have no social function. They are medieval caricatures of selfishness and sensual gratification (the gluttonous Sponge wants to eat the peach, Spiker can only smell ways of making money out of it) – a fact we must appreciate to understand, by contrast, the sophistication of the wise women in Dahl's cast (Miss Spider and the Ladybird), who guide James across the symbolic sea of enmity.

These women are enlightened creatures of skill, wit and breeding. They can spin silk (Miss Spider – 'with a mile of thread inside her' – and the Silkworm provide the rope to catch the sea-gulls), they defy convention (the Ladybird has left 400 children behind in England), yet they are also respected beldams, with a comically doomed value for polite society (the nine-spotted Ladybird tolerates her five-spotted cousins, but finds them 'a trifle saucy for my taste'). They preside, in effect, over a chaotic salon, whose members treat the picaresque irruption of magic into their world, with all its attendant evils and unconscious terrors, as an opportunity to restore in the long run balance, reason and hope. Selick is Dahl's ideal interpreter in this respect, drawing our attention to sudden, disorienting transformations so as to emphasise a deeper continuity. 'But I've changed!' James cries out, when he catches sight of his puppet-self in a mirror. 'We've all changed, James,' the eight-foot Miss Spider counters gently, and the pedestrian inevitability of such a metamorphosis is not referred to again.

On the peach, as in every fairy-tale family economy, everything and everyone has, or discovers, their own magical usefulness. The more extreme the apparent discord – the more violent the 'exaggerations of language' and characterisation – the more urgent this discovery becomes. Selick's cast delight in their supposed incompatibility. The Centipede, voiced by Richard Dreyfuss as a Brooklyn wise guy, infuriates David Thewlis's morose Yorkshire Earthworm. Old Green Grasshopper (Simon Callow) is a blusteringly exclusive toff. Even Miss Spider, wonderfully evoked as a beret-wearing Dietrich by Susan Sarandon, is mischievous enough to compare the taste of peach flesh to 'freshly caught Ladybug'. In a tight spot, however, the bugs pull together: the Centipede gnaws through the stem of the peach to speed them away from Spiker and Sponge; the hapless Earthworm serves as juicy bait to attract the seagulls; and, in a terrific sequence of melded stop-motion and digital effects, the Ladybird defends her adopted family, from an iron shark that fires fishy torpedoes, with the aid of her reinforced handbag.

This last conflict is an addition to the original text, but it makes good sense inside Selick's loosely historical frame. Although the flight of the peach is primarily a *rite de passage*, it is also, in this interpretation, an evacuation from wartime Britain, where James collects old maps and tram tickets, and where bellowing rhinos could, and did, fall out of the sky to kill one's parents. As a pilot in the RAF, Dahl, too, fell out of the sky in a Gloster Gladiator, and had his nose driven into his head. Dangerous but miraculous flight is therefore a constant refrain in his children's books. When the huge peach tumbles to earth, it appears to threaten atomic disaster – 'Strong men turned to one another and said things like, "I guess this is it, Joe"' – before making a rude landing – 'There was a squelch' – on the upturned finger of the free world.

By delicately suggesting the nearness of Dahl's ripest fantasy to the lived experience of a wartime generation, Selick emboldens the fairy-tale importance for which it argues of 'getting carried away'. A place of real safety, James discovers, may also be a place of soaring, comic distraction. As a serious little boy, with no rhymes to amuse him, he is a prisoner in a hill-top ruin (the film makes the Spiker-Sponge household look like Bates Motel), but as a silver-tongued, far-fetched adventurer, he is given a home (the peach stone, erected in Central Park) and a vocation. The distinction of mood is important, because, although Dahl's books for children contain occasional cruelties, the cruelty is itself contained by sophisticated wit. Selick misses the very best example of this by omitting James's fight with the Cloud-Men (substituting for it a fight with ghostly pirates), in which the Centipede is immobilised by rainbow paint and the crew suggest various ways of removing it:

'Now if he stuck out his tongue,' the Earthworm said, smiling a little for perhaps the first time in his life, 'if he stuck it out really far, then we could all catch hold of it and start pulling. And if we pulled hard enough, we could turn him inside out and he would have a new skin!'

There was a pause while the others considered this interesting proposal.

In other words, it is not just the cool pragmatism of his portage across sea and air that earns James his reward, but the liberating cheek of its narration – a cheek mostly preserved by Selick in this joyful adaptation. For James is, of course, the 'author' of the book (and now the book of the film) 'you have just finished reading'.

# Anne Ridler

Anne Ridler, *Collected Poems* (Carcanet)

From the epigraph to 'The Runaway', first published in *New and Selected Poems* (1988), we learn that Barnard's Star, a red dwarf 5.9 light years distant, is speeding towards the earth on an uncertain trajectory, in gravitational thrall to an 'invisible companion'. Likewise, the light from Anne Ridler's *Collected Poems* reaches us fifty-five years after the publication of her first volume (*Poems*, in 1939), but on a beam warped and waylaid by darker stars: Eliot, for whom she worked at Faber and Faber; Yeats, Auden and the Metaphysical school of the 17th century. Eliot is there, certainly, in the priestly denials of 'A Matter of Life and Death', one of several meditations on infancy and its loss ('I did not see the iris move, / I did not feel my love unfurl'); Yeats and Auden, too, in the bleak personifications of 'The Rudiment is Single' ('A man coming in sunlight and sharp wind / down the moors, his heart cold and crazed / With life gone wrong'), but the devotional debt is harder to trace, obscured in part by the obvious signposts.

Two of the later poems, 'Traherne and the Long-legged Spider' and 'On 'The Glance' by George Herbert', name their sources. But Ridler owes as much to Henry Vaughan, in diction (the new-born and the love-sick are both 'parcelled' by clothes and affection) and philosophical sympathy. Like the light-obsessed Vaughan, she is a religious poet swayed by branches of hermetic knowledge, and like him she puzzles over perspective, the chief technical endowment in art that separates the modern from the pre-modern.

For the poet, perspective allows for convergence. Along its metaphorical lines, distant objects appear to meet and the leap of faith required to bridge the gap between the revealed universe and an unrevealed God looks less daunting when viewed through the wrong end of the telescope. In Vaughan, the distance is spatial. The love poems and hermetic hymns, such as 'The Constellation' and 'They are all gone into the world of light!', turn spiritual affinity into physical proximity so that 'wherever God is, all agree'. Three centuries later, the perspectival rays from Barnard's Star or the Star of the Nativity have become historical; the universe has again expanded, this time relativistically, and the vectors that carry us back in time are vexed by physics: 'In Old Moralities', Ridler writes, 'could be included / The entire structure of the world; we bound / To audit for a less rich philosophy / Add meagre figures, note / Tentative conclusions.'

'Old Morality' refers both to the moral geography of the medieval stage – one imagines Ridler's dramatic poems and discourses being performed on the same rake as, say, the *Castle of Perseverance* – and to a pre-Copernican world view. The paradox of modern scientific abstraction, Ridler maintains, is that it admits us to a world of portent and symbol coeval with our ancestors; they, too, speak in forced accents. Here is one of Ridler's magi, speaking in the second of two 'Christmas Broadcasts' for the BBC:

> Reasonable men, though we came in a wild season:
> We did not listen to angel songs on a hillside,
> Nor birds with guttural messages from the gods.
> These cold nights, too easy to imagine prophecies,
> With the glittering heavens splitting through the brain;
> We did not dream, we moved along the beam of logic.

Maybe this kind of erudite scepticism is nothing new. The idea of a consubstantial past and present, for example, still finds its most exquisite expression in 'Burnt Norton'. What makes Ridler unusual, and less easy to place, is her optimism, and the passion of her conviction that the mortifying tendencies of rational inquiry can only corroborate and strengthen faith. In the 'Dialogue between three characters and a chorus', the sceptic's element, fire, which burns itself, is God's too: 'Control is by definition; / And consider how the Son of God, how even Saint Paul, / Their God a *consuming fire*, consumed the world, / The antinomical, in a defined rational peace.'

Occasionally, the inclusiveness sounds forced. The competing echoes of mystery play and mythic music theatre in her masque, 'The Jesse Tree', are hard on the ear. At the same time, and in the same masque, Ridler's invocation of the Three Kings strikes unexpected sparks from early Christian chant and prayer, and (especially) the Breastplate of St Patrick: 'Bring him power, that power may be free of corruption. / Bring him knowledge, that knowledge may be free of arrogance. / Bring him grief, that grief may be free of bitterness.' But she is at her most original considering the intellectual trial of a faith that meets only failure. 'Free Fall', a late poem, tells the story of a French tailor who attempted to fly from the top of the Eiffel Tower in 1900. Film cameras recorded the whole farcical episode, and the poem – the best in a remarkable collection – spools backwards and forwards from the crowd to the tower, from the ignominious tailor to the viewer. It settles briefly on Daedalus, Christ in the desert and the modern suicide, before coming to rest 'Not in a myth, not a century back, but now':

> Ridiculous death.
> Yet as he stood on the tower,
> Shaking, shaking his robe,
> He mimed what each man must in private try,
> Poised on the parapet of darkness.
> Each in that crowd, and you, reader, and I.

# Fergus Allen

Fergus Allen, *Who Goes There?* (Faber)

Fergus Allen published his first book of verse, *The Brown Parrots of Providencia* at the age of seventy-two. This late flowering of harsh nature poetry (entropy and predation crop up a lot) and sceptical reflection (on violence, Irish genealogy, loneliness) has been justly admired for its intellectual catholicity. Allen's poetic touchstones are old-school and contemporary – illuminated manuscripts and Louis MacNeice. As a former engineer, he appreciates the scribe's intricate utility. Put the poet and engineer together and the result is a kind of pensive eccentricity: 'Thoughts slide out of thoughts, like an old brass telescope, / Lubricated with ambiguity, bent by time'.

The singularity and harshness are part of the same mood, which is one of disconcerting objectivity, a pretty relentless taking-up of the long view. When Auden and MacNeice put on dark looks, their talk of hastening ends and scientific over-reaching is leavened with defiance and humour ('Our end is Life. Put out to sea'). Of leavening humour in *Brown Parrots*, however, there was not much evidence. True, the last poem in that book is a witty reworking of the story of Adam and Eve – 'The Garden of Eden (described in the Bible) / Was Guinness's Brewery (mentioned by Joyce)' – but the wit is, as you might expect, calamitous. Allen's muse sounds battle-scarred and weary; our only hope 'in this world of confusion and error', the poet decides, is to storm the brewery and get wrecked.

The good news is that the wrecks of *Who Goes There?*, Allen's new collection, are more varied, and his inspection of them, across many continents, more precise. The poems feel active, even when they are reflective. Several deal with archaeology and the detritus of past civilisations. 'Foreign Fields', a parody of a visitor's guide to an exotic site, addresses the tourist's self-deceiving sense of exemption from history. A local fever – death in the here and now – spoils the sightseeing trip; but, the guide reminds us, since the whole world is a reliquary, geological if not cultural, wherever we go 'there will be no shortage of remains / Broken columns and reassurances / About a sort of life to come'. Culture clashes with geology again in 'Near Naples', in which a Neapolitan fresco, depicting hell, is restored after an earthquake. It is not always clear to which hell – Hades or Vesuvius? – the poem's narrator refers. The point is that calamity itself may be buried 'under words like ash and pumice', until the next eruption or tremor. We like to forget.

There's something refreshing about this lack of faith in the restorative properties of an art it has taken Allen all his life to put between covers. Words are public things, he avers, and subject to collective abuse; they may too easily become 'flags waving along the frontiers / of authoritarian states'; they can bury, as well as disinter, sense. This is also the way into reading and writing any mature poetry: the most commonly observed emotional responses (falling in love) or states (of war, of nature) are the least expressible; so certain conventions (rhyme, metre, stanzaic form) are necessary in order to remind us that it is not the experience itself that poetry captures, but our realisation of separateness. It is good to be galled by language, Allen finds. Too much is written that seeks to draw us into untransmittable experience. What we need is more of the stuff that keeps us out.

The reluctance to overdescribe and identify typifies the best work in *Who Goes There?* 'A Time for Blushing' warns of the dangers of looking for significance in love where none exists: 'From lairs in mock orange and dogwood, spectacled eyes / Interpret my movements, read my lips and note my lies,

/ And remotely controlled bees employ their working hours / Dictating my sins into the corollas of flowers.' That's marvellously sharp. The ornithologist as spy and insect as cyborg poke fun at the idea of the poet lying in wait for some Keatsian epiphany. But their appositeness is mined with irony. Being too sharp, too clever, too good even, may mean that you never show yourself as you are, or that you fail to express anything important. Observe the unspeaking world this closely, Allen implies, and your observations will come back to haunt you: 'So it's silence for us, my love, it's silence in bed – / And what I was about to say had better not be said.'

A similar dumbfoundedness afflicts the poet-deity of 'Sunday', who, having spent six days creating the world, finds himself obliged suddenly to 'name names':

> Abstract nouns prove difficult
> ('I am doubtful if beauty
> Would serve any real purpose
> And remain very much
> In two minds about God . . .

He seems to regret his power. (And: to Whom is he making his excuses?) At any rate, he evidently prefers the MacNeiceian drunkenness of things being various to strict taxonomy: 'Python, custard apple, pig / Date palm, clay and salt. / I relish smoke and poppy / And, for a bit of fun, / Shall nominate the fossils.' The delight in variety is Carroll-esque, energised by weird and faulty logic, and that is what makes Allen's catholicity so appealing in this second volume. It is intoxicated, not wrecked, by its own limitations.

# Annie Proulx

Annie Proulx, *Close Range: Wyoming stories* (Fourth Estate)

Of the eleven tales that make up *Close Range*, Annie Proulx's second collection of short stories (the first was *Heart Songs*, a decade ago), seven or eight are very good, and at least three are off the scale. The collection's subtitle, 'Wyoming stories', hints at plainspoken folksiness: hard life in the wilderness, endurance as a test of belonging, all the turned-over virtues of American pastoral from Henry Thoreau to Willa Cather. And with the latter, certainly, Proulx has something in common, not least her sense of enchantment before a high-plains dawn ('the endlessly repeated flood of morning light ') and her prophetic feeling – the staple of pastoral – that people are bound by their early memories, that there is no migration without the fugitive promise of homecoming.

Cather, not usually a sentimental writer, found this idea reassuring. Father Jean Marie Latour, the French priest in *Death Comes for the Archbishop*, fashions a Midi-Romanesque cathedral from New Mexican rock, and the earth is seen to reward his deserving ambition. In Proulx's work, the same idea survives as far as *The Shipping News*, her second novel, in which Quoyle, an ugly, emotionally stricken newspaper hack, heads for the frozen territory of Newfoundland, land of his forefathers. Life is hard, but little by little the environment yields, love builds its house. Nothing so neat and pretty troubles the new book, where the washed-up ranchers and cowboys are on 'dangerous and indifferent ground'. 'Against its fixed mass', Proulx writes, 'the tragedies of people count for nothing although the signs of misadventure are everywhere.'

In Proulx's Wyoming, the pathetic fallacy is put into lurching reverse: nature doesn't reflect man, it brutalises him. Characters may be bound to their barren plot, but only because they have been stripped of the will and, often, the physical ability to leave it. They are reduced to raw materials or base elements. In 'Pair a Spurs', the broken-boned Car Scrope, with a 'morbid passion' for his birthplace, is held together by metal pins and plates. A frozen corpse at the outset of 'The Blood Bay' has its legs sawn off to satisfy an ill-shod passer-by ('That can a corn beef's wearing my size boots'), and numberless bronco riders, ranch hands and faded rodeo stars, all of them 'torn up inside', leak horribly into their saddles. Passions are dehumanised, made squally and ungovernable; men are either impotent or violently priapic. For a moment, it looks as though Proulx might be making a point about the superior female instinct for self-preservation – 'Men had that flaw in them, Inez thought, to go over the cliff of events and fall precipitously into moral ruin' – until the same luckless observer is catapulted through a windscreen, 'mouth open, plowing the red dirt with her teeth'.

Humour – the humour of relentless exposure – caps these atrocities, which in the hands of a lesser writer could imply glibness or, worse, irony. 'This's a miserable place,' mutters the barfly blonde in 'A Lonely Coast'. 'My God it's miserable.' She dies in a highway shoot-out. Elsewhere, a rueful narrator wonders briefly about somebody's absentee husband: 'Nobody knew where Mr Freeze was – killed and kicked under the rug maybe.' Moreover, everyone sounds like death, or hoof-rot: Leecil Bewd, Car Scrope, Red Touhey, Roany Hamp. The names belong to pulp fiction, but the mishaps of these miscreants are something else, visions from the pit. What looks, at close range, like the sensational compression of mutilation, inbreeding, natural disaster and libido is revealed, at the end of each tale, as a plateau of sparse incidents, dwarfed by time:

You think about the sea that covered this place . . . millions of years ago, the slow evaporation, mud turned to stone. There's nothing calm in those thoughts. It isn't finished, it can still tear apart. Nothing is finished. You take your chances.

It is the spaces between settlements and acts that give them a dramatic foundation. These spaces are unreachable and unspeakable, and Proulx does not try too hard to describe them (a restraint she hasn't always shown in her novels), but they're always there – ready to swallow people whole – behind the fantastic impermanence of desire, ambition, gesture. Lives, being details in a landscape, are poignant. Dull matter suddenly matters because somebody saw it. The reader is unexpectedly engrossed by the brutal economics of ranching, by the genetic deterioration of men and stock ('The Governors of Wyoming'), by doomed business ventures in long-sprung tourist traps ('Job History'); and, in 'The Mud Below', the magnificent story of a pint-sized prize bullrider, by the ministrations of his rodeo doctor, 'a local sawbones swinging one foot and smoking a cigarette'.

'Brokeback Mountain', the novella that ends the collection, has already been published separately and represents, according to Proulx, her best work to date. Hard to argue with that. The unlikely tale of two hard-up cowboys, alone in the bare hills, whose intimacy 'deepens considerably' one summer, is technically perfect. An extraordinary tension between its percussive descriptions and strangled conversations shows how the clearly seen must often (in art as in life) go unsaid. But it is also tenderly transforming, placing the other stories' far-flung, freakish phenomena in their proper psychological context, the waking vision, the only one capable of uniting them:

The stale coffee is boiling up but he catches it before it goes over the side, pours it into a stained cup and blows on the black liquid, lets a panel of the dream slide forward. If he does not force his attention on it, it might stoke the day, rewarm that old, cold time on the mountain when they owned the world and nothing seemed wrong. The wind strikes the trailer like a load of dirt coming off a dump truck, eases, dies, leaves a temporary silence.

# Edmund White

Edmund White, *Skinned Alive* (Chatto and Windus)

Comedies of adolescence are all about affectation, but the comedy of gay maturation, particularly that of the average Edmund White narrator, is additionally self-conscious. The affectation is stress-tested and competitive. Marginal, repressed, smarter than Einstein, that's White's type; clever enough to know that while intellectual pride may be trying to turn a growing awareness of difference into aloofness, the effort can only make erections more painful. Being cute about desire in this way is also the essence of camp humour, and White is at his funniest on campus, both in his previous novel, *The Beautiful Room is Empty* (the sequel to *A Boy's Own Story*), and in 'Watermarked', the final story in *Skinned Alive*, the new collection, which catches a gaggle of University of Michigan drama queens at a low ebb in a café, feeling 'sick from the endless cups of coffee, the bottled fruit sauces and the ambition to be as bitchy as the dialogue in *All About Eve*'.

Repartee and literary swagger, the survival tactics that help White's characters aestheticise their 'pathological longings', also confirm his aesthetes in their isolation. Theirs is a sexual and cultural identity in waiting. At the end of *Beautiful Room*, the unnamed narrator watches this identity emerge from hiding as the drag queens in New York's Stonewall bar barrack the police, but the first stirrings of a conviction that 'gays might one day constitute a community rather than a diagnosis', are retrospectively stilled by the contemporary shadow of AIDS.

Of the stories here, 'Palace Days', a moving tale about a couple who flee the epidemic in the United States to make their home in Paris, is saddest and wisest about the brevity of liberation. As Mark, a gay travel agent and sometime community leader, falls cautiously in love with Hajo, a more innocent German film producer, the former's memories of 1970s New York – 'losing consciousness in leather harness, the smell of poppers, his legs coated in grease' – well up from the backroom subconscious to perturb their courtship. That's all the 1970s warrant, a wistful parenthesis, but White deals beautifully with his generation's sense of dislocation by making it geographically explicit, and by emphasizing its characteristic, American restlessness. Crevecoeur's 18th-century pioneer wished for a 'change of place' in which to farm and thrive; Mark and his long-term partner, Ned, have returned to Europe, looking for somewhere new to die. The apartness of the adolescent is the homelessness of the adult, and coming to terms with the end of sex turns out to be much like the awkward avowal of first love: 'the skill for enjoying a familiar pleasure about to disappear was', White says, 'hard to acquire'.

The recall of a non-virulent era is partial, and painful. From the chemically assaulted vantage point of the HIV-positive, it's sometimes easier to run away altogether. Many of the characters in *Skinned Alive* are travellers. The bereaved partner of a corporate image-maker disappears to Crete, where his lover's last words 'You have to look after yourself' return to haunt him in the faltering accents of a beautiful youth ('The Oracle'). An introvert goes hiking with his high-school hero in Minnesota lake country, where everything, including sexual longing, is teenage border country ('Pyrography'). And in the title story, one of White's famous unnamed first persons is smitten by a formidably brainy nightclub bouncer on a trip to Morocco.

For all the scene-shifting, the mind is the only place these characters can really call home. Critical as he is of adolescent posing, White likes its willed separateness. He feels that it's the lodestone of all future experience and that this is not just inevitable but probably a good thing: a safety net, in time of plague, as well as a comic distraction. Desire is unpredictable, equivocal, often treacherous (and then disappointing), but intellect is insatiable. Tokenism and pretension are another matter, of course, and merrily dispatched. At a Kabuki play, in 'Reprise', the narrator recalls that 'we hadn't paid for the earphones that would have given us the crucial simultaneous translation since my mother said she always preferred the *gestalt* to the mere details'. But the real thing is everywhere in evidence, most visibly in the frayed encounters between the physically incompatible. When White's first person and the heroic doorman of 'Skinned Alive' find that their mutual regard for pain makes a sexual relationship impossible – they're too alike – it's somehow no surprise to find that Paul, the bouncer, knows what Derrida thinks about Heidegger and that, on balance, he prefers Ronsard to Shakespeare. Practically everyone has a PhD, or has read the Symposium in Greek.

Occasionally, a deeper disorientation tangles the web of reference and scholarly reminiscence. In 'Running on Empty', a former child prodigy and prematurely old translator, flies home to Dallas and finds his wits failing him as toxoplasmosis takes its toll. Luke is poor, but the currency in which he really trades is intellectual confidence, and AIDS has bankrupted him: 'The translation he was working on would be his last. Translating required a hundred small dares per page in the constant trade-off between fidelity and fluency, and Luke couldn't find the necessary authority.' Fear eats away at these pages, and the grisly price of a certain kind of unreal academic dignity, the adult equivalent of that teen vanity, is paid in full.

White can be severe about professional pomposity and egotism: the famous biographer in 'His Biographer', who agrees to meet his own chronicler, only to find himself entertaining a second-rate hack with a $25,000 debt to pay off, is duly humbled. He can be self-deprecating: the narrator of 'Watermarked' winces at the memory of an Ionesco-inspired first play about homosexuality and race relations. He imbues sex-on-the-page with physical, erotic truth; and, like Thornton Wilder, the writer he secretly admires, he is a master of slow-burn metaphor: 'The rain steamed the sweetness up out of the mown grass and the leaves of the big old shade trees kept up a frying sound; when the rain died down it sounded as though someone had lowered the flame.'

Rhythm, cadence, proportion, his prose has it all. So why the metallic aftertaste? The compassion we are meant to feel working in the core of a letter to a first love – a letter which half-mocks, half-celebrates the staginess and 'ambition to be bitchy' of his narrator's theatre years – flickers like a dying filament. It's private rather than personal, like the discovered correspondence you wish you'd left unopened. 'Remember how I was so horny in Wales I had sex with the village idiot I picked up at dusk in the public toilet at Caernarvon?' Yes, of course. Then again, no, sorry. But we remember that word *idiot*, because of the person it uses and elbows aside, and the pain of his silence.

# Making Books

Neither of my parents read much and certainly not poetry, but from some other far-sighted relative they inherited a copy of *Peacock Pie* by Walter de la Mare, so I read that. I can't say that I remember many of the poems in it, or even any of the better lines. He is out of fashion today, and besides his Georgian contemporaries, never mind the later Modernists, the verse is threaded with fustian. Its Wordsworthian yearning sounds hollow within earshot of the First World War, titles and rhymes express a somehow anxious formalism, and the ear is tuned only to the past. Anyway, I loved it: De la Mare treats the natural world as a magical realm, a stage for transformation, where shadows solidify (they are always being *cast*) and words become things.

It is a poetry of unfeigned Romanticism. Moonlit nights and slippery-cold pre-dawns are especially good times to observe these rituals of creation – and to join in. For some reason, I felt that a book of poems was something I could make, too; and so, for a while, I got up at six in the morning and made books before school, cutting leaf-shaped pages out of jotters and stapling them together. The only plain paper in the house was a pad of Basildon Bond Blue and I couldn't use that, which meant settling for lined. It would have to do. Then there was the writing itself – the easy part. Cats, moonlight, shadows, trees, Time, God, cataclysmic destruction. You don't have many loggable memories at the age of seven or eight, so your subject-matter is whatever you can call to mind, together with the slightly dementing perception of power that such early efforts at invocation produce. I had no idea that I was doing anything unusual, or clever, and indeed

I wasn't. This was writing as play, influence without anxiety. I made books and gave them away.

Experience and reading teach humility, but their combined weight can be crushing. How one marvels at novelists who always knew they wanted to write, aren't happy unless they're working on a novel, write a thousand words every day, have a laser-printer, an understanding partner (also a writer). Well, I have written two novels and worked at the *TLS* for eleven years and I have no more idea what I'm doing now than when I started out. I find writing mystifying and difficult. I couldn't say whether it comes naturally to me or not. Certainly, I have never held a critical opinion with lasting confidence – an awkward truth that put an end to my career as an overnight reviewer as soon as I discovered that the unstable opinion is too often liable to become the overstated one.

But there have been heartening moments, among them the surprising discovery that I do, after all, have a few things to say in fictional prose, and that they are a funny-serious result of the way I put things together, the associative impulse. I find dialogue easy, for example, because I can hear voices, and I know that the turns of a conversation are unpredictable: it has purpose but *not the purpose it thinks it has*. In the same way, a book is a shape held in the mind before it is written, and my job is to glue the scraps together to make that shape real while recognising that, as I work, the shape changes. Like, I suppose, a lengthening shadow. Form is important (is formlessness possible?), but it isn't a jelly-mould (Elizabeth Jennings's nice phrase): it is coeval with speech, plot, character, description, cats, trees, sex, Time, God, destruction, and all the rest of it.

A fear of insufficient seriousness urges me at this point to make a brilliant distinction between prosaic and poetic creation. Sadly I can't; for me they are horses in adjoining stalls. At the heart of writing is curiosity: we are taught by what we find. The instruction afforded by that curiosity will always trump the instruction of the academy, of other writers, great works, colleagues and friends. And what we find, we have to give away.

This is the mire of good intention on which I have set up my own publishing house, Brockwell Press. Its first published author – me, because I had no money to pay anyone else – has just put his name to a collection of poems, *Small Hours*, in a limited edition of 300 copies, on plain Canaletto paper in monotype Bembo. If all goes well, and even if it doesn't, there will be another limited edition by another poet towards the end of the year. I am hoping that it will be by Peter Porter, whom I revere, and who little suspects my plans for him. It took me a decade to write the fourteen poems in *Small Hours*, and I am aware that there are ice shelves calving themselves to death in half the time. But it is the making of *Small Hours* which I chiefly remember, not the writing of it: the rifling through swatches of Fabriano Ingres for the cover, the collaboration with a master typesetter (Stan Lane of Stonehouse, Gloucestershire) and with the engraver Edwina Ellis.

I did it not to support my own standing, but because I wanted once more to feel that a book could be beautiful. Reputation and esteem are abstractions. Books, on the other hand, stay real long after their authors have been forgotten. That is why, thirty years after I first sat at a wobbly formica table in a room with a stuttering gas fire on Miser Rate, I have started making them again. I stand to lose money, of course – though, interestingly, not as much as you might think (if I sell 150 copies at £10 I will make my money back; if I sell more than that I go into profit; so if you can't afford £10, make me an offer). But I have my own first principles and instincts – Romantic ones – to regain.

# Danny Markey

It is famously not the purpose of modern visual art to console. The most suspect of effects, consolation carries with it a fear of sentimentality and gutlessness: either the artist is coating the pill or we're looking for easy assurances. Danny Markey's painterly touch is light without being at all soft. His drawings, watercolours and oils are plainspoken to the point of introversion; they cast no significant glances at us, the world or each other. The fact remains that they are very consoling indeed, and one wonders why.

Their subject-matter is simple, like a straight blues riff: suburban landscapes and night scenes, which at first sight appear lonely until one registers, almost everywhere, the residual presence of humanity. Cars nestle in driveways, a solitary camper van looks out over the bay, a river of lights drifts down a Welsh valley. Even when the humanising strokes are few, so that we're more aware of absence than presence, the effect can be soothing, though not perhaps comforting, cars and vans and cement-mixers making a kind of wide-screen still life with the natural world for a backdrop. Figures must be hereabouts, we think, indoors perhaps, or to one side of the scene. Or behind us.

Markey is a tonal adept, too. But it is no use getting writerly about it and listing the colours of an expanded rainbow, the mauve-grey of thunderheads, that dab of turquoise amid the pebbledash. The subtler colourists – like Bonnard, like Diebenkorn, and Markey – aren't that bothered by the question of range and don't think of colour as an aesthetic device. It's more akin to a reflex technique: the right shade of purple solves a problem of form and accurately conveys the vanishing point at which solid high ground becomes night sky. Sometimes the technique brings with it a fresh, unsettling insight. If you look fearlessly into the blue of the New Mexico horizon, you'll find that there's a hint of black in the top slice of the visual field, presumably because that is what the blazing azure becomes in the top slice of the earth's atmosphere. You can see, or sense, at the periphery of Markey's swiftly drawn 'Desert Places' series, and even in the brightest of his blues, a metallic reminder of that same darkness.

It's a way of looking at things that owes a lot to instinctive draughtsmanship. Part of the energy of these works comes from their directness. They deftly notate forms and colours, places and landscapes and then export that deftness into other media, from conté crayon to oil, say, with no loss of immediacy. It argues a quickness of perception that is not unrelated, I think, to the underlying mystery of Markey's emotionalism, and of why I love the two drawings that I own so much and go to them every day.

When I look at them, I feel I am being told the truth and treated as a grown-up. They are records of whole perception from which the perceiver has removed himself. Very little art can bring itself to do this. More often, what one is schooled to admire is the illusion of honesty, the aptness of the scene or the forced economy of the line or the brave boldness of the idea, all of which seem to me to be troubled, necessarily, by what they've left out – inconvenient parking, those bloody cement-mixers, feeling, skill (which is neither a traceable quality nor an asserted talent, but something less certain and more inevitable: the writer Ann Quin called it 'involuntary commitment').

Markey's inclusiveness isn't exhaustive. He isn't a merciless realist. There is still selection at work, or he wouldn't be an artist. The point is that he accepts what he sees and doesn't wish it away. The view of Falmouth bay from the inside of the car, with a rear-view mirror and air-freshener exploding in the sky, is less a calculated effect (though that effect is funny and pleasing) than an acknowledgment of the fact that it is raining, and there is nowhere else to go. He hasn't sought either to get around this or to ennoble the bleak outlook with aggressive artistic purpose. This is what we have to look at today, his paintings tell us, and the view is always provisional. It amounts to a letting-go of preconceptions, and in letting them go we're freed to discover something else.

# The Greville Press

*A Field of Large Desires: A Greville Press anthology, 1975–2010*, ed. Anthony Astbury (Carcanet)

The Greville Press, founded in 1975 by the Warwickshire poet Anthony Astbury, grew out of his friendship with George Barker, author of the first Greville chapbook, 'Seven Poems', and W. S. Graham. Its quickly developed intentions were to publish poets new and old in pamphlets with an affectionate regard for the principles of clear typography and design; to revive reputations (the Press is named for another Warwick man, the courtier poet, Fulke Greville) and to expand the circle of lyric friendship, making welcome, as it were, the friends of friends (Sally Purcell's sensitive romantic-historical sketches one year, and her tougher translations of the 16th-century Gaspara Stampa the next); to be consistently and amiably broadminded.

These are honourable aims, indicated, with forgivable sleight of hand, by the title of this new anthology, *A Field of Large Desires*, a selection of poems culled from 190 publications. The suggestive phrase is Greville's, from Sonnet 102 of the sequence *Caelica* (1633), and it is a definition of youth rather than broadmindedness. The poet goes on to say that youth is the condition of being convinced of oneself, and that this fiery conviction is always attractive, drawing others into its sphere of influence, to the benefit of all. But it's also narrow-focused, of course – a kind of opinionated self-love, which people must be prepared to, and generally do, indulge.

Editors are like this, too, Astbury hints: apparently open-hearted and full of fine-sounding convictions, actually ruled by a personal taste which is as much a matter of instinctive

97

attraction as analytical judgment. And so it proves in this mercurial, odd and occasionally maddening volume, where a wide variety of styles, forms and poetic registers, and translations, appear to advantage as expressions of a singular editorial sensibility. It is a thoroughly enjoyable book, even when its inclusions are baffling, even though the alphabetic ordering of very different poets feels forced (it would have made much more sense to present them in order of publication, since the evolution of the Editor's taste is what unites them). The experience of reading it is a little like that of glancing at a friend's bookshelves and spotting Adam Smith next to Delia. One is strangely gratified by the juxtaposition, without being better informed by it.

A picture emerges, in Astbury's case, of an editor and publisher with strong and equal interests in the less celebrated Elizabethan lyricists (Greville and Thomas Campion), in those 17th-century metaphysicians and divines who are neither Donne nor Milton, in late-Victorian unearthings (the fine, Rossetti-ish Elizabeth Daryush), in Symbolist-Surrealist odysseys (Apollinaire's 'Zone', beautifully Englished by Oliver Bernard as a sort of Zoroastrian invocation, and 'Poem of a Day' by the great Spaniard Antonio Machado), in versions of classical myth and light verse acidulated by melancholy, in narrative poetry and irreducible squibs. All these styles and sizes have their good exponents, but the most striking poems in the book are the ones that bear the imprint of intelligent selection – that echo and choose each other, whispering across the room, because they are liked by the same person.

These poems fall into three categories: translations, poems by the neglected or currently unfashionable, and (broadly speaking) expressions of a near-religious or at least metaphysical ecstasy. Purcell's translations of two sonnets from Stampa's *Rime* (1554) are extremely good. Though unrhymed, their relatively terse lines achieve an emotional compression which feels like rhyme, as if a mind were continually turning over the circumstances of heartbreak, repeating another's crime to itself, and looking for a way to transform despair. Here is the whole of Sonnet No. 141:

> Love, standing by my side,
> keeps saying to me, 'Poor girl,
> what will your life be now he's gone,
> who gave you such happiness?'
> And I say, 'Why did you show him
> to me that first time, there
> for a moment and gone again,
> if you only meant to kill me?'
> Then he sees he is in the wrong
> and says nothing, and I go on grieving,
> my heart knows how piteously!
> My prayers are no good, if I pray,
> because I send them all to him
> who cares little or nothing for my pain.

In her short life, Gaspara Stampa suffered the loss of an adored brother and was abandoned by her lover, Count Collaltino di Collato. Her poetry preserves the immediacy of grief with something like triumphant regret. This is pain and passion newly reasoned into artistic understanding, the high calling of the Renaissance, and Purcell, who was herself a subtle poet and a scholar of the period, attends to it with sympathy.

Purcell calls to Stampa (both women died young); Stampa, in her turn, calls back across the centuries to Antonio Machado (1875–1939), also bereft of a brother, and in Charles Tomlinson's elegant stepped tercets similarly seeking to end the repeatedness of sorrow. In both Stampa's sonnet and Machado's 'rural meditation', we notice that the source of grief is only partly loss itself. The other part is the breathing vacancy of contemplation that succeeds it – a companion but not companionable silence.

> But, clock, is yours
> this time of mine –
>   are mine your hours?
> (Tick, tick)
> There was a day
> (tick, tick) that passed
> and that which I
> most loved
> death made away.

This is almost naïve, like a folk-song, but the plain-dealing voice of the lyric, cutting across history and expectation, unseats any objections. It has the lulling power of the Corpus Christi Carol and the ability to spring an emotional surprise (boredom reveals itself to be mourning in disguise) that we find in another of Astbury's restorations: the Englishman Henry Reed (1914–1986), best known for his war poem, 'The Naming of Parts'. Reed is not widely read now, but his appearance, here, as the author of a long narrative poem, 'The Auction Sale', is a useful corrective to our sense of him as a poet and playwright imprisoned by influences, Hardy and Eliot especially. 'The Auction Sale', about a provincial stranger who bids for a painting in a room of snobs, is wittily distinct, with an ear for the dignity of absurd types that looks forward to Larkin's 'Show Saturday' and perhaps also Fenton's 'Ballad of the Shrieking Man'. The young stranger squares up to a couple of London gallery experts, and pushes the price for a genre painting of Venus, Mars and Cupid sky-high until he is forced to withdraw. The poem is funny but sinisterly intense; a shadow falls, and it ends on a ghostly note, with echoes of Gethsemane, the disappointed man seen 'crying bitterly' in a grove of 'sodden trees'.

Reversals of fortune and expectation also govern Astbury's metaphysical and religious selections: Henry Vaughan ('Peace'), Thomas Traherne ('Shadows in the Water'), George Herbert ('Sin', an atypically gloomy work) and Rochester ('Upon Nothing') from the 17th century; Anne Ridler, instead of T. S. Eliot, from the 20th. There is a serious point at stake here. The starriest names of poetry are not necessarily the most influential. The example of George Herbert was more important to both Vaughan and Traherne than that of Donne or Milton. Ridler, who was Eliot's amanuensis for years, absorbed more from Vaughan and Traherne than she did from her famous employer: the beautiful rapt images, in Traherne, of a world inverted in a puddle are re-used by her to convey the perspective of a small child:

> He rows about his ocean
> With its leaning cliffs and towers,
> A horizontal being,
> Straddled by walking people,
> By table-legs and chairs;
> And sees the world as you can see
> Upside-down in water
> The wavering heights of trees
> Whose roots hang from your eyes.

But it seems possible that this call-and-response story of poets and poetic influences is not the point Astbury is making, or at least not deliberately. Rather, he is skirting the problem that inheres in organising any selection on the grounds of individual taste alone. How reliable is that taste? And is the 'I like this poet' say-so of an editor publishing individual pamphlets good enough when it comes to anthologising?

Anthony Astbury has set out to provide a representative selection of work published by his Press. His criteria for selection are therefore quantitative, as well as qualitative, and in the context of an anthology (which is all about the creation of context) he risks seeming inattentive to the claims of demonstrably great poets as against those of well-intentioned but minor practitioners: Emily Dickinson's single, buoyant inclusion, for instance, seems dragged down by comparison with Harold Pinter's trio of not-quite poems, or even Ian Hamilton's blown 'Rose'. The weaker voices are flattered by selection, the stronger ones almost unfairly diminished, as though Astbury were trying not simply to revive reputations but keep a few in check as well.

Perhaps I'm wrong. The secondary distillation of work by less well-known contemporary poets, from already slender pamphlets, makes them potent. B. H. Fraser's 'Business Centre', a fagged-out hymn to the conference-world of the mid-1980s, is a shining example. (Think Frederick Seidel in a cheap suit.) The selection is also beautifully produced (though one of Greville Press's characteristic block prints would have made a better cover). And perhaps we can, this once, agree to a pollarding of mature reputations, as also to a broadmindedness that occasionally fences us in with the justly neglected. We are among friends. The field is large enough to admit a few thwarted desires.

# Dan Burt

Dan Burt, *Certain Windows* (Lintott Press)

The centrepiece of Dan Burt's second Lintott chapbook collection is a tense, often brilliant prose memoir of his formative years in the post-war, working-class, Jewish district of South Philadelphia. In particular it is a portrait of his parents, Joe Burt, the youngest son of a carpenter from the Pale, and Louise Kevitch, the daughter of 'tough Jews' who ran the Tenderloin's numbers racket and its associated prostitution, gambling and protection operations for half a century until the action moved to Atlantic City.

Our sympathies are subtly but firmly directed towards Joe, a brawler and semi-pro boxer whose fights seem emblematic of a wider social and ethnic struggle for survival. 'Lust and rage beset his every age,' the author writes, with a feeling mixture of revulsion and pride, before reassuring us that 'bullies and every form of authority were [his father's] targets'. At the age of ten, he fells a lout with a lead pipe. Scarred by the Depression, Joe drops out of school (his brother stays on), becomes a butcher, struggles to keep the family business afloat, but is saved by wartime trade and the deals he cuts with black-market slaughterhouses. Justice is rough. When an anti-profiteering inspector asks to see the coupons for the meat being sold, Joe pitches him through a plate-glass window. When Louise stalls the car in front of a tram and the tram driver insults her 'sex, intelligence and parents', Joe runs to the tram, hauls out the driver and beats him unconscious. A lot of this instinctive, retributive violence is complicated, and in part explained, by its proximity to the Kevitches, a clan of Jacobean monstrosities – and murderers – from whom Joe does his best to shield Dan, but on whom, of course, the family also relies to get Joe off the hook after the defenestration; to pay off the IRS, to 'protect' its own faltering respectability. They are a frankly terrifying crowd, shooting state legislators, gunning down delinquents, denying everything, and their mad annexation of mob loyalty to aspirationalism is contagious, so that when Joe finally wins $250 in a crap game and blows it all on a model-train set for his two boys, Dan and Rick, we sense the gesture's doubleness, the guilt behind the quick, jarring generosity.

Some of that doubleness also blurs the otherwise transparent style of *Certain Windows*. It is a striking account of intimidation and struggle, for the most part simply told, which would come over as plainly true were it not for Burt's odd, pre-emptive strike against doubters at the outset. The 'dishonesty and danger of romantic reconstruction', he says, 'is reason enough to try and record as accurately as possible what we saw, if we record at all.' It is as if he does not quite believe it all himself, and gives his tale a hint of those *voyages extraordinaires* whose narrating witnesses, like Watson in the Holmes stories, are always astonished into reporting the wild facts. At the end, too, after a thrilling and moving last chapter devoted to Joe's second career as a Jersey coast charter captain, the author tells us that his purpose has been to find out 'how vision forms, how I come to understand what I do of the world and whether that understanding is sound'. But it isn't certain that this is what he has done, and there is some collapsing of categories, here. The birth of the adult artist is missing from these pages. Why did the scion of mobsters and a poor meat-trader become a poet? Impossible to tell. Why did he also become a very successful lawyer and high-finance businessman? That much we may deduce.

For the facts, we have a prose recollection; for the truth, or for invention that is true, we turn to the poems that bookend the pamphlet, and which variously foreshadow and echo its themes of brutality and loss. Burt is a painstaking and able poet. Most of the verse in *Certain Windows* is enjoyable, and some of it exceptional. The commemorations of Louise ('Death Mask') and Joe ('Ishmael', 'Who He Was', 'Trade'), as of the wider American-Jewish experience of self-definition ('John Winthrop's Ghost'), are formal and learned – but their wealth of allusion, to the myth of Tereus and Procne, to Spartan mothers, to the Old Testament and the authoritarian early history of Massachusetts, never seems forced. They are a part of the 'vision' and a proof of William Empson's chattily shrewd theory that 'the reason for writing verse is to clear your own mind and fix your feelings'.

The best poem is called 'Rosebud', after the totemic sled, and uses Burt's favourite, Tennysonian tetrameter – a tricky rhythm, because it only *seems* innocent and therefore inclines either to false naivety or irony – to revisit his father's tenderness. It is a fine narrative elegy, an act of filial invocation couched inside the story of how young Dan coveted and was given a Raleigh bike for his birthday, only to lose it at once:

> So long a dream it slipped my mind
> Till I walked back to school at nine
> And saw it hanging, bent, flensed,
> A skeleton on the school fence

Into those simple stresses the verse packs a world of wartime horror, already past but not yet conceivable from the child's point of view. It's delicately done. The boy goes home, bikeless, fears punishment and lies awake all night. In the morning, Joe 'shook me, eyes red / Free from my twisted covers / To find a second virgin racer'. At this point, Burt relaxes his grip on the meter, its stresses bounced farther apart in longer lines, and with that relaxation comes the right kind of doubleness, for which one feels the poet has long been reaching and

searching, and by which he is rewarded – a lovely accuracy of
emotional statement that comprehends mystery without trying to understand it:

> We never spoke about those Raleighs.
> Perhaps my desolation recalled the
> Depression corner where he hawked apples
> with his father, memory of an older brother
> pedalling past to high school while he walked
> to work, or something from his favourite film,
> *Citizen Kane.* Now I cannot know. Old myself,
> when I survey the wreck we make of life
> he comes to mind and the vessel rights:
> in balance with what's worst, two bikes.

## Wildlife

Richard Ford, *Wildlife* (Vintage)

The plot is simple: the adult narrator, Joe Brinson, recalls the year (1961) he moved with his parents to a new town, Great Falls, in Montana. There, falsely accused of theft, his father loses his job as a golf coach and leaves town to fight a fire in the hills. In his absence, Joe's mother begins and ends an affair with a local businessman, Warren Miller. His returning father tries burning down Miller's house. His mother walks out, and then comes back. They're a couple united, and spared, by the brevity of their passions.

It's avowedly a recollection. These are so many events that happened in the past. We don't know how old Joe is now, because the present is not specified: we assume that Joe is talking to us as we read, and the relationship Joe establishes with us, in what we might call the moment of recall, is important.

A first-person narrative often constitutes a witness statement, of sorts: 'this is what I saw, heard and felt, and my direct address to you is a guarantee of its authenticity'. But Richard Ford's use of it is subtle: time and again, the characters (and the narrator) tell us how much they don't know. Joe's frankly incomplete recall bears witness to the strangeness of others, especially one's near relations, and to the compassionate understanding such an awareness of strangeness entails: we may not judge, because we do not fully know.

And Jerry and Jeannette are here doubly unknowable: both as youngish parents in the early 1960s, negotiating a crisis in a way that is mystifying to an adolescent boy, and as people the adult narrator can't quite remember, or chooses to remember in partially idealised ways: 'I don't know what his [Jerry's] ideas were for himself then, but he was a man, more than most, who liked to be happy.'

Ford uses this potential idealisation not to sentimentalise the events of the novel (which are largely inexplicable) but to suggest something of the nature of forgiveness, of love working at an historical and physical distance. Adolescent Joe is separated from his father by the geographical reach of the forest fire just as Joe the narrator is separated from him by mortality and time. But the two separations are really one: because of course age is a physical barrier, too. The fire is life passing by: not a burdensome symbol, but a smouldering inevitability; and neither turns out to be controllable (the fire in the hills is never put out; the fire that Jerry tries to start, at Miller's house, refuses to take hold). It may even be significant that one misreads the title from time to time: *Wildlife* could so easily be *Wildfire*.

At one point Jeannette and Joe drive out to see the fire for themselves. It's a strange, almost shamanic, rite of passage. The 'line of the fire' is another sort of line of demarcation – the point of transition, perhaps, from adolescence to adulthood. Though we should be hesitant, as Ford is hesitant, about reading too much into the incendiary fact of the blaze, which is inherently without meaning. Ford can be read alongside a number of recent American and Canadian writers in this respect, particularly Annie Proulx and Cormac McCarthy, and even Alice Munro, for all of whom nature is inevitably 'the wild'. Could it also be that the net effect of such 'wildness' is actually to reinstate a kind of romantic heroism in the most unpromising circumstances, with the characters tempered by unfeeling nature – made 'wildly' vulnerable, precisely because they can't affect the world around them?

The town in which Jerry loses his job and, for a while, his marriage, is 'Great Falls'; but powerlessness throughout the book weighs lightest on Joe's narrow shoulders, and its tenderest expression is in the dinner with Warren Miller to which the young man is dragged by his desperate mother.

The seduction of Jeannette, and its aftermath, is a tour-de-force of awkwardness, the centre of which is Joe's wandering self-banishment. While his mother dances with Warren, Joe goes to the businessman's bedroom, rifles through his drawers, sees his condoms, ponders his limp (there is a sort of brace in the wardrobe, behind all the suits) and then looks out of the window into the neighbouring house:

I had nothing to do in the bedroom. All the lights were on. The windowpanes were shiny and through them I could see into the house next door. An old man and an older woman – older than Warren – were sitting side by side in chairs watching a television in the dark. I couldn't see the screen, but both the man and the woman were laughing. I knew they could see me if they looked around, and maybe they could even feel me watching them, and would think I was a burglar and be afraid if they saw me, so that I stepped away from the window.

There's a quiet emphasis laid on how visible or invisible Joe is. Part of this attaches to his age: we all feel semi-visible as adolescents; we all wonder how much we matter to others' lives, and how well we understand our own actions. But of course it is the parents who don't understand their actions, in this book – and who make no bones about it – and Joe who tries to account for them.

Joe is, arguably, made to stand in for his father. He is invited to witness his mother's affair, and it's hard for us to resist the feeling that he is being made to suffer in place of Jerry. Is Jeanette taking her disappointment in Jerry out on Joe? Perhaps. The stroke of genius on Ford's part, I think, is to conceal the possibility from Joe himself. Both as a young man, and as the older narrator, he fails to accuse either of his parents of what seems to us to be clear manipulation. Or does he merely refrain from accusing?

The young Joe's bewilderment becomes the narrator's forbearance. *Wildlife* is a brilliant exercise in the precise cancellation of censure through the use of first-person recollection. Perhaps this is the point, and the meaning, of the book: not knowing why we do things, or why they are done to us, doesn't stop us acting, or the things from being done. But a lack of awareness of clear intention is attractively human and, from the reader's point of view, crucial to the novel's emotional plausibility.

## Situation

Angie's daughter, Stella, doesn't want to collect her order from Pizza Pizza. She doesn't want to go inside. She's thirteen, sensitive to the approach of adulthood and wary of adults for that reason. She has on her new white platform shoes and a short, flared skirt. She saved up for the shoes – her first serious purchase. They cost $130, of which she had $100. Angie made up the difference. She sits outside the take-out restaurant. 'It hasn't come,' she says, when we drive to fetch her. 'You have to ask, darling,' Angie says, gently, 'so they know you're here. How would they know otherwise?' Stella hugs her knees and looks to one side. 'I don't like to.'

I think I know how she feels. I wish I could tell her that being grown-up isn't anything to be scared of, but I can't. First of all, it's not a state you reach, it's a deferred prospect. Second, it is scary, because becoming anything means leaving behind something else, like childhood, just as – in my case – coming to Australia means leaving home and the UK.

Angie is the reason I first visited Melbourne, fifteen years ago. She was getting married, I was working at the *TLS* and feeling fraudulent about my pretensions to write. I needed three clear weeks to push a first novel towards completion and I got them. The wedding was a joyous occasion, even for a gay gooseberry like me. I danced with her disreputable Auntie Marge and got sent off for foul play. On the same trip I met many new friends, went out into the Victorian bush, heard new and exotic birdcalls – the sonar-beep of the bell bird, the melodious argle-gargle of the Australian magpie – and sat out under the spilled Milky Way at night, enjoying the bounded freedom of the tourist who indulges a fantasy of self-recreation.

A lot has happened since then. The new and immediately

familiar milestones click past: death of a parent, change of career, end of a relationship. I'm a sanguine person, it may surprise my friends to hear, and when Antony and I split up I decided there was nothing to stop me coming to Australia for a long stay. Melbourne has been good to me: I've written chunks of three books here. I canvassed opinion. Give it a go, was the broad consensus. I remember David Malouf saying he'd gone to Italy in the 70s to 'see how he was' in another country and had come home ten years later with five or six novels, including *An Imaginary Life*, his best, a shamanic fantasia on Ovid in exile. So, for the first half of 2013, I busied myself administrating the move 10,000 miles south-east of SW2 and didn't stop to think about what the effects of moving – the disorientation, the dreamlike sense that the things one has done previously don't count and might actually have been unreal – would be like.

Because that's the substance of Ovid's story in the Malouf novella: distance is a journey in time, which makes everyone vanish. The immigrant is conspicuous, but feels invisible. You have your memories, for a while, but you're becoming someone new whether you like it or not, and those memories and psychological props, though sometimes sweet, are also out of place. To begin with, everything speaks of the past. Melbourne is a city of elms, those beautiful trees which in blossom look like a single elderflower and no longer exist in Britain. In Muscle Shoals, the record shop on Lygon Street, in the inner northern suburb where I now live, the proprietor plays King Pleasure's version of 'Little Red Top', which my father used to sing along to. More profoundly, of course, the past speaks in the civic acknowledgements made during public concerts, readings and performances to the peoples who first lived here. Australians themselves exhibit a version of this what-has-been-lost vertigo, which goes along with a sense of being both the colonised and the conqueror.

But it's six months since I relocated, and it's getting harder to ignore the signs that I am no longer merely elsewhere. Accepting a present shorn of the past can be chastening, like trying to ride a bike in the path-blocking squalls of a Melburnian winter (impossible), or coming across graffiti – 'Hipster Scum Get Nothin' Done' – that suggests a reckoning is imminent. Mine came just a few weeks ago, on a walk to Merri Creek, which runs south into the Yarra and is a barometer of the changeable weather – now low, now full and roaring. There I sat down on a bench, on which someone had carved the words 'You Are Here' and I realised, a bit late, that the answer to my mid-life jitters was just that.

In the car coming back from Pizza Pizza, Stella kicks off the white platforms and relaxes, hangs her legs over the back of Angie's driver's seat. The slice of pizza in her hands bends at the same angle as her calves. Angie, looking like she's wearing some sort of neckbrace or safety-harness, diagnoses my stuckness with the ease of a good reader. 'You're overplotted, darl. Stop worrying about the outcome, get interested in the situation.' I whine something about feeling I'm waiting, and Angie says, 'Welcome to the party. Waiting is happening.' And she's right. Easily the most devastating moment in the *Odyssey* is the encounter with Argos, Odysseus's faithful dog, who waits for ever for his master's return and then can't support the shock of getting what he wants: he dies, because the waiting is what mattered. Peter Porter's last poem, 'River Quatrains', is about waiting in bed for the end, and even that vigil turns out to be alive with boat races, bars, chat, music. The whole point of suspense and comedy is that the set-up is what counts. Plots are premeditated and that's the problem: they don't allow for what *happens*. Aristotle says that there's a difference between 'something happening after certain events and happening because of those events', i.e. narrative events should be consequential, but I'm not sure. Order tends to reveal itself, come what may. You think your diaries are orderless? Take another look at them. Most writers lie about the planning, anyway.

You write, you wait and see. That's how it goes. The coincidences that crop up, mysteriously, while you're waiting are proof that things are happening. Rhyme, in poetry, isn't so much about imposing a shape on language as showing how things in the real world chime with each other. Right now, for example, we're in Lorne, about two hours down the Great Ocean Road, and we can't get into town because there's some kind of fancy-dress swim carnival – from Angie's house on the hill I can just see a banana running up and down on the beach – and the place is gridlocked, so we have to wait. 'Come and see the Bowerbird,' says Eddie, who is enthusiastically ten. He takes me into the garden, and over to a hide behind a laurel. Inside we can look out at a patch of shady forest-floor occupied by a shrine to waiting.

The bowerbird is a medium-sized passerine, with a unique claim to artistry. It is the only bird that builds an artifact, a work of art, other than its nest, to impress the ladies. The bower is a graceful passageway construction, made out of thin but stiff grass and slender twigs, with tall sides, curved at the top like the lip of a lily. Around it in a sort of galactic disc is an explosion of bright blue odds and ends the bird has painstakingly collected – feathers, plastic straps, bottle-tops, glass fragments. It's a brilliant feat, to no certain end, because the female might not show. (She might get a better offer.) What's left is the situation, the thing the bird's amassed. 'I am what is around me,' said Wallace Stevens, nicely capturing the sense one has as a writer that to observe others is to be hidden oneself. 'He's there,' Eddie says, 'but you can't see him.'

When the bananas have crated themselves up and gone home, we go down to the beach and I buy a book by Stephen King (*On Writing*) in Fowlers, the excellent local second-hand bookshop. In this essay, King says that his stories are found objects that need careful extraction from their surroundings, like fossils. I don't know this at the time, of course; I read about it and write it up later – *now*, as it were – and I suppose I could be inventing the whole thing. But what is definitely happening is that Angie is organising an expedition to get food, because we ate most of Stella's pizza for her and she's still hungry and so are we. Eddie has an idea. He's a brave, experimental cook – some fungi had to be set aside yesterday – with a thing for weeds. He has a colourful book called *The Weed Forager's Handbook: A Guide to Edible and Medicinal Weeds in Australia,* and he wants to make Weedy Pasta. 'Or Pizza,' says Stella.

We begin looking and the ingredients reveal themselves: plenty of prickly pear (a Mexican native) whose knobbly pads can be fried (the taste is tart but more-ish); wild brassicas (mustardy-hot cabbage), milk thistle and – almost everywhere – clumps of Fat Hen, which is a kind of spinach. All these plants are introductions of course, but Fat Hen comes with a story. Its Old English name is Melde, and until roughly the turn of the first millennium, the Derbyshire and Cambridgeshire family which eventually lent its name to the Australian city was spelled Melde-Bourne, because they grew the weed so prolifically in both counties. A weed you don't want, a crop you do. With a bit of patience you can sometimes turn one into the other.

## The Odyssey

1

Being away from home, feeling its slide into the past and one's concomitant ghostliness in a land which, whether it welcomes you or not, cannot be familiar, challenges the wanderer to start again, to build on different foundations, to make new friends and routines, or to find peace in solitude. Freedom *from* something, from oppressive circumstances, from the confines of the known, is the impulse behind the Desert Fathers' retreat into the wilderness, and behind Henry Thoreau's desire for 'simplicity!' in a hut in Connecticut. But each flight *from* is also a going *to*, and an encounter with statelessness. The freedom *to* do something new with one's life in a new place may be a dubious freedom; it may in fact be, or feel like, the reverse – an exile, imposed or self-willed.

And what is the feeling of being exiled from the self, from all that has been real and familiar, if not a sort of rehearsal for death – or at least a facing up to the fear of what it might be like to wander for ever? In a lovely early poem, 'Remorse for Any Death', Jorge Luis Borges puts this fear of no-longer-being in the context of its more attractive opposite, transcendence: 'Like the God of the mystics, / whom they insist has no attributes / the dead person is no one everywhere, / is nothing but the loss and absence of the world.' The wanderer in literature tastes something of this plight: adrift, he is 'no one everywhere', and his actual vitality, whatever joy it brings, is sometimes experienced as a half-reproach to the real elsewhere he desires, the place to which a ghost gravitates – his home.

Probably the most famous homing ghost in literature, half in and half out of his experiences not least because of the amount he drinks, is the original master of divinely assisted disguise, the wily beggar-King and teller of tall tales, Odysseus. In Book Nine of *The Odyssey*, we hear from the hero's own lips of his grisly encounter with Polyphemus, the 'man-mountain' Cyclops. Book Nine of Homer's epic is deservedly remembered as a high-note in a song of continuous high-notes: funny, revolting, and thought-provoking, and the careering verse translation by Robert Fagles is thrillingly, necessarily, over-the-top.

First, we laugh: the Cyclops is a herdsman dairy-farmer. Odysseus and his men steal his cheeses, offering a portion to the Gods but eating 'the bulk ourselves'. Once the men are trapped in his cave, however, things turn sinister and then nasty. '[You] must be a fool, stranger,' observes Polyphemus, 'or come from nowhere, / telling *me* to fear the gods or avoid their wrath!' Only the scion of a God would dare to speak this way, but Odysseus doesn't notice. Having invoked his stranger's rights to hospitality to no avail, he goes on to lie about his ship so as to protect it, claiming that it has been smashed to pieces by Poseidon; and the story backfires, because Polyphemus is Poseidon's son and a natural heir to the sea-god's rage. The poem is being subtle, I think; the Cyclops is not wholly *sure* of his parentage – we glean this from his ringing curses at the end of the book – and perhaps it is Odysseus's inadvertent reminder of his lawless father that drives him mad:

> Lurching up, he lunged out with his hands toward my men
> and snatching two at once, rapping them on the ground
> he knocked them dead like pups –
> their brains gushed out all over, soaked the floor –
> and ripping them limb from limb to fix his meal
> he bolted them down like a mountain-lion, left no scrap,
> devoured entrails, flesh and bones, marrow and all!

Odysseus's weapon of retaliation and means of escape are complex. He gets the Cyclops drunk. He tells him his name – 'Nobody – / so my mother and father call me, all my friends'. He cuts a long stake from the giant's club, roasts it in the fire and plunges the tip into the monster's 'broiling eyeball'. His men flee the cave clinging to the underside of the giant's sheep, and Polyphemus roars to his neighbours that 'Nobody's killing me now by fraud and not by force!'

We tend to remember the marvellous trap-springing play on words, but not always the context in which it is said, the truths it tells us about Odysseus – and Odysseus about himself. Of course, a supremely physical warrior has got the best of Polyphemus, but at the same time our hero has been reduced to a voice: a tale borne on the wind and henceforth *only* a tale that must remain invisible to the one-eyed, now blind giant. For Plato, we recall, a thing is not seen because it is visible, but visible because it has been seen, or witnessed. Odysseus becomes invisible on the island of the Cyclops – and not only there, it seems.

When he says that his family call him *Nobody*, he is being ironically truthful: like the Cyclops, neither Odysseus's dead mother nor his father Laertes can see their son any more. To Laertes, though Odysseus *may* be alive, he is also dead, passing out of sight and, possibly, mind. And where he really is, while he tells his tale, clearly prompts him to reflect on his faded state, his invisibility. He is sitting with King Alcinous and his daughter Nausicaa, on Phaeacia. He is spinning a yarn, sensing 'the loss and absence of the world', as Borges put it, and he feels guilty. His response, both in the nightmare world of the Cyclops, and at the table at which he's speaking, is to do something simple: he lays it on thick.

To Polyphemus, he reveals himself in an aria of self-praise. On Phaeacia, he submits to winning flattery and carries on with his story. It's boasting, yes – but it's also a piece of trail-finding, a way of becoming not just a tale-bearer but a real person again, which is to say a person with a rich inner life whose wandering indirection has a purpose, if not a conclusion. The shades in Homer have thin, bird-like cries; they are the concluded, 'burnt-out' ashes, or echoes, of being. Bards have an endless purpose: they sing themselves to life.

This is the pendulum swing of *The Odyssey* on which the hero rides – moving 'at will', as Fagles has it, 'from self-effacement to self-assertion, from *mê tis* to *mêtis*, from Nobody to Odysseus, the wily raider of cities'. The movement is more than a push for self-actualisation in performance; it is a means of survival in a world that in time will not know him or us. What seems to be at stake is the point, the *telos*, of Odysseus's life: is there a final position of rest for it, a home full of people and things that will corroborate his professed desire to be there, or is his drive to get home the thing that matters – a dynamic conception made in the present that assembles itself from set-pieces as the need arises and doesn't need a resting place in order to be true? And if it is the latter, what happens to the actual home he has left behind? Can the two sorts of belonging, the fixed truth and the portable one, be made to coexist?

Odysseus longs for home, for Ithaca, for Penelope. While he longs, he has fantastic adventures with the Lotus-Eaters, the Cyclops, Aeolus, the Laestrygonians, Circe, the Kingdom of the Dead and the Cattle of Helios – tales with which he entertains the Phaeacians. They happen again in the telling, and of course this second odyssey is an important part of the poem's meaning. It tells us, as will Shakespeare's Prospero 2,000 years later, that art and imitation are also forms of experience and not merely indices of the real. And in so doing it says something vital about the nature of the voyage home – because while Odysseus is with Alcinous on Phaeacia he can only *think* about getting back home; while Alcinous's hospitality detains him, he can't set sail. Home, like any object of hope, is kept at arm's length, 'over there'.

At the same time, it is a constant mental preoccupation, a fact of the inner life. Now, as Odysseus speaks, the 'real' Ithaca is forsaken and overrun by suitors. The home of his imaginings is an idealised, almost childlike vision, and yet the burning desire to be there is real, and in its flame the lost place becomes a found cause, something that compels a new encounter. The reiterated longing beats a path to a realisation at journey's end, which is that the actual and the imaginary are as day and night to the soul, but neither has an absolute claim on reality. They are complementary aspects of lived experience.

For the hero, Phaeacia is a physically 'stuck' present; it needs an animating vision, a narrative momentum, for things to get moving again. Conversely, on Ithaca, we have a stuck past: Penelope waiting, weaving and unravelling her tapestry, a tale that does not progress at all. She needs something to happen *now*. If Odysseus is to win back Ithaca and Penelope, he will have to throw out the old story, the idea of going *back* anywhere, and spring some effective surprises. And so the poem's conclusion is less a resolution than an extension of the voyage, in which the hero battles to bring his homeland out of suspended animation; to devise; to be once more the 'man of twists and turns', of nimble reactions. One kind of stasis, on Phaeacia, is 'actual' and present; the other, on Ithaca is narrative and past, but both are real. One kind of dynamism is fabricated from stories and flashbacks, the other is a response to clear and palpable injustice, but both propel.

One point of the Homeric epic is to caution us against thinking that we know what our experiences are or have been; to counsel against trusting or mistrusting the image we have of ourselves, of our words and deeds. For something greater than self-expression and self-reliance is in play throughout *The Odyssey*, and it is Homer's pre-emptively Shakespearean task to demonstrate it: to show us how the mental and physical realms interpenetrate; how thinking *is* doing; how a galvanising mental agility, favouring the truthful over the simply true, can create a metaphysical order of reality that is accurate and expressive, even if it is rarely consoling. When you tell a story about the world, you don't just add to that world, you change it; you also show how the original model was arguably incomplete.

Homer throws light on the nature of memory itself (and on the current psychological and cognitive-neuroscientific debates on that subject). It is not a series of repeated snapshots to which we can return as to photographs in an album; nor is it a pure, endless construction, but a combination of the two. In a recent essay ('Electric Sheep: the myths, constructs, and integrity of memory', *TLS*, Nov. 30, 2012), the philosopher John Sutton twines these Penelopean threads: 'The constructive processes involved in present retrieval or simulation of past and future processes alike are just those that ground our abilities to generalize, recognize patterns and update our understanding of self and world.'

In other words, what we remember is shaped to carry a meaning that has a bearing on how we act and think now, the significance of which is two-fold: first, it is possible to fabricate (or fabulate) a memory in the present without falsifying its past (that is, I can remember something in essence, and truthfully, while also reinterpreting it); and, second – which is of equal importance to Odysseus's homecoming – to have 'created' a memory does not, as Sutton puts it, 'undermine the ordinary realism about the past that is implicit in our understanding that we sometimes get the story wrong'.

Here we begin to perceive the consequences of putting the actual and the imaginary on an equal footing. It isn't just a piece of aesthetic convenience. It's what Plato worried about in *The Republic* (Books III and X), when he proposed the eviction of the poets from the city: if you imitate, you concede i) the 'truth' is not as stable or convincing as it ought to be, and ii) the flawed nature of the work of art suggests that the ability to get things wrong the first time is reproduced, not corrected, the second time around. This is either a shame, or a revelation, depending on your point of view. It could be, for example, that getting things wrong, being at times *un*convincing, is an inevitable part of right-perception. Educative, as Aristotle might say.

2

Sometimes, a person disappears, or is hidden, in ways that are more interesting than the putting-on of a disguise. There are two kinds of 'Nobody' in Odysseus's life. There is the man of overt craft, the soldier who vanishes into wordplay or dwindles into rags and a stoop before the addled suitors, the better to emerge victorious. And there is the entity, the man-in-the-crowd, or the mind at play, who is for ever missing, concealed by whatever happens, whose whole purpose is a leap into expressiveness – into art – that is also an 'escape from personality' (T. S. Eliot, on poetry), personality being the trap of the privately incommunicable.

This second Nobody is the 'Odysseus' who disappears into the force and colour of his memories and inventions so as to make them not just *his* story, but a part of everyone's daily experience. Even so, occasionally, he materialises in front of us, like an actor pricked by his own emotions. He is hard to identify. I hesitate to call him 'the author' or 'Homer', because that is to categorise him unhelpfully. Instead, let us *feel* for his piercing presence: it is like hearing, as I once heard, a busker play a wheezy reduction of J. S. Bach's Passacaglia in C

Minor on a small accordion; wrong, in 'fact' – if ever a piece of music needed a four-manual organ and a large baroque acoustic, it is the Passacaglia – but right in its sincerity, like a lyric voice speaking through a wall of special effects. The critic R. P. Blackmur once said of Thomas Hardy's late style (in 'The Walk') that it seemed 'reduced to riches', and something similar is true, here. How remarkable that it exists at all, in the Ur-epic, outside the grand sweep! It's as if this Nobody were saying 'but most of my life means nothing: the truth is bitter, briefer, a fragment'.

We see this Nobody just twice: he's a Hitchcock cameo, the man caught staring back at the work that is his life! Both times come after the hero has returned to Ithaca. Both times, the fabric of reality around the moment warps and shimmers. The first appearance is in Book 17. Odysseus is about to enter the palace with his loyal swineherd, Eumaeus, when he sees Argos, his old dog. Or rather, it is Argos who sees him – sees through the raiment of rags – and so, *pace* Plato, makes him very briefly visible, the kind of visibility that stands aside from the theatricalities of magical assistance, clever disguises, plotting and revelation:

> here lay the hound, old Argos.
> But the moment he sensed Odysseus standing by
> he thumped his tail, muzzling low, and his ears dropped,
> though he had no strength to drag himself an inch
> toward his master. Odysseus glanced to the side
> and flicked away a tear, hiding it from Eumaeus,
> diverting his friend in a hasty, offhand way:
> 'Strange, Eumaeus, look, a dog like this,
> lying here on a dung-hill . . .
>  [ . . . ]
> With that he entered the well-constructed palace,
> strode through the halls and joined the proud suitors.

> But the dark shadow of death closed down on Argos's eyes
> the instant he saw Odysseus, twenty years away.

Like many acts of recognition, this is an encounter with something already deeply and wordlessly known. What Argos illuminates, for an instant, is not the King behind the 'shameful rags' (Argos is only a tired dog, so the disguise holds), but the thinness of that other disguise of which we're not normally aware, a daily vanity, the ordinary dogged unconvincingness of everything we do, glances that betray the words we utter, stories we tell in excess of what we believe or feel in our hearts – stories which are not without their own truthfulness to a desire to seem plausible or even mildly heroic, but which, having run their course, can't allay the wanderer's fear, the *mind*'s fear, of being brought to a halt.

Beneath such vanity is the self we gratefully move beyond in art and all manner of daily invention; for a moment, and only in a certain light, our undisguisability lies exposed. Perhaps this is one way of interpreting Eliot's reality of which, famously, humans cannot bear very much. With a flicked-away tear, Odysseus acknowledges it and moves on, deep in his own sustaining fiction.

But his steps are now ghosted. He has witnessed a rehearsal for the end, a reminder of the equivocal prophecy uttered by Tiresias in the Kingdom of the Dead (Book 11) – that, yes, the returning hero will gain peace, but peace with more wandering in store and a final journey to propitiate Poseidon, carrying an oar inland. At the end of *that* journey – what will happen? The dog shows us, in a scene that takes us nowhere in the plot but tells us plenty about the various ways in which we wander. It is a novelistically apt detail, this parting between dog and master. Injured dogs will indeed wait for the return of their owners before they die. And if it borders on anthropomorphism to speak of dogs seeking permission to depart, it's less of a stretch to see Odysseus's offhand recoil as a reaction to what he now realises it is in his power both to bestow, and to receive.

He stands right next to Argos on the dung-heap. But he is 'twenty years away'. He has travelled unimaginably far, and now, so close to home, the dog shows him that he has travelled only in time, not space. Homer offers us a moment of lyrical but also novelistic poignancy, a turning point in the drama that leads inwards. He wants us to understand that, soon now, all journeys will take place in time alone, in an Ithaca of the mind, and that Odysseus will travel as only the dead can travel, in others' memory – ours, perhaps. That is why Tiresias commands that he carry the oar inland, to the earth, his grave. The gift the hero brings home, the consummation made visible, is Death.

After Argos dies, something odd happens to the blood and thunder of the *Odyssey*'s last quarter. The recognition scenes and the patient plotting of revenge, the biding of time, the stringing of the bow, the shots fired through the axes, the acts and speeches pregnant with a meaning but dimly available to the suitors (and then too late) hum with tension. By comparison, the slaughter in the hall (Book 22), when it comes, feels insubstantial. Am I the only reader to have missed the presence of Nobody behind the scenes, now that Somebody and his son are putting the Bright Young (or Not So Young) Things to the sword?

And Jorge Luis Borges, with whose delicate portrait of an eternal wanderer we started, turns out to take a somewhat similar view, in a poem that beautifully captures the questions raised (but not answered) by Book 23:

> Now has the rapier of iron wrought
> The word of justice, and revenge is done.
> Now spear and arrows, pitiless every one,

Have made the blood of insolence run out.
For all a god and all his seas could do
Ulysses has returned to realm and queen.
For all a god could do, and the gray-green
Gales and Ares' murderous hullabaloo.
Now in the love of their own bridal bed
The shining queen has fallen asleep, her head
Upon her king's breast. Where is that man now
Who in his exile wandered night and day
Over the world like a wild dog, and would say
His name was No One, No One, anyhow?

Borges catches (in Robert Fitzgerald's translation) the authentic, half-comical note of exhaustion in the love-making that brings Odysseus and Penelope back together, the falling away of threat, of doom-sayers, violence and pretence. But the Nobody who is banished here is only the first kind of Nobody, the master of illusion. Behind him we feel the presence of the second, the servant of the daily illusory, alert to the paradoxes in Borges' question: where can the man be who was no one? Has he lost the best part of himself, now that he is someone? And, for the wanderer, is coming-to-rest a second, profounder disappearance?

These are intractable questions with roots deep in metaphysics. For creatures in the Heraclitan river of time, to be at rest is as contradictory a notion as asking a mind to observe itself – tricky, since, as Dorothy L. Sayers once put it, the mind doing the observing is the thing it wishes to observe. The problems of home (a place, or a feeling?) and mind (a state, or a becoming?) are really those of time: has it a bare minimum value – a discrete state – or is it all flow?

They are almost logical antinomies, to which Homer presents no solution, though he does admit an occasional bias in favour of those jarring moments when the hero concedes his commonest artifices and affords us a glimpse of the Nobody who is always there, but visible only for an instant, like the bright interior of a soft metal, a bare-minimum-state human.

Our second impression of such an entity comes in the last of the recognition scenes, in Book 24, as Odysseus confronts his father, Laertes, on his farm in the hills. Rather than 'pour out the long tale' straight away, Odysseus decides to 'probe' and 'test' his father, employing the tried-and-tested device of posing as a stranger and asking after a long-lost friend. He praises the old man's industry – we find him tending an orchard – but remarks on his shabby appearance and asks, pointedly, 'whose slave are you?' This has struck some critics as a cruel gambit: after all, we know from three sources (the goddess Athena, the shade of Odysseus's mother, Anticleia, and Eumaeus) that Laertes lives now in a state of pitiful abjection; but in his commentary on the last book, Bernard Knox defends the decision: 'Clearly, this is a case that calls for careful handling if Laertes is to be extracted from the prison of grief and self-humiliation in which he has closed himself off from the world. What Odysseus does is to bring him back to consciousness of his own dignity as a man and a king.'

This is well put, but arguable. Because the deeper point of the scene, the source of its emotional power is surely not just to show Laertes to himself but to make his son feel, in Thom Gunn's euphonious phrase (used of W. B. Yeats), 'the strain of all that rhetorical striving'. Odysseus, still in the rut of being no one, says he'd like to see Laertes' son again, some day, at which point –

> . . . a black cloud of grief came shrouding over Laertes.
> Both hands clawing the ground for dirt and grime,
> he poured it over his grizzled head, sobbing, in spasms.
> Odysseus's heart shuddered, a sudden twinge went shooting up
> through his nostrils, watching his deaf father struggle . . .

> He sprang toward him, kissed him, hugged him, crying,
> 'Father – I am your son – myself, the man you're seeking,
> home after twenty years, on native ground at last!

When darker suspicions and failings gain ground, they are suddenly *in* the ground, *in* the earth around us. States of matter are inverted, the air is a weight – 'Light thickens', Macbeth says – and gorgeous palaces evaporate. Everything is hurly-burly – Elizabethan for commotion, turmoil – and all of life is in uproar. That is Laertes' world, of course. But it is his son's as well, because it has taken this amount of uproar and confusion for our second Nobody to cut through into the light, for Odysseus to stop falsifying his emotions, to see things as they are. Fagles's assonantal cloud and shroud are marvellous touches, though the masterstroke is an active detail – the 'sudden twinge' in the nostrils and the time-travelling collapse through the years that it precipitates.

The revelation at hand is not a simple product of narrative technique or question-and-answer inspection. It is an unargued sensation. Odysseus, master of exploits, has a plan for revealing himself to Laertes, and it must give way to the detail, the citric moment that throws all of the rhetoric, all of the wandering, into sharp relief, but which could not have come about without them. The last engine of recognition is both short and long-term, a physical and a poetic thing, a nasal embarrassment and a mental strategy, a whiff of home and a crisis of statelessness: 'being home, being someone, is this all that I am?' We should be careful not to underline too heavily the metaphors of home and artistic wandering, and that is because Homer himself treats them with such care: Odysseus is not just a soldier who drops anchor when justice is served, nor yet a figure of the poet who lives to speculate another day. Rather, he exists in that metaphysical realm in which we, too, exist, bounded by the facts of birth and death;

freed by memory – which remembers nothing of either – to consider an alternative. The light thickens and pulses about them as Odysseus and Laertes embrace, then shrinks to this point. We can only recognise what we have always known, says Homer; but if home and mind are things we never leave behind, then there is no going back to them, either.

# The Problem of the Image

The crime novelist and Dante scholar Dorothy L. Sayers, most readable and concise of lay philosophers, once summarised the empirical approach to words: 'all language is metaphorical' (*Mind of the Maker*). That is, all of human language relates one experience to another – one experience in the 'real' world of objects, thoughts and feelings to another experience on the plane of description and articulation.

Of course, language is itself a real experience, and often a frustrating one. It lacks dimensions. Saying 'a walk in the park' is not the same thing as going for a walk in the park. Then, too, the conceptualisation of a walk in the park is suspect: how far is it a non-verbal, non-symbolic feat of primary cognition – of intuition – and how far an effect of language, an idea shaped by the terms in which it is expressed? Would you want to go for a walk in the park if the words to convey your meaning did not exist and had not been developmentally embedded in your brain?

The pragmatist will object: just go for the walk. Picture the intention. Act on it!

But: how do I know what the picture means?

The pragmatist heaves a sigh and, sensing the presence of an aesthetic rather than strictly philosophic mind, invokes the spirit of W. H. Auden in 'Writing', his aphoristic prologue to *The Dyer's Hand and Other Essays*, published in 1956. There is a class of primary image, Auden says, that is 'drawn from sensory experience'; which transcends even as it precedes the verbal, and can therefore be translated with ease from language to language, because it is not linguistically derived. Earlier in the century, the Imagist poets had famously sought a similar kind of immediacy in things, objective or subjective.

This looks sensible enough, until the interested observer spots the weasel phrase 'drawn from'. An experience, even at the preverbal stage, is still being siphoned off from Auden's realm of the senses (or Sayers's first real world) and converted into meaning. What is the process of that conversion? Even if we allow for an imagistic proto-language that doesn't use words but is a more direct utterance, there still seems to be an element of interpretation going on that looks suspiciously like language – of baseline information processing and presentation. But what is it?

When William Golding (first published as a poet, in 1934) wanted to give his Neanderthals in *The Inheritors* (1952) just such a proto-language, he conceived of it as a series of 'pictures', passed from individual to individual with a kind of semi-transparent immediacy, something akin to telepathic communication. 'I have a picture,' says Lok, who transmits, rather than describes, the movement of a log he has seen in the water. Lok finds that the pictures do not always readily transmit, however – they contain obstructive, peculiar information not shared by the group – and then the Neanderthals are confused. Even a picture has got in the way of – not managed to be – the object it depicts. The cry that issues forth from the upset creatures is a cry of separation. The origins of language are two-fold, Golding is saying: 1) a need for direct, communicative indication, and 2) a realisation of loss: 'I am separate from the thing I have seen, separate from your interpretation of it, and separate from you.'

Auden, who liked categories, might say: State 1 is an Eden of naming, knowing, and effortless community. State 2 is the Fall into self-awareness.

Different generations of poets, especially, have always wanted to find their way back to State 1, to the Platonic world of pre-linguistic forms, in an effort to refresh their sense of proximity to life. They want, every now and again, to do something urgent and vital; to rescue a true means of expression – and, often, its concomitant, idealist-Romantic political truth – from stale usages, cliché and rhetoric.

A School emerges, various *dos* vie with various other *don'ts*, and quite quickly everyone falls out. It's always the same. But the question of why this happens is interesting, and leads us to the possibility, at least, of understanding the origins of poetry and lyric, perhaps of language itself.

Anti-rhetorical poets, like the Imagists, do their exercises in, and are exercised by, language. (It is the most exquisite form of poetic justice.) They seek a bright rightness in the lines they write, so that the language used may strike the reader as uniquely apt: in this line, in this poem, now, the words could not be improved upon. The grail is the precision of State 1. A poet such as Ezra Pound, for instance, wants to get to the thing, the real object or feeling, behind the veil of language. 'By good art,' he writes in 'The Serious Artist', ' . . . I mean art that is most precise.' And we might refamiliarise ourselves with an example of what he means by remembering his most famous poem, 'In a Station of the Metro':

> The apparition of these faces in the crowd;
> Petals on a wet, black bough.

It is wonderfully well seen, is it not? One looks through the lines at the faces, which lead us to the petals. The petals are an image, yes, but they are less of an 'apparition' than the faces, the real things that occasion the comparison; and this consideration of the image brings us back to the framing lines, which seem all at once to indicate a secondary, but actually obvious, beauty – that of being themselves beautiful.

The by-product of precise indication is an aesthetic thing. Words rather than things are reintroduced to the forefront of the reader's attention. Or rather, the words turn into things in

their own right, and nested within, say, a lyric of unimprova-
ble clarity, like Pound's couplet, is the philological revelation
that the individual words have become, as Auden nicely put
it, 'little lyrics about themselves'.

A circularity is introduced. The drive towards clarity of
expression produces a beautiful form, and that beauty invests
the form with a degree of self-consciousness which is poetry
as much as the 'intentional and emotional complex in an
instant of time'. One feels the effort, the strain, on the part
of the poet. He or she is caught in something like Wittgen-
stein's trap of language: 'A picture held us captive,' say the
*Philosophical Investigations*. 'And we could not get outside it,
for it lay in our language and language seemed to repeat it to
us inexorably.'

The pressure per square inch of some poetry is bedevil-
ing: the concreteness of language seems to impede as well as
direct the attention. An apt image can lead us to what the
poet wants to say – can open, as it were, a perceptual door
for the reader – or be the kind of distraction that dazzles and
forestalls further decision-making, like a too-beautiful sign-
post that forgets its main purpose. In a similar manner, the
limpidity of form which allows Pound or early Lowell ('why
not say what really happened?') to 'present' experiences, can
get gummed up – become formalism.

The problem is one of tension, of insistence either on brilliant images or shape; the poet is trapped by the desire for
words to be pure indicators, pure shapes. We say of both
some late Modernist inheritors and a reactionary movement such as the New Formalists that they are purist. This
is not to say they are bad: Marianne Moore's syllabics and
Anthony Hecht's facility in rhyme are both enlivening, up
to a point. But when that point is reached, we may find that
beyond it lies the snare of wanting to transmit 'a complex'
in Pound's 'instant of time' – to get it across straight away,

almost angrily, in its entirety, in just this way, with no loss of amplitude.

Yet the Lyric, we notice, speaks very often – *very* often – of loss, and it does so because the thing it is trying to get across unfolds in time, and is therefore always lost. It seems somehow 'filled with the intent / to be lost' (Elizabeth Bishop, 'One Art'), as if a pair of lungs had filled up and emptied with a bellying inevitability (in-out, in-out) that is indeed the source of both rhythm and rhyme, patterns of sound that first made the world memorable*; that goes on and on and is both poignant and practical, individual and universal.

The thing that fills Bishop's line is the thing that fills our lungs; the thing the Neanderthals had in common with us, and which 'draws' images from sensory experience that they might be remembered. Neither the seen nor the act of seeing, but the thing that sustains the body while it is seeing. It is our breath, and the instrument it inspires is the origin of language and poetry: the human voice.

---

* Writing is a specialisation: there is evidence that it emerged in the Near East as an outgrowth, in agricultural society, of the necessity for counting and exchange. Articulate language predates it, and its origins are complex, hidden. But some scholars think they may be poetic: in rhythm and rhyme that helped societies prioritise, that is, remember important things; and as a survival strategy in choruses that made small voices sound much bigger and helped to ward off predators. The one cry from, as it were, the One Art.

# The Lord Is Listenin' to Ya, Hallelujah!

If memory serves, I was trying to write a poem about the middle reaches of Sydney Road in the Melbourne suburb of Brunswick, where the shops and butchers and Turkish cafés and semi-abandoned bridal boutiques face each other across a patched and uneven surface clogged with traffic. Trams clatter up and down the street as they have done for more than a hundred years. The late Victorian buildings, many of them, retain their coloured plaster facades, like cake decorations with pink and brown piping. The more I looked at them, the more they refused to obey what Thom Gunn has powerfully called the 'occasions' of poetry, which are not moments of great inspiration so much as the sorting of real and imaginary experience in favour of the happenstance, the inner prompting that presents itself as a found object or an unexpected idea.

I'd injured my back and was in a fair amount of pain. Helpful distractions included the energy and beauty of my surroundings, the birdlife, the markets, the sounds of flyscreens slamming shut in the wind, the kindness of the people I met, the Polish lady on Lygon Street who took me under her wing, the odd way in which my relocation to Australia had both banished and revived childhood memories, because of course memory is dynamic – a conversation between past and present in which the retrieved event serves the needs of one's current predicament. Memory is meaning in search of form.

That search is a treacherous thing in both prose and poetry. Too strenuous an attempt to fix the results on the page can produce something aggressively personal or inert – the writer getting in front of the camera or in the way of a more unresolved and therefore interesting image. But if you can slide past a declared aim and speak in an aside, then the 'adventures in writing' (Gunn again) can begin. I am taken with the notion of asides: they are, in early modern drama, the convention whereby people – liars especially – let slip the truth. I write a lot of them. They are part of the flow of a scene or narrative, but relatively unplanned, quickly ushered in. When we find ourselves digressing or speaking in asides, we are often saying what we really think but would be embarrassed to own. There is something Proustian about even the most trivial examples. It is almost as if we can tell the truth only when it doesn't matter.

This is by way of introduction to a poem I wrote, unusually for me, with few corrections. It is somewhere between an aside and a soliloquy, and there is plenty in it that strikes me now as peculiar – that 'helium-filled Titanic', for instance. But the strain in the image is part of the overall sense of unburdening that came with staring at the shop-fronts on Sydney Road, and the heart of that staring was a revelation of indebtedness. I wanted to tell my father, who loves listening to music, how much his example has meant to me. I listened to music as I walked up and down Sydney Road, and for a while I listened every day to the American jazz composer Carla Bley, whom we both admire. I associate her gospel instrumental, 'The Lord Is Listenin' to Ya, Hallelujah!', with Dad, with Melbourne, with the smell of meat in Brunswick market, with the dramatic monologues of U. A. Fanthorpe and Billy Collins, with the Psalms of thanksgiving.

> The Lord Is Listenin' to Ya, Hallelujah
> *for John Eaves*
>
> Gary Valente's on trombone and you're mixing acrylics.
> The sound is that of a lone magisterial goose laying
> about itself in cycles of wide-eyed, tearless grief.

The other farm animals stare at it in dismay.
'What's got into her, apart from extra corn?'
Lately, people have been telling me I should stop
writing about my childhood and move on. Where to,
they do not reveal. And how can I,
when it follows me down Sydney Road,
in even these blue nethermost latitudes,
flapping its weird relic wings in despair
at all my pointless running about?
I could try, I could for once just *try*
listening, as I do battle with phone companies,
internet cafés and robot ladies grateful for my abuse,
to what the music is saying, however painfully
long the passage of recall might be on the way
back to mornings of hopeless pleasure in a room
filled with light and colour, your paintings
streaming on every side like pennants on a standard
or the *tricolor* plastic strips at Dewhurst the Butcher.
Perhaps that's why the goose is so frightened:
though even in the grip of the most plausible terror,
knowing full well what goes on behind the curtain
where the rosy-cheeked lads let fall their arms,
the noise she makes tells a different story.
Instead of trying to sound beautiful, let it blow.
Live as though you were already dead and free
to wander the brazen rooms of this honking solo
which lifts off like a helium-filled Titanic
and floats effortlessly upwards laden with coughs,
barks, distant alarms, cheers, dropped glasses, sleep apnoea,
locked-ward chatter from the audience and every other song
of inadvertent praise you can imagine hailing from the top deck.

## Executive Decision

A bearable preposterousness is what one wants from a hijack action movie – the reassuring feeling that what you are witnessing looks credible but could never happen to *you* – and yet, as so often, getting what one wants is an odd experience. In the 1990s I worked briefly as a reader for Warner Bros. I looked at scripts as they came in and wrote a report. I didn't read *Executive Decision* (and have never since heard of its writers, Jim and John Thomas), but I did attend an early screening of the finished film and I saw some of the test audience's comments on a pile of unusually full and emphatic response sheets. Veteran editor Stuart Baird's first movie as director divided opinion. Some people loved it, and others felt furiously short-changed. Here is a partial synopsis, followed by (from memory) a few of the sharper comments, to which I have added my own belated replies.

A group of terrorists takes over a 747 on a transatlantic flight bound for Washington DC and demands the release of their imprisoned leader. But US defence analyst Dr David Grant (Kurt Russell) has intel that this is a cover for a more sinister purpose: the detonation of a nerve toxin bomb over the capital. Dr Grant persuades the military that the 747 cannot be allowed to enter US airspace. An interception is planned by Lt Col Austin Travis (Steven Seagal), using a stealth bomber adapted for air-to-air transfers, and a special ops anti-terrorist squad, including Grant, attempts to board the 747 undetected. The interception is half-complete when injury and accident force Travis to abort. He is killed and the stealth bomber lost.

It is left to Grant and the remains of the squad, with no equipment and no radio, to locate the bomb, disable it, neutralise the terrorists, and effect a rapid recovery of Oceanic

Flight 343 before the Pentagon scrambles its F14s and brings down the airliner.

*Steven Seagal was great in* Under Siege, *and here he's toast inside 20 minutes. I don't know about Kurt Russell. He has weird hair.*

Steven Seagal was indeed excellent in *Under Siege*, and has played a variety of elite operatives with martial-arts expertise to wide acclaim, but it is nevertheless possible to make the case that Kurt Russell is the better actor, and (in the way of actors who are familiar without being too famous) a more plausible Everyman – Mr Seagal's limitation in this respect being that he looks like the megalith from *2001: A Space Odyssey*.

And: perhaps the removal of the action-movie hero is meant to heighten the sense of jeopardy? Who will rescue Dr Grant now that the hero is fish-food? It allows the film to become a canny hybrid, in which disaster must be averted as usual but by the wrong person – because there is no alternative.

*Executive Decision* is truthfully insistent on this fact of life. In crises, the circumstances are by definition rarely pro-pitious: we are miscast, our abilities are of limited use, we don't have the right tools, people don't trust us, and the line of command is unclear. One of the more boring clichés of American cinema is the veneration of the President as the Commander-in-Chief. But in the Thomas brothers' script, he is unhelpfully missing. It will be the President's 'executive decision' whether or not to blow the 747 out of the sky, and yet, like God, or Mr Seagal, he has disappeared. When one of the passengers, the unhappy Senator Mavros, demands to speak to his boss, the Secretary of Defense snaps: 'You can't. He's out of the country.' Or playing golf. There is no execu-tive to make the executive decision, it turns out, and at this point in the film I could feel the hairs on my neck rise up in sympathy. The absurdity of bureaucracy is a constant and believable thing. The people in charge are useless and never *there* when you need them.

I agree with you about Mr Russell's hair, which seems long even when it is short, though again its dependable weirdness is a sort of overturning of expectations and a sign that our hero has yet to fulfill his destiny. Notice that when he finally enters the cabin in the last ten minutes, his hair has changed. It has been smoothed back, its demi-wave has crashed, and he looks like – *qui d'autre?* – Steven Seagal.

*What is Dr Grant even doing on the plane? He tells Travis everything he knows in the Pentagon meeting. He confirms the voice identity of the chief hijacker Nagi Hassan (David Suchet) and that's it. The only photo of Hassan is thirty years old. He can't identify him by sight and he's an inexperienced liability. Why would Travis bring him along?*

Madness, I know. But I found this completely convincing. Remember the prologue: Travis, acting on US intel supplied by Dr Grant, tracks down a consignment of the nerve toxin to a Chechen mafia safe house. In the ensuing bust, one of Travis's men is killed and the elite operatives with martial-arts expertise discover that the nerve gas has already been shipped out. Travis bears a grudge. He wants Grant along on this mission as payback. He would like him to experience danger. Pettiness of the first order. But if you want to know about pettiness, bad feeling and backstabbing, go to elite operations – to boardrooms, cabinets, privy councils, the Pentagon, and FIFA. And in addition, the decision bears out the tactical wisdom of the great Carl von Clausewitz (1780–1831). Military leaders (like Napolean, or Mr Seagal) need carefully selected fall guys – adjutants with real but unpopular ability on whom everything except a medal can be pinned.

*The main character has no depth and the terrorists are all clichés.*

Yes, and maybe.

The history of the novel, which is the history of art with psychological depth, sometimes leads us to expect the wrong things in onscreen heroics and to be confused about our actual requirements. Action films are a species of workaday epic. The characters in epic are not there to be sympathised with, or related to: they are there to be recognised, to be thought and talked about, to be debated. What Dr Grant and the terrorists have in common is that their characterisations omit unnecessary detail, and this is what makes Grant a hero and saves the villains from obscene stereotyping. 'Who *are* you?' whispers Hassan, when Grant appears at the end, and Grant replies, 'Me? I'm nobody.' Which is what Odysseus says to the cyclops Polyphemus when he is trapped in his cave.

The more dramatic his circumstances, the more an action hero must vanish into the things he does. The situation is paramount. The last thing we need from him is a long, searching account of his education and lonely childhood. He's a PhD smartass and a desk jockey. That's all we need to know. To see what happens when you bring the requirements of the novel to the action movie, look at the overburdened reboots of *Batman* by Christopher Nolan and the 'realistic' Bond films starring Daniel Craig. When Batman and Bond become rounded characters, we are left with the glaring difficulty of the ridiculous things they do. The same argument does not stick so easily to the villains because they supply the premiss for the movie: we need a sense of why they are doing what they are doing, and we want that explanation to embody a principle of wrongdoing (so that we can experience catharsis) with sufficient but not distracting depth. The terrorists operate in a mid-1990s context that includes the disarmament crisis in Iraq (with an emphasis on Saddam Hussein's biological weapons programme), the massacre of Muslim Bosniaks at Srebrenica, territorial gains by the Taliban in post-Soviet Afghanistan, and the growing conceptualisation of global jihad. The short-hand for this in *Executive Decision* is that the terrorists want different things: the hijackers think they are bargaining for the release of their leader El-Sayed Jaffa, but their onboard chief, Hassan, is really a lone wolf intent on a strike against the Infidel West using a plane weaponised with Russian gas. It is a reduction, but an intelligent and prescient one.

The film is not widely shown or networked because, though thrilling as an action adventure, it is also alarming. The script is full of sinisterly repeated actions: a bomb that has to be defused twice, a search for a 'sleeper' terrorist that goes wrong twice, two attempts to land the crippled plane. Nagi Hassan, at the centre of the turmoil, repeats himself a lot – and repetition is the essence of prophecy.

*Halle Berry is a good actress but her role is embarrassing. She even looks embarrassed, several times.*

True. Halle Berry is the stewardess with whom Dr Grant establishes a line of secret communication by appearing in the dumb waiter and putting his finger to his lips. She is also, as you say, a fine actress, with too little to do as Jean, and no surname. But, like all good performances by women in these – yes – embarrassing roles, hers is a sort of meta-struggle, both with the terrorists and with her script, which serves the purpose of reminding us that we are watching a fantasy from the studio of Joel Silver, not the pen of Katherine Mansfield. She speaks a little hesitantly throughout, as if not quite able to believe what's happening or what she is being asked to say. 'Oh, who *cares*?' Jean cries, leafing through the flight manual in search of instructions for landing weaponised 747s, 'just *fly the plane!*' Exactly. Who has time to reckon the finer points of altitude and approach velocity? And yet, when she steps out of the wreckage, moments later, wearing an expression of puzzled relief, we can feel her wondering why the same emergency vehicles she saw pelting down the runway at Dulles International airport, where the plane did not manage to land, are suddenly here at Frederick Field, where it did. (When Jean writes her own two-word disaster movie, it will be called *Continuity Error*. Stuart Baird will edit it, and we will all complain that it is difficult to follow.)

Never mind. Berry's is the performance that inoculates us against actual anxiety, or generic boredom, whichever it may be. The effect of her double-edged frustration is to produce in us, and in the film she inhabits, a tension that is half-serious, never ironic, and pleasingly hard to explain.

# Trees and Sympathy

Some of them are still alive and some, most probably, are dead – forgotten in dried-out pots, uprooted by the new owners of an old house, eaten by squirrels, mummified by hot summers and clay soil, self-mortified by a barren attachment to the wrong part of the garden. Why do I grow them, knowing my husbandry is amateur and insufficient, accepting I haven't room for them in my back yard, barely noticing when I give them up? It isn't a matter of hope (hope: the great peril). It isn't in pursuit of a generous holism such as Derek Jarman's, whose garden, planted in the double shadow of AIDS and the nuclear reactor at Dungeness, spread like some radicalised trefoil across aesthetic and mortal boundaries; or the less uplifting organicism of the gardener and painter Neal Jones, who hates practically everything about his life, but makes an exception for 'the reaching arms of plants'. Trees don't 'respond'; we can't tell if they care or not.

This simple point is often borne in on me by nature writing that ploughs an old Romantic furrow of surreptitious ego, reinstating the pathetic fallacy where it's least welcome: 'nature is wild, but here I am again, noticing it.' The tendency is everywhere, like a weed. (Like sycamore seedlings.) The writing may be good or bad, but something in the feeling-tone, the soulful exceptionalism of an attitude that seems to agitate for nature so long as it comes between attractive end-papers, feels wrong, or at least inadvertently funny. Liking trees, which I do, isn't the reason I like them. I like their anatomical irrelevance to me (they don't have arms), and the fact that they belong to the unidentified long term. Biologists are extending back in time the origins of the oldest trees on the planet, and even native specimens on these islands – the yew, the oak

– may be much older than hitherto suspected. Some ancient yews take us back almost to the last retreat of the ice sheets.

They will probably exist long after us, too, unless the planet enters a Permian-like phase of drought and desuetude, and it's in the prospect of this much later, more distant fruition, by trees or similar structures of as-yet-indeterminate identity, that part of the interest seems to lie. The philosopher Samuel Scheffler, in *Death and the Afterlife* (2013), has apt things to say about the far future in specifically human terms: we will die, and life will carry on, a source of consolation perhaps. But, on inspection, that consolation – the sense that life has a purpose now because of the imaginable continuation of our families and networks, of the tracery of relationships that starts with us – doesn't derive from those intimate relationships alone. In fact, Scheffler says, the emphasis is elsewhere: 'the coming into existence of people we do not know and love . . . matters more to us than our own survival and the survival of the people we do know and love.'

It's a salutary argument about the importance of the (very) long term to human activities in the present. Much of the value of what we do – procreate, write books, conduct research, play music – depends on it mattering in general to people we will never meet. This is the essence of working in a tradition; but also, perhaps, more mysteriously, of our pleasure in doing anything well, fixing the roof, being surprised by a good fuck, or having an ice cream: even instantaneous and sensual personal delight rings a bell that is social and future-historical. The idea of unknown others doing likewise enriches our pursuits, and that enrichment depends in turn on a dawning acceptance that we as individuals will not always be around to experience it. Scheffler's cast of mind is benignly Stoic. It also underlines what I've always found arid about Camus-grade existentialism, in which ego reigns and other people are just the handmaidens to self-awareness.

On the contrary, what Scheffler and the Stoic tradition (at least as it comes to us via Marcus Aurelius) seem to be saying is that the value of much of life, to us as individuals, depends on it not being available to us as individuals. It has to be remotely beyond our experience – and not in the sense of a personal afterlife or of a fantasy of roboticised eternal life, both of which deal with mortality by dodging it. No: for us to feel sure our actions matter, they must come to an end and be taken up by others. We are fragments: tiles in a temporal mosaic. Now, for Scheffler, the 'beyond' in which others do this taking up – the edge of the mosaic, as it were – is still human, their like-minded carrying out of tasks part of a super-historical flow of art, science, politics, sex, bickering, and so on: but does it have to be? The problem I have with this reliance on human continuation is that I suspect it of smuggling in a desire for personal immortality by the back door, as if we can have individual temporariness alleviated in some way by a collective 'confidence' – Scheffler's word – in the species' survival.

The view from the closed factory floor doesn't warrant that confidence, in part because we seem to be doing very little to avert ecological catastrophe, but also because the probability that we're already in an extinction event should tell us something about our progressivist linear view of history, which is that it's wrong. That isn't how deep time works. Scheffler waves this away – most people do – as being something beyond our comprehension. We can only understand a human time scale, he says. But that is wrong, too. It is a matter of practice, like all discomfiting thought experiments. Everyone should be gay for half an hour (more, if you're cute) so that they can see their partner get off with someone else. The world does not end. Everyone should do a semester of geology, so that they can get a feel for the nature of deep time and see what's coming. The world will indeed end, for us, but evolution will not. Microbes and extremophiles – insensate entities who hang around billowing vents in conditions of sulphurous toxicity – will be fine.

The large-scale warp of time is broadly cyclical. A season of life, of convergence and abundance, gives way to a perishing, and we are back to the beginning again. Palaeontology confirms what Sumerian, Celtic, Norse and Amerindian mythology knew before theological teleology got involved: things die out and are succeeded, not revived. I sometimes wonder if the longing for a personal afterlife isn't a sort of gross statistical confusion brought about by ancient innumerates who muddled up the improbability of a particular unexpected thing coming to pass with the (very high) probability of something unexpected happening: we don't come back, and neither does Jesus, but *something* does, and on the human scale once again, where we can at least attempt to familiarise ourselves with these disconcerting concepts, if you're gone for any amount of time that something will be a tree. Trees.

Into the brickwork and pointing they come, these alien opportunists – first the buddleia, then the hazel and elder, then the birch, the holly and the oak – reclaiming territory, dismantling our history. Perhaps that's why councils hate them so much. They don't respect borders, or appreciate our efforts to make them welcome in garden centres. Sometimes, like epiphyte or 'flying' rowans growing out of other trees, they even co-habit without changing identity. We can be very eloquent about their exotic beauty and serenity, but they don't seem to notice. With a residual classical fetish for memorialising, we plant them in memory of the departed, skirting around the uneasy realisation, bound to hit us sooner or later, that trees are memento mori, not memorials. When Malcolm's army takes up the branches of Birnam Wood and advances on Dunsinane at the end of *Macbeth*, the creepiness of the denouement has an edge seldom remarked on. The fulfilment of the witches' singular prophecy is trans-historical; the sinister aspect is its literal truth. All woods come to Dunsinane in the end. Civilisation has no roots.

It's easy to be sentimentally misanthropic about nature, to come close to suggesting that its gorgeous unfeelingness is a rear-guard virtue. This flinching from the human is often either puritanical in origin, or the corollary of an egotistical position that sees the subject-object distinction – me plant-ing or conserving a tree, T. H. White or Helen Macdonald training a hawk – as the point of sympathy or its absence. To identify with someone else. To relate. (If I had a pound for every blogger who demands relatable characters, I could retire.) But that is a misunderstanding of sympathy, and the cracked-bell sounding note of our age. Sympathy is the effort to forget oneself, an unseating of what one expects of others in terms of reciprocity, and by extension a letting-go of the illusion that we can feel their qualia, their pain. Real sym-pathy opens on a void, as anyone who has watched someone die will know, and that is not as desperate a predicament as it might sound.

It comes down to accepting that our commonality – not just the political or interracial or intercultural flavours, but the transhistorical, transhuman and interspecies varieties, too – is not the set of characteristics and traits we share, or can imagine metaphorically, but the bigger category of un-elidable differences. Death and trees are useful things to think with and against in this respect. The truth about death is that we don't know anything about it: no one experiences it (we're alive and then we're not), but we have good observa-tional evidence that it happens. It's utterly alien to each one of us; unifying and real. Trees coincide with, and overcome, human intervention. Our whole sense that they are alive in a way we are not depends on them being inaccessible to us.

This is the essence of the panpsychist movement in

contemporary philosophy of mind: the extension of sympathy towards beings that live differently, unknowably, leads inexorably to the cosmic appreciation of consciousness – that it's everywhere, instinct in all matter, in an 'all good things around us' kind of way. I'm not sure about this: I feel it's nudging at transcendentalism and a property dualism it can't quite admit to, whereas the old belief-system it most clearly resembles – animism – puts the idea more bluntly and, well, sympathetically. Neal Jones, in *My Art Shame* (2015), his brilliant swipe at painters' careers and fancy gardens, writes: 'The ethical problem with the archaic idea of Animism is that human beings become equal citizens to animals and plants, so that there's a moral imperative to treat all life with respect.' It's a problem because it involves a redistribution of sympathetic capital. To the life we can identify, not the life we identify with.

Being selfless – forgetting ourselves – is impossible, but more interesting as an imaginative proposition than being reluctantly unselfish, and we could start on the road to that selflessness by growing trees, or indeed letting them grow, where there is no harm done to others. As an illustration of what happens when we get our sympathetic priorities wrong, we have the conveniently near-to-hand example of Southwark Council, currently removing twelve acres of woodland habitat in Camberwell Old and New Cemeteries to accommodate – or rather to sell – new graves. It's quite the irony, and metaphor for mistaken emphasis, that we should kill so many of the living to lay the dead.

# Music and Friendship

I miss my piano, which I bought with my grandmother's legacy (£1,500), and I miss playing Bach on it. The piano, a Pohlmann baby grand (*c.*1935) with art deco legs, now resides in Streatham with a cabaret artiste, whose own legs have a certain shape and style to recommend them, and there it will stay. The understanding is unspoken; friendship should be non-contractual. I shall buy a new piano when my employers at the *Brixton Review of Books* increase my quarterly rate by 10,000 per cent, but times are hard and I shouldn't pester. I miss clambering my way through the *Well-Tempered Clavier* (aka the Forty-Eight Preludes and Fugues, in all the keys from C to B minor, *c.*1722–1742) because I have no keyboard on which to do the clambering. It doesn't follow that I miss the music, however. As with a lot of Bach's 'exercise' work, and perhaps with contrapuntal harmony in general, the relationship between sound and idea is complex, dazzling as a mesh-like aural artefact, but just as beautiful in its conception.

Bach himself makes the relationship mysterious in his title page to the autograph fair copy, which reads 'For the Use and Profit of the Musical Youth Desirous of Learning as well as for the Pastime of those Already Skilled in this Study'. In other words, the pieces are for young and old, for instruction and delight, and it is not obvious that by 'study' the composer means performance, or even execution. He means, rather, exactly what he says: the study and skill should constitute a 'pastime' – *ZeitVertreib* – a pursuit unbounded by considerations of professional brilliance. I love solo Baroque music and played a lot as a teenager – piano and organ – and I never improved, or became proficient, because I didn't have the ability. And I didn't have the ability because I lacked the patience. Besides, the study gave me the pieces fully, internally, and in a form I could carry about with me like a download on a pair of Platonic headphones.

There isn't a recording to match my private rendition of the fugue from the Fantasia and Fugue in G Minor BWV 542, which seems to shout 'all is forgiven' in ways I can't explain. It's my favourite organ piece. I want it played at my funeral, or obscenity trial, whichever comes first. The fine mesh of manual invention lifts to reveal two clarion chords (VI–V at the beginning of the final pedal entry) and everything ends with a *tierce de picardie* – a way of sharpening a minor triad so that it springs a major surprise – but of course there's more to it than that.

The music isn't a test of skill; it's 'already skilled' – sufficient in itself and, therefore, a test of one's ability to submit to it. It reminds me a little of Fielding's observations on Miss Quested, ostracised from society for telling the truth at Aziz's trial, in *A Passage to India*: 'Although her hard schoolmistressy manner remained, she was no longer examining life, but being examined by it; she had become a real person.' And the reality, in this case, seems to be that in music like Bach's, performance – one's own examining – doesn't have the last word. It is not, *pace* Andras Schiff (a great executant), about cleansing one's palate in the morning, being ostentatiously the servant of the music, or any of that falsely modest stuff you hear being peddled on BBC Radio 3. It's about bringing nothing else to it; skill as statement, not demonstration. Keith Jarrett, the jazz virtuoso, concedes as much in his very practical interpretation of *WTC* Book 1 for ECM. His articulation is fine, without being austerely choppy; there's a minimum of ornamentation. It's not plain, but merely unassisted style; playing that preserves the intrinsic potential of the composition and is both surprising and logical given Jarrett's reputation as an improviser – surprising because improvisation surely implies stylistic freedom, logical because musical improvisation (especially in the baroque era) is freedom *relative to* (not freedom *from*) constraint. You can't have no constraints. See also: free verse.

The 'nothing else' in this approach to Bach matters, because his music is the kind that absorbs one's technical failings – you can have a stab at it in a way you cannot have a stab at, say, Liszt or Steve Reich – and we can see in that absorption, if we choose, a metaphor for the spiritual relation to formal perfection that interested the composer. But if we choose not to, we find something just as valuable in our more ordinary acceptance of sausage-fingered mistakes, which is a disposition not to judge our deficiencies too harshly or be unrealistic about them.

John Milton writes about this in Sonnet 16, the famous poem that is either about the onset of his blindness or a later retrospective meditation on its lessons (the date is contested). Or rather it is about both at once, because the physical failing is also presented as a characteristic and characteristics don't so much change over time as become more and more themselves. Again, the context is religious – 'God doth not need / Either man's work or his own gifts, who best / Bear his mild yoke, they serve him best' – and also sceptical, radical. No praise, no offerings, no Republican or Protestant fervour. *They also serve who only stand and wait.* That last line suffers, as poetry and Bach both tend to, from over-interpretation. But it is entirely literal. Patience is speaking in the poet's ear. She says: sometimes the most useful, the very best, thing you can do is nothing.

'Not being able to do what one wants,' writes Wolfgang Sandner in the sleeve notes to the Jarrett recording, 'but wanting to do what one can.' This is a way of stepping back, creatively, of finding expression (as Jarrett himself goes on to say) 'without adding'. It is also the liberty enjoined on us by friends, in whom the slightly boring facts of the matter are more valuable than endless interpretative arias. And those facts are emotional ideas, minor revelations and reverberations, as much as solid examples. Friends are like unassuming monuments to themselves. Statues on a far-off Easter Island. They're there, even when you don't see or recognise them, which is just as well given my talent for sailing straight past in the opposite direction.

But I didn't miss, couldn't have missed, Simon. Simon Smith – clay-pigeon shooter, radiographer, and rhythm guitar in Tone Deaf, the covers band of our shared youth. A month ago, he was standing outside Bath railway station looking pretty much as he looked thirty-two years ago, bar the grey hair and the thickened mid-riff: sports jacket, dark shirt, glasses, jeans, a bit taller than I remembered. We used to go swimming at Bath Sports and Leisure Centre. Simon seemed always to smell pleasantly of soap and chlorine – an 'always' I find myself inventing, or at least pressing, to mask the shock of no shock on seeing him again and the almost total collapse of time into one instant. I sat next to him on my first day at Beechen Cliff Comprehensive, in the old secondary modern buildings on Wells Road. The Bee Gees and the Sex Pistols were both troubling the charts. He had an enviable amount of hair on his upper lip and a disconcerting stare. 'I've got a lazy eye,' he said, and went back to drawing mazes and practising his signature.

All this came in the moment of recognition, which, as the word, and *Oedipus Rex* (and *Star Wars*) suggest, is a confirmation of something already known but not expressed. We went to the nearest pub and began talking quickly. Simon glanced away from the table and, following his cue, I looked out of the window at a couple having an argument in the street ('I never!' 'Yes, you *dead! I seen you!*'). 'I've got a lazy eye,' he said. He wasn't even looking out of the window. So much to catch up on, and very little of it tellable as a story. His lovely Mum, a foster carer for forty-odd years, received an MBE. His qualifications notwithstanding (two A-levels), Simon was allowed to train to be a therapeutic radiographer because of his background experience as the child of a carer. We ran to the station, I got the last train home, sat down and burst into tears.

Probably I don't recall much of what we chatted about because the content of our friendship is objectively slight, like my ability to play Bach, and thirty-two years of nothing at all happened to it in between leaving school in 1985 and going to the Pulteney Arms. Re-reading my digest of that evening, I see that I've given what psychologists call event-specific knowledge (sensory images) against a peculiar and shifting background (the 'knowledge base') that I sort-of claim for my own but which is derived or adopted – the kindness of his mum, for instance, and his stare (also mine), and the music (I wasn't in the band). One of the interesting discoveries about shared memory is that the point-of-view is frequently mis-attributed. We think something happened to us that hap-pened to someone else: everybody with siblings can vouch for this. Another is that we are overwhelmingly more likely to misattribute the point of view in a shared memory when the experience was a positive one.

I tried and failed, many years ago, to play the Fantasia and Fugue in G minor. And when I say I carry it around in my head, I am exaggerating – building something up from evidence that's importantly suggestive but far from defin-itive, and in its very incompleteness shared. In the matter of conscious feeling, we are always finding that the behav-ioural grounds for supposing another person feels a certain way (flowers, dinner, letters) are not wholly reliable and that our own successful ability to control a particular emotion can't disguise from us its inner reality. That is not to say that behaviour, and skill, and evidence for feeling, are not important. On the contrary, they are indications, vital to our progress through life, of how necessary it is not to over-interpret signs and cues, and of how wise our friends are to let the relatively few public exhibits in our lives together stand on their own, unmolested, like the study of a score that is skilled in itself, or the instantaneously unfolded history of a smell.

# Ken Kiff

It is very hard to write persuasively for others about the works of art that one loves unreasonably and irrationally. 'I am a Jane Austenite,' said E. M. Forster, 'and therefore slightly imbecile about Jane Austen.' In Forster's case, the childish imbecility perhaps conceals an element of self-satisfaction: 'I have been inducted into the ways of this writer or artist and I can only feel sorry for those who are too sophisticatedly stupid to feel as I do.' An actual child would see things differently, without apology, and it is the work of a lifetime for many poets and artists to think their way back into that state of mind which encounters the world, and consciously ferments the encounter into a communicated response, for the first time.

It is Wordsworth's subject, of course: the deep love of being that trumps learning, as learned as he might be. He's sceptical about it, which is interesting, perhaps because he knows that this 'under-sense' of replete identity with something (usually nature) is apt to sound pretentious, or even like a disavowal of adult responsibility. He calls it an 'overlove of freedom' in Book VI of *The Prelude*. At the same time, it is indubitably real and important to him, because it represents the mystery of artistic immersion which he experiences as a 'treacherous sanction' of the critical. Better than any explanation, and worse, because it is not to be trusted.

The work of the painter Ken Kiff (1935–2001) confronts this head-on: his is a riotous, protean imaginary of sexual archetypes, shadows, surreal encounter, landscapes and artistic anxiety that takes seriously (though not sombrely) the whole business of love, the personal, sharing beyond words, and how hard it is to give a reliable account of these things to others. The open-ended summation of his, on the face of it, very un-English, wrestling with the Psyche, and with Jung (Kiff was in analysis for some years), is a 200-image serpent of continual making called 'The Sequence'.

He began it in 1971 at the age of thirty-five. A beautiful sketch, with an Uccello-ish dragon bottom left, and a tree dividing the page like a pale green fuse, was left unfinished at his death at the age of sixty-one. The paintings are mostly acrylic and pastel on stretched paper, with the gummed tape around the edges preserved as a reminder of their essential provisionality. Walking round the astonishing exhibition of sixty or so paintings, at the Sainsbury Centre for Visual Arts in Norwich, is like visiting Regent's Park Zoo with something from the reptile house as your anima and guide – a salamander, say. Kiff likes salamanders. Symbolic and actual, clearly emanating and signifying from inside the head, but smooth and scaly to the touch, a highly proprioceptive fantasy.

There is nothing like these paintings anywhere else. They do not belong to the main outgrowths of European Surrealism, with its manifesto-led disaggregation of narrative elements, its collage and taboo. They are not Abstract, although two abstract geometrical forms – a blue spike, like a tooth, and a flying parallelogram, like the Phantom Zone from the *Superman* comics – find their way into compositions otherwise made up of anthropomorphised animals, floating heads, defecating or spitting bodies, lovers, smiling naked figures, and darkly observing or listening shapes who might be the painter or his analyst. They don't seem aware of their own facility, which is the problem with Chagall, and even Dalí, whose idea of the unconscious was heavily branded from the start. They're not *faux*-naive, either, or archly primitivist, in that way you can't help laughing at when artists find a shtick and can't stop waving it (painting onto frames). They're not unaware of the rest of art – far from it – or trying to be singular. In *Spitting Man* (1976–80), a seated thick-set figure, pink and monumental, expectorates other smaller figures. The heaving up is a reverse-engineering of Goya's famous Black Painting, *Saturn Devouring His Son*, and like that image, which started out as a wall painting, Kiff's fleshy acrylic has an air of the built about it – of plaster and blank, wall-eyed permissions. They are happy to refer to things. In *Talking with a Psychoanalyst: night sky* (1975–80), a tremendous dramatisation of the scene of analysis, but in a real room with proper curtains, the two breast-like hills outside the window are Uccello again – the Fiesole hills in Florence.

But, in referring to things, to ideas and other artists, to writers (there is an astonishing drawing of Vladimir Mayakovsky blowing his brains out), and to himself, Kiff never feels as if he is drawing on a store of decided knowledge or material that has been corralled from another discussion or medium. What comes up for him in the process of painting is the unaffected recreation of passion and erotic delight, the importance of colour as a ground to which every other question of formal invention and planning is subject, and in both the passionate and colouristic manoeuvres he is convincingly childlike, without being creepy. The paintings resemble those semi-ritualistic, incrementally developmental games that children play as they discover for the first time, and with a never-to-be-recaptured combination of hesitancy and sweeping confidence, their relationship to the external. That's why the donkey's legs (*Donkey*, 1976) are so accurately seen, the soft kink of the hind legs, and the scale of the animal so intuitively grasped before a mark is made. That, too, is why the sun is smiling. It's not kitsch. It's a matter of stepping into the moment. *The world exists before my eyes, and I am making it.*

Idealism agrees, and so would Jung. For the great symbolist analyst, the psyche was individual and irreducible to anything else. This is also broadly the position of philosophers like Thomas Nagel and John Searle, for whom the mind is physical but not in ways we currently understand; for whom the subjective viewpoint, our looking-on at the world, is not a skim on the surface of objective reality but a puzzling part of it. And inextricable from it: this may be the most important point to consider, Kiff suggests.

Before we recruit him to one side of the subjectivist debate or another, we need to remember that he is an artist and a maker before he is anything else, and that artists do not feel they are transcribing or representing or interpreting the world. They're just in it, and they're in it more comprehensively for their willingness to have an experience that doesn't try to isolate the understanding. The problem with the language of symbols in artistic activity – the sun is the mother principle, the shadow challenges the ego, the tree recalls Ygdrassil, and so on – is that the attribution of meaning takes place after the event, when one is only looking on or looking back. One wants to ask: how can unconscious meaning survive into consciousness? Here is the logical obstacle in the path of psychoanalysis. To get at meaning, we need to relive, not describe, and experiencing art, Kiff thinks, is one way of achieving this.

We want the kind of absorption in all our contemplative activity that neither stiffens into description nor threatens a psychotic episode in which objective distinctions disappear (Wordsworth's 'treacherous sanction'). Kiff puts it best himself in a long and sensitive letter to his friend, the writer Ian Biggs, dated June 10, 1998: 'My position is to emphasize that the unknown is the unknown. That the unconscious is unconscious. "Self" is an unknown, as "wholeness" is an unknown ... Painting evokes the sense-data by which we read the world, I suppose ... It is an independent thing, however, because it isn't the servant of our conscious activities, nor is it merely a product of our unconscious activities, nor is it a mirror. It is a highly developed medium with a continuous logic.'

In other words, painting isn't a record; it's a kind of pattern-forming attentiveness, in which things that are seen change as the painter looks at them, and in a way that feels logical and sensible, however unlikely the changes. It's striking, as one moves from painting to painting, how genially unperturbed Kiff's dramatic personae seem to be by all the psychic chaos. Nothing puts them off their stroke; there is illness and fear (a man throws up), but there is also comfort (another man, rising out of the ground, comforts him). Domestic routines are done naked. It's Eden, or the 1970s, or both, maybe.

In *Posting a Letter* (1971–2), a beaming male nude strides towards a smiling red post box with an envelope in his hand. He is lifted up above the ground, above his own shadow; he walks on air. Behind him, to the left of the sheet, a bowler-hatted commuter disappears behind a tree. Both figures are regarded with total self-possession by an ant-eater, where one might possibly have expected a dog or a squirrel. The surprise is like the bend in a pencil when you put it in water and the memory of the first time you looked at that phenomenon. It is a real thing, an image, and a piercing emotion all at once. Emma Hill's excellent catalogue to this rejuvenating show – the most enjoyable I have seen, anywhere, in years – reproduces an email from Kiff's former student Emma Bosch, who remembers him at work on this painting. Kiff was a great correspondent, and he talked, Bosch says, about 'the excitement of leaving a letter in the postbox and then waiting for the reply'. Hope is often an unreasonable and irrational feeling, of course, but it's sentimental to think it always without foundation. The man in the air could fall. At the same time, he is buoyed up, right now, by sheer communicative delight.

# A Diptych

1

Visitors to my father's studio in Bath are commonly struck by the view from the bay window: a panorama of the city in which Georgian terraces, Victorian spires, Brunel's railway and the complex interventions of the 20th century combine to suggest something other than architecture. On a bright morning, the effect is dazzling, a curving wall of hazel and grey stone, windows turned to stars, shadows that cut buildings in two, detail everywhere and a teeming quality – cars crawling up the arm of the hill – that's felt rather than seen, or felt-seen, perhaps. The eye is forced to 'graze', as Paul Klee put it, on abundance. There follows what psychologists probably still call a 'moment of separation' – a brief, not unpleasant hiatus – as the visitors turn back from the cityscape to the studio itself, which at first sight is so different. Music is playing (mostly jazz, mostly – in my recollection – Georgie Fame or Carla Bley), and the cool of the room, with its assorted finished canvases and works-in-progress, is irradiated by a second contemplative mystery, something other than light or glowing colour.

The relationship between that view and the abstracted landscapes that have preoccupied my father for five decades has always puzzled me. Growing up, I had the sense that the two were separate; that the picturesque mosaic of streets and crescents could not be further removed from the lavishly non-descriptive, largely blue-and-red paintings that came and went on our walls like temperamental frescoes. An encounter, on a trip abroad, with some of Paul Cezanne's Provençal landscape watercolours, made me less sure, and there – in Aix, within reach of Mont Sainte Victoire – I realised for the first time how the fullest descriptive content of such intimate works – their whole sense of place – belonged not so clearly to the visible terrain as to the desire of the painting to evoke it, to be a part of it. Modern painters want their marks to be everything at once – statements, representations, expressions of feeling – and why shouldn't they be? But the 'wanting' to join in, the desire to add, is involved, too, not least because it discreetly acknowledges that art is built out of personal responses to a collective achievement. Ambition can't exist without the example of others, and talent is a pursued inheritance.

I'm fairly sure – though we've never discussed it – that Cézanne is an important painter for my father; as important, maybe, as the expressionist Emil Nolde, to whose mythically inflected North German scenes he continues to pay practical tribute. Cézanne for the relationship between forms, Nolde for the elemental paradoxes of colour, with their huge collisions of earth and sky (often captured on scraps of paper): both are painters of abstract landscapes if by 'abstract' one chooses to mean an essential sample, or excerpt, of the whole. That, at least, is how I think of my father's approach. His chunks of colour and slanted lines don't have scale so much as suggestive mass. They're dense seeds, rather than fragments. Whether a given title is referential or not, the paintings almost invariably allude to essences: geological strata, the vanishing point of trees in a dark forest, of light under water, or between rocks. There is no concerted effort to represent, but the desire to express formal arrangements is striking. When you look again at – or imagine – the railway, roads and terraces from the studio window, you see how they gather, in tectonic waves, on the canvas.

These arrangements are not quite 'primitive', although that was how the Irish painter William Scott, who taught both of my parents at the Bath Academy of Art in Corsham in the 1950s, preferred to describe (if pressed) his still-lifes – widely spaced domestic objects on tables that are also picture-planes (or perhaps cave walls). But the word still carries unfortunate associations of false naivety. Simplicity of gesture, even after Rothko and American Minimalism, is too often confused with lack of sophistication, as though the chief characteristics of primitive art – which so impressed my father when drawing Stonehenge – were not precisely its monumental complexity and ambition. Perhaps 'primal' is better. There is certainly the idea, in most of his paintings, that our relationship to colour is primal: an original and constant responsiveness, wherever we find ourselves, whatever we may be looking at. It is hard, in fact, once the eye begins to think, not to see colour everywhere.

And because every painting (certainly every big oil) I remember is a variation on that responsiveness, there is an important large-scale sense in which all views from all windows are continuous. This is both topographically true and aesthetically accurate, since one of the original functions of image-making is to confirm our presence in the landscape; to distil the sum of our sensual histories into simple way markers – the line, the dot, the curve. Scott may have been thinking about this when he ruefully claimed always to be painting 'the same subject whether it be still life, figure or landscape', and I think my father would agree with him, though he might put it more optimistically. Apart from anything else, his way with colour is characteristically upbeat. The studio is rarely silent, and one of the sounds I associate with it – even above the jazz – is laughter. The paintings are fewer now that my father is losing his sight, but they still turn the air blue, red, green, pink, and every shade in-between.

It is hard not to see colour everywhere – and it is particularly hard when the spectrum has been reduced to black and white. We have an apparently irrepressible urge to infer tint, to colorise nebulae, to concentrate on just the two book-ends of the spectrum and still see the rainbow on the shelf. The world may be a sphere of colourless particles and forces, but that's not the way it seems for us, or not when we're looking at it; so charcoal or pencil drawings are, among other mysterious things, a kind of challenge to the human. A representational sketch may of course depict things and people in the ordinary way, but it is also negatively capable in two others: it suggests both the hidden extent of colour (of perceptions not granted, or not this time, not on this page) and – odder still – what the world looks like when we've stopped looking, or disappeared altogether. Much more than paintings, drawings are our trace fossils. We say they're 'sensitive', in part because they show how vulnerable the human perceptual apparatus is, and by extension how easily removed from the whole picture *we* are.

I have a folder of drawings made by my mother, mostly in her fifties and sixties, that contains many good examples of this suggestiveness. The images are small-scale sketchpad notations of extravagantly shaded fields and inventive gardens, harbours, boats, hillsides, and houses in outline only, fascinatingly (to me) stripped of their hue and made to blaze with reflected sunlight. Their composition has its own ambition, quite different to my father's, because it is a response to different wants by a differently constituted creature, balancing conflicting impulses. The empty walls of the empty houses are so many blank faces, but they can be lit up, and they are surrounded by an enormous natural world brought close with a remarkable continuity of tone. In that clash of full naturalism with geometrically reduced line – William

Townsend meets Ben Nicholson – I can't help seeing something of the artist's search for expression, energised and complicated by the experience of poverty in the 1930s, the habit of thrift, and by her selflessness as a parent. Some bewilderment and frustration, too. To whom should she address these creations? What is she supposed to do with her talent?

One of the things one notices about men who are inspired by colour, and prepared to investigate their feelings (for which colour may sometimes be a substitute as well as a means of discovery) is the simple fact that they feel able to lay claim to emotion, the way they have of clearing a space for themselves. In a revealing conversation with the curator John Elderfield, Howard Hodgkin finishes by saying, 'Alone in my studio, working on my pictures, more than anything, I long to share my feelings.' I can see my parents smiling now. They admired Hodgkin and studied at Corsham together. But it takes self-assurance to be able to say that kind of thing, and to underwrite one's sensitivity in so decisive a fashion, not to mention money and the blessing of assisted solitude. In *A Room of One's Own*, Virginia Woolf famously wished that blessing on women with literary skill who wanted to develop their art and escape the 'measurers', the taking of sides, the 'pitting of sex against sex, of quality against quality'. Hard to disagree with that, politically and morally, or with her conclusion that 'it is much more important to be oneself than anything else', except when it frays at the edges as one looks closer at her argument for creativity as an androgynous act, because: if one doesn't have to be one gender, why does one have to be one kind of self-motivated artist?

In *On Being An Artist* (2015), Michael Craig-Martin talks about setbacks and the exposing nature of any art practice in which one is wholly identified with one's work, his implication being that such identification is a precondition for being taken seriously. It may be, but the case is not thereby made for its being necessary to the art, or making you good at it. There are a lot of serious idiots out there who could do with being a shade less convinced by themselves. Most people struggle to find the time (and money) to do things they want to do, and the quality of what they produce doesn't usually suffer because of it. Their frustrations are just a part of who they are, expressively. (Van Gogh.) Being oneself means being conflicted and pulled in many directions, many of them non-artistic, or not obviously so, although the nature of the subconscious imagination is such that we often find in obstacles to reflection a kind of disguised, or delayed, motivation.

My father acts joyfully on what he sees or remembers seeing, adds to it, goes out to greet it. My mother did, too – her gardens are full of imaginary foliage, palm trees and spiky red-hot pokers – but she also stayed in. Her beautiful drawings, even as they look to the distance, are full of nearness, the quality we associate with still-life, and quiet reminders of those obstacles to expression in her own life – fences, barriers, gates, windows – which then allowed for, or opened onto, a late flowering. In one picture, just four inches by seven, she considers a farmhouse in a grassy declivity. There is an almost abstract stockade in the foreground, around the edge of a ploughed field. Are the black stumps fence-pilings, trunks, cut-back vines? Nearer still, in five white lines striking through the image from top to bottom, are the traces left by running water on the glass – the glass through which this austere world is being soundlessly observed. There has been heavy rain, but it is over now. Her line is definite, confident, soft; sometimes achieved by rubbing-out and repair; but to the resting (not grazing) eye unbroken, threadlike, as though the graded contours of hills and the winding of roads were part of some cheviot wool blanket, and like a blanket both practically made and hugely loved.

# Q&A with nothingintherulebook.com

*Tell me about yourself, where you live and your background/lifestyle.*

I live in London, at the top of Brixton Hill. I've been in the area now for nearly thirty years, though I come from the West Country (Bath) originally. I went to a comprehensive school: I think it's the best kind of education there is. Far from perfect, but fair. It is absurd to talk about freedom of choice, in education or health, if choice is something only the rich can afford. Of course, environment has a lot to do with contentment at a young age, and the setting was beautiful. I liked cross-country rather than contact sports – I was small and thin – and the weekly runs that the bigger kids hated (because of all the hills) took me through a kind of paradise of beech forest and meadows. While the PE teachers repaired to the staff room for a well-deserved fag break after all that fiddling about with whistles, we ran through Rainbow Wood and then down through the grounds of Prior Park towards Mike Casford's house, where we'd stop for coffee and biscuits. I can't run any more, which is a shame, but I can remember – well, I conjure up – the trees and thistles on those runs, and the view, and the freedom. The teachers smoked, we had coffee. Fair enough. There was some bullying at school, but nothing too bad. I was conscious of being small. I still think someone is going to push me into the road. On the other hand, I could be sharp, and I learnt to answer back. I don't mind being taken to task, or disagreed with, or even disliked. I mind being exploited by the dull and fortunate.

*Is writing your first love, or do you have another passion?*

It is a habit, more than anything else, with an element of developed automatism about it. Jorge Luis Borges felt it was an adequate way of passing the time. I think of it as the sum of things that leads to a poem or a story or a book (though those things can be ends in themselves). I've always liked trees, and seeing seeds I've planted come up in the spring. Music, too: I played the piano and organ as a teenager; I liked the sociability and solitude of both those instruments; I can sing a bit. I enjoy acting. If I could afford it, I'd have a house with a music room. I was a latecomer to sex, and then had a great deal of it for twenty-five years! I've loved being gay. Even the bad experiences have been good, because you meet such different people. I've been properly in love twice. The last time was eight years ago and completely changed me.

*Who inspires you?*

My aunt. She is ninety. She left the United Kingdom in 1947, at the age of nineteen, and went to New York, where she taught at the Central School and met her husband, Bob Bollard, who was a Broadway composer and director. She got to know Sydney Pollack and Harry Belafonte and became involved in Democratic politics for a while. Bob died of cancer in his thirties and Priscilla was completely stuck, no money, three kids. But she got a government grant to go to medical school and became a doctor. An ear specialist. I, too, listen carefully: but have never heard her complain about anything. I dread losing her. She is ten times the person I will ever be, but I try to follow her example. She liked *Murmur*, and if it passed muster with her, well, that's good enough for me.

Writers – the scribes of the Exeter Book, Shakespeare (especially the late plays and sonnets), Montaigne, Jane Austen,

S. T. Coleridge, George Eliot, Flaubert, Christina Rossetti, W. H. Auden, William Golding, Penelope Fitzgerald, whoever I happen to be reading (Patricia Beer), Elmore Leonard, Thom Gunn. Also, many comedians and comic writers – Victoria Wood, Lily Tomlin, Joe Keenan, Billy Wilder, Paul Rudnick. Musicians and composers – Bach, Poulenc, Chopin, Stevie Wonder, Aretha Franklin.

And my father, John, who is a painter. In a Borgesian vein – he's losing his sight – he has found it necessary, or acceptable, to keep going. His approach is very much 'do what you can' in life, which is sensible (and kinder than 'do your best').

I also admire my friends for a variety of reasons.

*The Absent Therapist and* The Inevitable Gift Shop *have been praised for their fragmentary form. Why did you structure your work in this way?*

I like the way speech patterns and conversations derail themselves. Good dialogue, like most things in life, is a combination of determined response and wild digression or misprision. I like the moments in arguments when people suddenly hear themselves yelling, or realise they've lost ground, and try to shut things down by changing the subject or feigning emotion. Or play dumb, or defend people who don't need defending and infuriate everyone else. This is as much as to say that there is a difference between what people want to say and what they find themselves saying, or, similarly, between a deliberate act and its unintended consequence. (Patricia Highsmith's plots are combinations of the two misunderstandings.)

Anger is often dangerous in life, but it's also the essence of comedy. I was frustrated with my life, just before I started *The Absent Therapist*, and felt I'd run aground. Nothing more to say. Which was a kind of turning-point, because when you have nothing to say you start listening, and *The Absent Therapist* is really a short book about listening – to the people who interrupt each other, the people who sit quietly and take mental notes. The little monologues are both external and internal, and often seem to be about recreating a moment or justifying a position in retrospect.

Memory is dynamic. It isn't the retrieval of discrete bits of information, but a sort of paradoxical jigsaw puzzle in which the remembered image changes with the piecing-together. I think that's what I was trying to get at in *The Inevitable Gift Shop*, which was an attempt at an honest and therefore slightly discontinuous (and critical) memoir. I was also in terrific pain at the time, and pain has a way of completely fracturing the mind. You don't lose your mind. In some obvious ways, the qualia of mental experience are massively heightened. But the intensity of pain can be distracting. It disaggregates your normal capacities, and you find not so much that you've lost the ability to do X or Y, but that the order in which you might have done these things has had to be abandoned: how are the experiences to be put back together? My scientist protagonist grapples with this problem throughout *Murmur*.

*The idea of collage as an artistic form is not new in the visual arts, but do you think it increasingly an influence on writing – or the literary industry?*

There does seem to be a fashion for it, yes. But I wonder if the difference between collage and continuous narrative isn't overstated. For example, a lot of ancient text is fragmentary – all that's left after the ruin of the ages – and the suggestive reconstitution of those fragments (the Psalms, the surviving tragic drama, the Exeter Book, etc.) has helped build the Western canon in its long and short forms. All writing is collage, or perhaps tapestry, in the sense that it is a composition of elements. The distinguishing property, as I've intimated above, is the ordering of those elements – whether the collage serves one story, or image, or many; and often the 'one story', on closer inspection, *is* the many. The parts may be related *en masse* without being joined. Or they are broken up and joined, as in philosophical narrative, or Proust. Proust is long but kaleidoscopic, motes in one immense shaft of sunlight.

I think that a lot of the fuss about 'experimentalism' is slightly embarrassing. If you step back from the collage, you rediscover a sense of its cohesiveness; the edges are indeed joined. A political metaphor – and a reflection of something we discover if we look at our diaries and unrelated experiences: order reasserts itself, though it may not be the order we expected, and it may take a while, like the contemplation of a mandala. The poet and critic Eric Griffiths – no stranger to disorder – puts it well: 'Human experience is in time; our experiences therefore form a series. Various frustrations, surprises, incoherencies may arise from the elements of the series not coming in the right order. Our experiences also may form a sequence as well as a series . . . [A] 'sequence' is a pattern of significance which unfolds in time but in which arches of interrelation are sprung across spans of time to join together in meaning occurrences which are separate in time. A good example of this [unfolding] distinction between "series" and "sequence" is a poem.'

Another example might be the reading of an enciphered message.

*We know that life does not run in linear patterns – and rather comes in flashes, moments of clarity and inspiration. As Daniel Dennett says in* Consciousness Explained, *'We tend to conceive of the operations of the mind as unified and transparent, [but] they're actually chaotic. There's no invisible boss in the brain, no central meaner, no unitary self in command of our activities and*

*utterances.' Is collage – or fragmentation – a more natural way*
*of organising a piece of writing than traditional methods, such*
*as – in fiction – plot?*

There are lots of different questions, here. I think we need
first to clear up something about linearity – to distinguish
between the nature of time, as it affects the objective world
(and the body), and the nature of mental reality.

It's an exaggeration to say that 'life does not run in linear
patterns', because of course it does have a marked linearity
for humans: we are born, we live, and then we die. That is
the plot of life. But that is only time as we conceive of it his-
torically; on closer inspection, time as we really apprehend
it mentally is rather different: a thing that is experienced
both as a linear process (we see its ageing, history-producing
effect) and as something that can be reconfigured in (see
above) the dynamic of memory. The odd thing is that this
psychological dynamism – a property of the consciousness
that Dennett and others consider to be an effect of ordinary
material processes – turns out to be quite a good description
of the way time operates at the level of the equation, where
physical law describes real-world outcomes but doesn't itself
discriminate between the past and the future because an
equation works symmetrically in both directions. (Classical
physics and quantum mechanics give different explanations
for the existence of a direction in time, given this underlying
symmetry.) What this suggests to me is that consciousness,
like time – let's say, our awareness of time – is an amalgam of
experience and potentiality, of occurrence and (strange, statistical) law, in which the subjective component, the feeling
that we are going through something unique to us, is not an
illusion, or an ideation, but an aspect of that amalgamated
reality.

Dennett is a brilliant man, but 'we tend to conceive of the

operations of the mind as unified and transparent' seems to me to be wide of the mark. I have never met anyone who thinks of their mind in this way. The homunculus language of psychology – the 'boss in the brain' – is a cartoon. Unless we are on powerful drugs, we normally conceive of minds as being complex and irreducible, as they may well be. My own feeling is that consciousness arises from material processes but cannot be reduced to them (the No Way Back Paradox). The fact that it cannot be reduced without losing its USP – the personal vantage-point – tells us something about our inadequate grasp of those ordinary material processes and their relationship to time.

I don't see how a fragmentary narrative could be 'more natural' than a unitary one because both are artistic constructions. But is fragmentation more realistic? Possibly.

*Your most recent book,* Murmur, *puts us inside the mind – the dreams – of the codebreaker and logician Alan Turing during his chemical castration. What processes do you go through to depict the most intimate and painful moments in a genius's life?*

I'm glad you feel that the experiment worked: thank you. It's hard to say what one does. Writing a book – and perhaps especially a book about a dreadful transfiguration – is a little like having a protracted fit. Once it's over, there's no way to retrieve the feverish actuality of the creative moment. Thank God. I just remember not enjoying it very much, and feeling exiled from myself – a dissociative condition I couldn't very well moan about because I'd chosen it. It's a short book, but it took years to write, mostly because it coincided with a period of restricted movement, and of course I wonder about the relationship of that period to the anxieties inherent in the subject-matter. I also had to continue working as a teacher to pay the mortgage and the bills.

I was nervous about tackling Turing. I'm not a mathematician so I had to work hard to understand the meta-mathematics of Gödelian incompleteness (*Godel's Proof*, by Ernest Nagel and James R. Newman, is the classic guide), the *Entscheidungsproblem*, etc, and I hope I haven't made too many errors. (The mathematician Anna Aslanyan read the whole text very carefully.) For fictional purposes, Turing had to be his own avatar: I couldn't allow myself to put words into the mouth of a genius. That would have been wrong. But I think my overall wager is sound. *Murmur* tries to find a dramatic paraphrase for Turing's physical, mental and political predicament. It asks: how does one fit the personal experience of trauma into a material conception of the world? The story's scientist, Alec Pryor, discovers that the outward responses one gives to the world are not necessarily related to the inner life, which may be crying out, in great distress. At the same time, the novel resists that pain. It's the story of a man trying to overcome desolation and self-pity by objectifying the trauma.

*Do you feel any ethical responsibility as a writer?*

Yes. Ethics is the social dimension of morality. Lots of books have been written about the social role of the artist, and I don't wish to misrepresent the complexity of that commentary, because there are many different ways of making an artistic contribution to society. But, as I see it, my ethical responsibility is not to wear uniform.

Writing springs from a strange combination of personal aesthetic ambition, vanity, and guarded conviction. It is much more provisional than the artefactual solidity of a book might suggest: this book is what I have to say this time, and it will be a different performance next time. Ethics, for a writer, are unavoidable because publication is the social dimension of private inquiry. The process is, and should be, discomfiting. One way of producing bad writing, bad philosophy and sclerotic politics is to attempt to get art, argument and policy to represent a standard of conduct that already exists – an ideology, I guess. Writers should be wary of all that. If you find yourself expressly on the side of a political party, or a movement, fine, but be prepared to find yourself in disagreement with it. Soon. The most important thing about a conviction is the moment when circumstances threaten its validity.

*What role do writers and artists have in shaping culture – or influencing social conversations?*

This is an enormous question. There is one's ambition to do something, and there is the true state of play. There is the role one's ego perceives a writer to have – the role one desires, or fears, perhaps – and there is one's actual insignificance. How you think you come over, how you are. What you think you can do, what gets done. If one thinks of art and writing as one might think of anything else in life, then the answer must be that one shapes and influences one's surroundings in a piece-meal fashion, sometimes by design but mostly by accident, and of course the shaping and influencing are reciprocal. Often, it's the work and the actions that take place on one's blind side that count for most: the contributions to a local paper, the email sent at just the right time, the note to a coun-cillor. Nothing lasts, and that's fine. We rediscover art and culture and form and justice. Also, it's a mistake to confuse the public voice with the social voice. Private correspondence is social, too. The most important things I have written have been letters to people who, for one reason or another, needed some acknowledgment.

*What is the relationship between fiction and non-fiction; prose and poetry?*

A fruitful misalliance.

W. Somerset Maugham (in his postscript to *The Casuarina Tree*, 1926): 'A work of fiction, and perhaps I should not go too far if I spoke more generally and said, a work of art, is an arrangement which the author makes of the facts of his experience with the idiosyncrasies of his own personality.'

*A running theme in some of your books is Artificial Intelligence. We live in an increasingly technological world in which there are now computer programmes capable of synthesising prose and poetry. What role will human beings play in the future, when surrounded by early-form AI? Are you as sceptical about AI as, say, the late Stephen Hawking?*

I'm not sure Hawking was sceptical about it. He was alarmed. There are two issues. One is the sci-fi existential anxiety about conscious machines, which is obviously predicated on an understanding of what sort of thing consciousness itself might turn out to be. We don't know. We're not there, yet, and conscious robotics are a way off, because what we have so far is responsive machinery behaving in ways to which we may, if we choose, assign the properties of intelligence. But assigning such properties to a piece of technology is not the same thing as claiming intentionality for the machine itself – that is, the capacity to refer to things outside itself, to understand the meaning of the rules it follows, etc. Metaphorical language isn't helping, because we tend to forget that 'messages', for example, are conscious-user-dependent concepts. A computer doesn't send messages; you read them.

Conscious machinery will happen. But machinery doesn't need to be conscious for it to play a significant, symbiotic and destructive role in socio-economic development. Non-conscious tech – automation – has been around a long time and is becoming more sophisticated; the efficiencies/growth model of capitalism means that it will absorb most remaining manufacturing labour in the coming decades. What then?

The vulnerability of labour in a national context is the second problem. Our anxieties about borders and migration are displaced anxieties about borderless technology and the silent transfer of executive power from the defined state (a country with a border and jurisdictional limits) to the transnational corporation. Cyber warfare is a demonstration of the fact that states are losing their integrity: the more powerful countries use the 'freeflow' of cyberspace to advance their political agenda. But this goes hand-in-hand with corporatism, it turns out, because the media platforms manipulated by these countries, and flooded with bots and micro-targeting, are themselves mega-companies with enormous worker populations across the globe and the ability to pick and choose their tax liabilities.

I'm not sure how we wrest back control. Corporates create the tech, the tech crosses or cancels the border, the states survive in name only, the corporates stay in charge.

*How would you define creativity?*

Consequential wonder.

*Do you have a typical 'writing process'?*

No. I used to say 'start, then keep going', but I don't know what 'start' means any more. I try to nurture a habit of reading and annotation, hoping that the trail of scrawl will lead to an interesting, half-original thought, and so to a premise, and then some figures in a doorway . . .

*What does the term 'writer' mean to you?*

Not much. Journalism is a profession – and an important one. Writing is one of its tools. Writers are presumably people who write. It's too vague as a term to be of much use, though people do like to call themselves writers, don't they? It's a conversation stopper, that's for sure.

*Could you tell us a little about some of the future projects you're working on?*

I'm sorry to say that I can't, because there aren't any.

*Could you give your top 5 to 10 tips for writers?*

Read slowly and carefully. Write letters. Eat properly. Walk. Don't be afraid to stop: other people matter more in the end, and it's not a race. Resist jargon (George Orwell: 'ready-made phrases . . . perform the important service of partially concealing your meaning even from yourself'). Learn to spell and punctuate. Look up.

## Murmur

1

*Murmur* is a discursive novel that takes as its point of departure the last few years in the life of the logician and computer
science pioneer Alan Turing, who was arraigned on charges of
Gross Indecency with another male in 1952, and bound over
for a year, on condition that he submit to a regimen of puni-
tive hormonal injections – chemical castration, in effect. He
grew breasts, survived the ordeal, but died in 1954. Verdict:
suicide. My Turing avatar is Alec Pryor. As I've indicated elsewhere, it's important to understand that Alec is not Turing.
Turing's work and thought are subtle. I wanted to respect that
subtlety, and to avoid appearing to attribute to him words
and speculations that are mine.

The book asks: what does great bodily change (in this case,
state-sponsored torture) do to a person's mind? The novel is
bookended by extracts from a fictional journal that show a
brilliant intellect struggling to come to terms with the effects
of that change. It further asks: how does one become reasonable and objective about such events? How does a mathematician, so used to removing personal bias from analysis – the
*sine qua non* of scientific method – fit the personal experience
of pain/joy/love back into a neutral explanatory scheme?

The bulk of the book is a sequence of dreams and letters.
The dreams are reawakenings of key moments and relationships – Alec's love for a childhood friend, Christopher Moly-
neaux; his wrangling with the problems of 'decidability' and
computing intelligence; Cambridge before the Second World
War; torture and authority; the future of thinking machines;
his own likely fate. The correspondence is between Alec and
the woman he met at Bletchley Park – June Wilson (a version

of the real-life Joan Clarke). Together Alec and June try to break the code of the dreams. The letters are a *cri-de-coeur*, but also, perhaps, a cry of victory for personal integrity.

All writers like to think that their latest offering constitutes a departure from earlier work, and all delude themselves: the connectedness of one's output is a very minor species of discovered truth, but one that has non-trivial implications for how we think about (and experience) the vicissitudes of life.

It could be said, for example, that this novel is a formal synthesis of the 'fragmentary' approaches to characterisation and argument essayed in *The Absent Therapist* and *The Inevitable Gift Shop*. It demonstrates that the scattering or collage effects of a work may appear disordered and yet preserve hidden order in the same way that an apparently random string of data may turn out to be algorithmically compressible (Paul Davies's discussion of complexity and compression in *The Mind of God* is an important summary of this idea, which in turn echoes the Stoical cosmology of Marcus Aurelius and Lucretius). The fact that Pryor is perplexed and humiliated and disordered – and denied a conclusion, in my version of events – does not undermine the processual importance of his experiences. There is no way of knowing in advance if a mathematical statement in one system is provable from the system's axioms using logical rules.

This limit to determinism can be recast in aesthetic terms: a cultural preference for narrative sequence over series, for plot and teleology over exploration and digression, and for, everywhere it seems, the non-sequitur of 'results-based research', need not blind us to the reality of our experiences while they are going on. (Can we begin to see why the endings to most novels and films and plays are unsatisfying?) The dreams in *Murmur* have a sprung rhythm to them, because they are 'live'. They happen on the page. They are not arranged as blank verse – the formal lineation is hidden – but indeed that is what they are (Herman Melville's *Redburn* is iambic, too, as is Jim Crace's *Quarantine*). This turns out to be a literal fulfilment of Vladimir Nabokov's stylistic prescription for the novel as a 'merging of the precision of poetry with the intuition of science'.

*Murmur* doesn't offer reassurances, though some readers have found it consoling. We know that the world is unfair and that there is no redemption. We don't experience death. No one knows what an absence of consciousness is like. For that reason, we recognise real sympathy when we meet it because it's rarely soothing. It's a way of looking across a gap in understanding and not flinching.

What impresses me most about Turing, as I look back on the experience of trying to hear him, is his decency. Not a nice man, I suspect; impatient and rude, sometimes; but also loyal and honest, a sceptical patriot committed to the preservation of liberty. Famously he helped to break Enigma, the German naval communications code, in the early years of the Second World War. His example of service still matters.

2

It's hard to say how a book comes into being. Subject-matter passes before the sifting gaze every day and then an image comes into focus. I did my BA Hons at King's, Cambridge, where Turing was an undergraduate (and later a fellow). Back in 1987, word processing was still a relative novelty, but King's had a computer room: the Turing Room. I had no idea who Alan Turing was at the time, but I wrote my two dissertations on Willa Cather and 18th-century Jacobin radicalism in that room, under his technological gaze. I remembered the name.

Fast forward a quarter of a century, and I'm reading the touchingly brief memoir of her son by Sara Turing – writing in 1959, five years after Alan's death. His terrible wrestling with the personal and the scientific, the proven and the unprovable, struck a chord and reminded me of an observation by Italo Calvino which later found its way into *The Inevitable Gift Shop*: 'The more enlightened our houses, the more their walls ooze ghosts.' I take this to be an elegant reformulation by Calvino of the idea that incompleteness and inconsistency may be limiting features not simply of epistemic logic, as Kurt Gödel showed, but of all rational enquiry.

Alec is caught between fascination and horror, as he becomes a new version of himself. In the first year of writing *Murmur*, I found myself in a distantly comparable state of deterioration: I'd moved to Australia, to 'start again', and developed a chronic spinal problem, with no convincing diagnosis or prognosis, but plenty of pain. Pain is complex: unpleasant to experience, and distressing for others – for one's friends and family – to witness, not because they feel it themselves, but because they cannot feel it. The situation is intimate because it is remote.

The related question of how reliably complete a guide external behaviour might be to the *qualia* – the subjective part – of experience is at the heart of ongoing debates about the nature of consciousness. Turing was a functionalist. He felt that the point would come where computer responses to input/questions would be indistinguishable from human responses (the essence of the Turing Test, as given in 'Computing Machinery and Intelligence', 1950). Human-like behaviour would be enough to presuppose the presence of intelligence: the plausible response to a stimulus would be all that matters. But *Murmur*'s scientist discovers that intelligence and consciousness are not synonymous – that his behaviour does not corroborate his experience – and in so doing he stumbles on the reality of mind.

# What Is Ability?

We like to think of ourselves as creatures with willpower and rights of self-assertion, but it is surprisingly hard to think for oneself.

Original thought always involves non-compliance with precedent, and in a systematic society and economy that is tricky, both practically, because it is for example hard to run one's life offline, without the various permissions of web-based administration, and emotionally, because it's a way of saying no to authority. Refusing the known produces feelings of uncertainty, the possibility of disappointing others or being disappointed by them. It's an old problem to do with hierarchy and the individual. Explicit examples, in narrative literature, are Abrahamic myth, *The Tempest*, and *1984*. But even *Pride and Prejudice* and *Persuasion* qualify. Austen's novels are not about romantic love; they are stories about the practical and emotional obstacles in the path of truth-seeking, and the way families and riches do not take kindly to daughters who disappoint them.

Creative ability is always a move beyond, or rather into, uncertainty and the fear of unforeseeable consequences. It's always an act of refusal or of resistance to something already established, even if you are adding to it. Extension is an outward trajectory; it involves a move away from security. In logic and mathematics, it involves accepting the profound consequences of inconsistency and incompleteness, the true propositions that cannot be proved from the axioms; in art, it requires the painstaking undermining of preconceptions, including the idea that writing a book or a poem is a question of deciding to write a book or a poem rather than discovering the form as you go. Scientific method and artistic construction are both matters of formal experiment and experimenting with form. (It still amazes me how few scientists and artists point this out.)

Ability is also resistance to oneself, what one has already done, one's effortful CV, one's 'skills', the carefully curated evidence of a thing called identity, as if identity were a set of emotional and behavioural cues on a plinth in a museum, or indeed a university staff card. It's in this sense of extension and resistance that I understand George Orwell when he says, in his 1946 essay, *Why I Write*, that literature is driven both by powerful personal motives, 'ingrained likes and dislikes', and by the constant struggle 'to efface the personality' in pursuit of the truth.

What, then, is the 'ingrained' component of ability? In her excellently clear book, *Heart and Mind* (1981), the philosopher Mary Midgley makes a case for the existence of innate gifts, not as quantities of intelligence feeding entitlement or its opposite, but as 'personal repertoires' of 'tastes and powers which can often startle both ourselves and those around us, which may find no path in our culture'. Her defence of the personal repertoire perhaps relies too heavily on unprecedented geniuses like the Indian mathematician Ramanujan, who had very little education. You can't infer a general truth about innate ability from such examples. We are not commonly exceptional. Yes, of course, we are different; but by degree, I suggest. If that were not so, we would be condemned to lead solipsistic lives, and others' abilities would be inappreciably mysterious to us.

I also think that innatism by itself is not enough to explain our changes in life, our adoption of trades, practices and activities that run counter to an apparent inheritance. This is more than adaptability; it's the will to change ourselves and the world by refusing something given. We may have a predisposition to draw or paint or calculate and yet object to doing so on emotional grounds (our parents did it!). What we later find, typically, is that the draughtsman's gift is re-expressed in another direction, mathematically or musically or paleontologically. As a species, we have learnt to do many things. Most animals do the same thing, but we specialise within the group, and even as we specialise we diversify: there are many tasks to be done and we can learn to do each other's tasks, up to a point (though always get a good plumber). What this doesn't alter is the idea of an underlying subjective dispo-sition – including the ability to have a go at various things in accordance with our temperament or in *defiance* of it.

Midgley is quiet about this second possibility. She dis-cusses abilities rather as if they were unique-to-user appli-cations, whereas I see them as conscious variables inclining, over time, to expressions of personality. This takes us away from innatism or biological programming to something more intriguing: the ability to educate ourselves, building not just on clear aptitude – the thing that comes naturally – but on what we can't do so easily, but might, with the right teacher, find interesting.

The word 'education' has two Latin roots: *educare*, which means to train, and *educere,* to lead or draw out. The sec-ond of these is the one that tends to be forgotten. Drawing out presupposes the ingrained or innate; it also suggests the hidden, submerged, and contrary. We're not just drawing out an obvious talent. Thwarting ourselves, steering away from what comes easily, is often at the heart of a breakthrough. The tussle is itself the expression of something. In this sense, the gift of an ability is difficult to pin down. It's often counter-intuitive, a kind of Turing-esque or Gödelian prob-lem, in which unprovable truths are at the heart of defined processes, in which it is simultaneously true that I can write novels and that I dread so doing, or that my attempts to avoid writing are themselves a kind of preparatory activity. Keats famously called this state of resistance Negative Capability, 'that is, when a man is *capable* [my italics] of being in uncertainties, mysteries, doubts without any irritable reaching after fact or reason'. Orwell is all irritable reaching by comparison, but his relationship with a talent that expresses itself uncertainly as the inverse of ability – debility, indeed – is one Keats would have recognised. 'Writing a book,' he says, 'is like having a long, horrible illness.'

2

Ability is both innate and shaped, determined and acquired, but it is in all cases the property of a conscious entity. That education appears now to be mandating acquisition of something off a menu called 'skill' over any real feeling for the experiential uncertainties of art, music, language, or indeed scientific method, is something that should concern us. The concomitant problem is not so much that machines will acquire conscious abilities, but that we are already some way along the road to forfeiting ours.

It is possible, just, to say no to systems like exams and SATS and phone upgrades and the tiers of administration in workplaces, but they are now firmly, normatively embedded in our lives, and by and large we do not stop to question them. We don't feel that we *can*. Technological systems owned by private corporations (in California, mostly) are essentially dominance hierarchies, like religions, or powerful families, and like those other institutions they greatly elevate the notion of control as a force for good. We are leading better lives by compliance, they say. We are in control by allowing ourselves to be controlled. We need this upgrade. Everything is easier if we just say yes. In such a long-lived protocol of submissiveness – Julius Caesar, Elizabeth I and Stalin would all have confirmed its utility – requests from an almost numinous electrical authority are to be understood as commands, and no command in practice may be refused. If you don't say yes, there will be consequences. You will be locked out of your bank account, you will not be able to order your medication, you will not get onto your degree course or be able to graduate. Notice in all cases, that the content of the account, the nature of the need, and the substance of your work and argument, your ability, are utterly irrelevant. It is simply non-compliance that signifies. Notice, too, that whoever is at the head of the hierarchy is usually exempt from these consequences.

In his Gifford lecture on 'The Religious Experience', the sceptical cosmologist Carl Sagan has this to say about codes of submission: 'Consider how we bow our heads in prayer, making a gesture that can be found in many other animals as they defer to the alpha male [. . .] We're enjoined in the Bible not to look God in the face, or else we will die instantly. In the court of Louis XIV, as the king passed, he was preceded by courtiers crying "*Avertez les yeux*! Avert the eyes. Don't look up."' I confess I've thought much the same as Sagan in various seminars, when no one looks up, or when I'm walking down the street, and I see students, everyone, myself included, bowing to the phone light.

It takes about three years to get the fear of God out of my students. To help them to see that getting a few low marks doesn't matter, that the fear of losing their place in the hierarchy of grades is an anxiety about power and influence deliberately fostered by one model of economics among many, that they are more than their earning capacity, and that the point of literature, as Auden said in his introduction to *Poems of Freedom*, is not to make us more efficient, but to make us more aware of ourselves.

The technological climate, in which capacity and influence

are so important, has confused freedom to develop the person *you already are* with the acquisition of power and status. Students want jobs; I hope they get them. They have loans to repay. But they also want to be *successful*; they tell me in their essays that they know they're smart, but that they're struggling to see the point of a second-class degree; and I worry that this generation, more than any other, sees recognised achievement – success granted by an authority, often an absent and quasi-religious electronic one – as the goal of learning. That is what they are being told, after all. That is what Nicky Morgan, the former Secretary of State for Education, means when she says that studying the arts holds pupils back. (Never mind that the creative industries are worth more than £80 billion a year to the UK economy. Never mind that the whole Renaissance humanist project – without which no rationalism, no economics, no Bacon, no Newton – was enshrined by the study of grammar, rhetoric, history, poetry and philosophy.) She means that there is no development without competition and, it is implied, reward.

It is the materialist-individualist creed, of course, and like every iteration of that delusion in every age, it never asks, simply and logically, what individuals will *do* with their reward, and how they expect it to shelter them from misfortune or make them happy – what relationship it has, finally, to the conscious inner life.

This is the point. Human ability is conscious and therefore intentional: it grasps meaning and has a felt, as well as reasoned, relation to the world in which it operates. It values what is being done *as* it is done: look at a toddler clapping its hands when one brick stays on top of another. It is not merely attributed or assigned relative to an observer, like a message 'sent' by Outlook; it is experienced, and experienced both by the persons with the ability and the people around them. It is the fact that we experience a great singer for ourselves that makes his or her ability so moving. If it were merely a matter of manifesting technique, there would be no need to involve a conscious audience. But in practice, and in all cases, ability, whether we choose to do anything with ours or not, is potentially communicative and reflective as well as personal: in someone else's unique gifts – let us at last call it their sensibility – we experience the emotional echo, and the limit, of our own, and that sense of frustrating limit is important in defining who we are. 'We are looking for freedom, not omnipotence,' Midgeley reminds us, and freedom – the ability to be ourselves – has mortal limits.

'Real gifts, in their nature, are limited.'

# A Journal of the Plague Year

Like a comet, its time has come again. Frantic and austere, the feeling for personal bewilderment running fast beneath the author's plain style, Daniel Defoe's *A Journal of the Plague Year* (1722) brims with recognisable situations – the wealthy thundering down the road to Oxford and safety, the poor condemned by the riskiest essential employments (searching, guarding, nursing, burying), the revelation of powerlessness in authority, the joy of deliverance, and the shortness of memory. It's tremendous in every respect, as an invention sprung from fact, as a dramatic monologue, as a composition disordered by its own subject-matter. To off-set its evil charms, I've tried reading it alongside Gustave Flaubert's *L'Éducation Sentimentale* (1869) – as different a novel as one can imagine – only to find strange resonances. In both books the act of fascinated witness has a sort of immu-nising property, and Frédéric Moreau wandering the streets of the 1848 insurrection in Paris is uncannily similar to HF, Defoe's narrator, making his way past plague victims scream-ing at their casements in London in 1665. In each description of chaos and disaster, the past tense is full of threat, because the past is where we're all headed. I imagine scenarios for a film version of *Journal* and then watch the evening news: like Defoe, I'm inventing things that have already happened.

It would make a terrific, if unusual, film. The novel is a quasi-documentary of the last great visitation in this coun-try, and it draws on a variety of reportorial (and sermonising) sources, including *London's Dreadful Visitation* (1665), which supplied the statistics and bills of mortality, and Thomas Vincent's *God's Terrible Voice in the City* (1667), as well as a not-too-remote historical memory of the capital as it was when Defoe was a young child – London in all its working vitality and stupid luxury in the middle of the gay restoration. (The devastating 1720 outbreak in Marseille also casts a long shadow.) Producers would want to know: whose story is this? But that is the wrong question to ask. They tend to confuse narrative fluency with heroism, and the two have no necessary relation to each other. Main characters are a secondary consideration when your main character is an epidemic. Protagonists are swept away, and Defoe drives the point home: 'It is not the stoutest courage that will support men in such cases.' The disaster tops the bill, so to speak, and like a villain or avenging angel, it doesn't look so bad at first, beginning in Long Acre in December 1664, appearing sporadically, but confined to St Giles, Cripplegate and adjacent parishes, until early summer, then breaking out and surging east across the city and the suburbs before raging south and north, and onwards, with the remnants of trade and waves of refugees, to other cities in August and September, when thirty thousand died in three weeks alone.

Look at the YouTube posts of the Boxing Day tsunami of 2004. The wave is a trickle of water, an uninterpretable swell, until we see it up close at the last minute, smashing boats and houses with a kind of lazy insistence. In the same way, the key to getting a screen adaptation right would be to reproduce the novel's air of delayed or haphazard suggestion, the filtered awareness of what's really happening at which humans and governments, alike frightened for their survival, excel. No period bile, no endless suppuration, no Matthew McConaughey and his blinding teeth (again, not usefully heroic: rotten 'teeth' killed 946 people in August and September, says Defoe). Much better to have people disappear in the night, as they do, and did; for the red cross to appear on the door and go unremarked. By day, people carry on, at least for a while: this is the British reserve in full muffled cry, and a proof of our natural tendency to exceptionalism. In one grimly funny scene, Defoe has a citizen boasting about the good health of his drinking companions, 'upon which his neighbour said no more, being unwilling to surprise him'. (Defoe is not, as a friend put it, the most 'huggable' of novelists.) Have the mayhem in long shot or parenthesis – the man who runs mad and naked into the Thames while others conduct business on the foreshore, the dead cart running down Aldgate with the driver in his seat but the reins fallen from his hands, a shop opening while the house next door is boarded up. Get it wrong, cast for charisma, and you end up with a 17th-century zombie movie, where survival becomes heroic, and we are once more at the predictable mercy of over-directed acts and motivations.

The presumption is still that stories should reassure us, and Defoe dismisses it. Yes, he holds the camera, but he keeps dropping it, because there are so many bodies in the way. Defoe wrote at speed (the book was finished in just over three weeks), and it contains contradictions, though they seem to embrace the predicament described. They're confusions that belong to panic: there were always enough people to bury the bodies; there were no people left in some streets to bury the bodies; the plague didn't reach the ships moored in the Thames; then again, it did. HF gives thanks to God, towards the end, when partial abatement brings people back into the light, but the homiletics are designedly unconvincing. Some things are so overwhelming they destroy our fixed beliefs. Surely what the Great Plague finally did, in a busy interconnected early-modern world, was to cremate faith in divine appointment of any sort. It fired up the engine of the Enlightenment. More powerful by far than HF's thanksgiving is his italicised outburst as the citizens break their quarantine: '*the best physic against the plague is to run away from it*'. The implied scepticism about divine protection chimes with the author's own vinegary Dissent but also gives an answer to the question that has bothered the narrator from the start, and which drives the whole story: 'Should I stay, or should I go?'

His younger brother leaves London early on, and advises HF to do likewise. HF stays to protect his business and property – he's a saddler – but trade packs up anyway, and he is left to make shaky memorandums of events, nervous forays across the river, brief appearances as an examiner of infected houses. The film, like the book, ought to be a caravan of episodes, made up of people going through the same horror in different ways. The route it follows circles back to the one central question. Some episodes are no more than quick, terrible visions. Once the houses begin to be shut up and watchmen appointed, the afflicted have no choice but to die where they are. Except that the sound are confined with the sick; torn between love and the love of life, they pre-empt the council men with the bloody paint, daub their own doors with crosses so that they will appear already to have been shut up, and then flee by night. But 'whither should they fly'? Many of the afflicted wander abroad in a state of disinhibition, dancing in the streets, kissing strangers, or bringing infection with them to inns of refuge where the maid forgets to attend until the morning, finds a corpse, and then perishes herself.

Two other sequences, assuming the larger proportions of a play within a play, are fully elaborated responses to the governing dilemma. In the first, after two weeks of self-isolation, HF walks to the post-house to deliver a letter to his brother. He goes further, testing the bounds of liberty, and comes at last to the river's edge, at Blackwall stairs, where he finds a waterman, whose wife and child are both 'visited', nearby, in a 'very little, low-boarded house'. The waterman makes what money he can from tending to the rich merchants and their families on board the ships at anchor midstream, and rows as far as Greenwich, Woolwich and 'farm houses on the

Kentish side' to buy eggs and butter for his family. He leaves food and money on a stone at a safe distance from the house, and is waiting, now, as HF finds him, for his wife to emerge. She has a swelling, 'and it is broke, and I hope she will recover; but I fear the child will die, but it is the Lord –'. Good writers know when to rest the pen; actors and directors, when to stop moving. The masterly handling of this scene hasn't much to do with the disease or the waterman's plight. It is just the shocking fact of his name, of there being someone to call it, and of our being allowed to hear it, adrift on the tide of anonymising destruction: 'At length, after some further talk, the poor woman opened the door and called, "Robert, Robert".'

The second major episode, an unlikely Utopian experiment, or parable, could be extracted from the novel and adapted on its own. It concerns three impoverished but resourceful men – an ex-soldier turned biscuit maker, a lame seaman and sailmaker, and a joiner – and has its dramatic roots in the preceding cataclysm of the Civil War. The skill and cunning of servicemen abandoned by the ship of state are brought back to life. The men leave the city, by circuitous means, avoiding checkpoints, thinking carefully about what they can carry (they are but 'three men, one tent, one horse, one gun') and how to get provisions, when they are met by wary villagers on the outskirts of Walthamstow. By wrapping sticks in rags to look like muskets and building a series of widely-spaced fires in the tall grass, the soldier (John) persuades the villagers that they are a large company and extorts from them plenty of bread and beef. On coming to Epping, the ruse is reversed. This time, John says, far from being a desperate company, they are pious and few. They win over the locals and establish a self-sufficient commune. In a further reversal, the commune is so successful it attracts the Epping villagers themselves, some of whom are already sick with the plague, and so the mirage of sanctuary dissolves.

HF counsels flight, but flight is an illusion, Defoe says, because fear of the stranger cuts both ways – the people offering refuge are strange, too – and safety doesn't lie at home, either. You can ask questions of the seeming well, but will you be satisfied with the answers, 'if the arrow flies unseen, and cannot be discovered'? The position of the citizens is pitiable, insoluble, but not to be wondered at. Their condition is not bleakly illustrative, as it is for the characters in Albert Camus' *La Peste*. (Like Defoe, Camus knows that lessons, philosophical or religious, tend to disappear inside the experience of catastrophe, but somehow, at the level of tone, the later writer finds them harder to resist.) Defoe's victims are subject to the dramatic irony of history, of course: we know, as they do not, how the disease was spread. Most guesses about transmission in the novel are wrong, though not wildly so – carrier 'insects' are briefly invoked at one point – and to feel that the characters act mistakenly, when they slaughter thousands of cats, the rats' natural predators, is to side with superficial narrative resolution. In fact, the book is remarkably open-ended. A film would be free to imagine survivors who were more than lucky – people who sold onions or pepper, or made strong-smelling oils for apothecaries, or who pursued noisy occupations, all rodent deterrents – but it would have to come back to the eyeless zeal of the pathogen itself, from which point of view objective cause and cure are limited by their expression in human beings. Terrible things come to pass, and then pass away. This is a fact. Now: what are we to make of it?

# Afterword: Broken Consort

For the last year or two, I have been collecting – reacquiring, in some cases – vinyl LPs from the books and music branch of the British Heart Foundation on Streatham High Street. The haul is varied, the sound always absorbing and moving, with an acoustic architecture (a sense of human performance and origin) generally missing from digital files, where even symphonies in large concert halls seem to lack depth. Here are many different families of instruments, voices, genres, cultures and emotions: folk music, church music, Monteverdi and Bach, Kathleen Ferrier, Tony Bennett, Stan Tracey improvising at Wigmore Hall, Michael Ponti playing Tchaikovsky's solo piano music, Aretha Franklin *Live at Fillmore West*. Nick Lucas, who runs the Soul Proprietors record shop just around the corner from where I live, has set me up with a reconditioned Pioneer turntable and radio amp, and on this new old kit the familiar listening experience crackles with novelty.

Two musicians have made a strong impression. One is David Munrow, founder of the Early Music Consort of London and multi-instrumentalist populariser of medieval and renaissance dance bands, early polyphonic song, and period performance. He achieved fame in the early 1970s with his authentic scores for the BBC television series *The Six Wives of Henry VIII* (1970) and *Elizabeth R* (1971) – a success parlayed into a recording career of scholarly vitality. To his LPs (and editions) of the 14th-century poet-composer Guillaume de Machaut (on *The Art of Courtly Love*), Thomas Morley's *First Book of Consort Lessons* (1599), and the works of Tielman Susato, Michael Praetorius, and Guillaume Dufay, among others, Munrow contributed many detailed, erudite and witty sleeve notes. For one of his later recordings, *Instruments of the Middle Ages and Renaissance* (1975), he wrote a wonderful accompanying book, describing and illustrating all the principal instruments in use during the period. I was not aware that Henry VIII had a collection of twenty-five crumhorns (apparently unplayed) or that the word itself – meaning 'curved horn' – first crops up on an organ stop in Dresden in 1489. There is no surviving English music for crumhorn, it seems; the whole repertoire for this once popular wind instrument is a continental European phenomenon.

The other find is Paul Jacobs, the virtuoso American pianist whose eight Nonesuch LPs, of mostly 20th-century solo music, are brilliant syntheses of technique and truth. If real dancers' feet can be heard behind Munrow's thrumming tabors and flutes, then something equally palpable, but perhaps less identifiable, comes through Jacobs's interpretations of Busoni, Stravinsky and Messiaen. It's a revolt against purity (which has little to do with authenticity, in performance or elsewhere) in favour of simple attention-giving: to the hymn-tune inside the mayhem, to pain and pleasure alike. Busoni's transcriptions of Bach's Chorale Preludes may be 'of transcendant difficulty', as Jacobs says, but in his playing you are only ever aware of the music, the swift summoning reality that Virginia Woolf found 'now . . . in a dusty road, now in a scrap of newspaper in the street, now a daffodil in the sun'.

David Munrow took his own life in 1976; he was thirty-four. Paul Jacobs died of AIDS in 1983. Together, their playing makes a kind of 'broken consort', the Renaissance term for a particular and varied instrumental combination, which was a fresh concept in the late 16th century, and comes round again on the turntable now.

# Author's Note

The pieces in this volume mostly appear in the order in which they were written. I have kept shuffling to a minimum because I couldn't find a thematic pattern to improve on happenstance chronology. My first book, now lost, was a substantial collection of film reviews, compiled in the white heat of adolescent conviction, when I was fourteen. I was very keen on *Bride of Frankenstein* (1935, dir. James Whale) and the Sherlock Holmes films of the late 1930s and 40s, starring Basil Rathbone and Nigel Bruce. I watched TV as much as I read: BBC2 showed b/w double-bills on Saturday nights, and I knew everything there was to know about Boris Karloff, whom I imagined having a torrid affair with Bela Lugosi. I liked arty movies and 'screenings', too, but my stint as a sixteen-year-old programmer for Bath Film Society ended in scandal. I ordered an Andy Warhol short, to show alongside Roman Polanski's *Tess* (1979), and received *Couch* (1964) instead, which is an hour of sex on a sofa. People wanted their money back. A local in the audience got up and shouted 'This is disgusting. When I was a young man, I made what they're doing last all night!' After that, I did some work experience for the *Evening Chronicle* and glowingly reviewed a Jim Jarmusch film I hadn't seen.

There were no more reviews for eight years, just a lot of acting, which is itself a kind of reading and criticism of life, I suppose. Then the *TLS*, stuck for someone to tackle a biography of Willa Cather, asked me to have a go at an in-brief. The paper liked it, and Lindsay Duguid (fiction editor) and Alan Hollinghurst (music) asked me to write more: the essay on Laura Riding was my first long article, in 1992, and Alan Jenkins guided me through the whole nerve-wracking process of rewriting and fine-tuning it. My thanks go to him, and to all the other editors at the paper, especially Michael Caines – friend, scholar, and multi-instrumentalist – to whom this book is dedicated.

Thanks, also, to the editors and publishers of the other journals, websites and organisations in which the contents of *Broken Consort* first appeared. They are: *Poetry Review*, *PN Review*, the *Daily Telegraph*, Chipping Campden Art Gallery, the *Wrong Review* at Vout-O-Reenees, the Universities of Warwick and Melbourne, *Nothing in the Rule Book*, the *Poetry School*, the *Brixton Review of Books*, CODEX: Leonardo at 500 (September 23-25, 2019), and the Royal Society.

W.E.

## ℂB *editions*

Founded in 2007, CB editions publishes chiefly short
fiction and poetry. Writers published in translation
include Apollinaire, Andrzej Bursa, Joaquín Giannuzzi,
Gert Hofmann, Agota Kristof and Francis Ponge.
Books can be ordered from www.cbeditions.com.